Adirondack Mountain Club

CANOE and KAYAK GUIDE: EAST-CENTRAL NEW YORK STATE

Includes Selected Waterways of Western New England

Kathie Armstrong and Chet Harvey, Editors

First Edition

Adirondack Mountain Club, Inc.
Lake George, New York

Design by Allison W. Bell, modified by Michele Phillips and Ann Hough
Cover photo © 2001 Vincent Woolley
Layout by Susanne Murtha, APROPOS Design Solutions
Page maps by Karen Brooks with updates by Ann Hough
Map page 109 by Adirondack Interactive

Funding provided by the Schenectady Chapter of the Adirondack Mountain Club helped
support the production of this book.

Published by the Adirondack Mountain Club
814 Goggins Road, Lake George, New York 12845-4117
www.adk.org

The Adirondack Mountain Club (ADK) is dedicated to the protection and responsible
recreational use of the New York State Forest Preserve, parks, and other wild lands and
waters. The Club, founded in 1922, is a member-directed organization committed to
public service and stewardship. ADK employs a balanced approach to outdoor recreation, advocacy, environmental education, and natural resource conservation.

Library of Congress Cataloging-in-Publication Data

Adirondack Mountain Club canoe and kayak guide, east-central New York
State / Kathie Armstrong and Chet Harvey, editors.--1st ed.
        p. cm.
Includes index.
     ISBN 978-1-931951-00-5 (pbk.)

1. Canoes and canoeing--Hudson River Watershed (N.Y. and N.J.)--Guidebooks.
2. Hudson River Watershed (N.Y. and N.J.)--Guidebooks. I. Title: Canoe and kayak
guide, east-central New York State. II. Armstrong, Kathie, 1932– III. Harvey, Chet,
1922– IV. Adirondack Mountain Club.

    GV776.H83A35 2003
    797.1'22'097473--dc20   96-034248

    12 11 10 09 08 07   10 9 8 7 6 5 4 3

"The canoe and the paddle are beautiful objects, graceful in repose. When united by a paddler, the whole becomes a dance; the water provides the music and sets the rhythm. To participate in this dance and follow the music is an art and a privilege."

—Marion Boyden

This guide is dedicated to Betty Lou Bailey, who arrived in the Capital Region in 1969 with a boundless enthusiasm for paddling and the goal of establishing a whitewater canoe group. Under her leadership, whitewater paddling in the Schenectady Chapter of the Adirondack Mountain Club developed a large and devoted following. For more than thirty years she has continued to guide, instruct, and inspire paddlers of all ages and abilities.

Use of the information in this book is at the sole discretion and risk of the paddler. ADK and its authors make every effort to keep our guidebooks up to date; however, conditions are always changing.

In addition to reviewing the material in this book, paddlers should assess their ability, physical condition, and preparation, as well as likely weather conditions before a trip. For more information on preparation, equipment, and how to deal with emergencies, see the Introduction.

If you note a discrepancy in this book or wish to forward a suggestion, we welcome your comments. Please cite book title, year of most recent copyright *and printing* (see copyright page), trip, page number, and date of your observation. Thanks for your help!

Please address your comments to:

Publications
Adirondack Mountain Club
814 Goggins Road
Lake George, NY 12845-4117
518-668-4447, ext. 23
pubs@adk.org

ADK encourages the involvement of all people in its mission and activities; its goal is to be a community that is comfortable, inviting, and accessible.

Table of Contents

Introduction 1
Paddling Safely 2
Respecting Landowners 4
Using This Guide 5
Paddlers with Physical Disabilities 7
Acknowledgments 8

UPPER HUDSON WATERSHED 10
Hudson River
Introduction 11
Newcomb Bridge to Indian River Confluence 15
Hudson Gorge: Indian River to North River 19
North River to North Creek 23
North Creek to The Glen 25
The Glen to Thurman Station 32
Lake Luzerne to Corinth 34
Corinth Dam to Spier Falls Dam 37
Spier Falls Dam to Sherman Island Dam 40
Sherman Island to Big Boom Road 42
Big Boom Road to Feeder Dam 43
Fort Edward to Fort Miller 46
Fort Miller to Stillwater 49
Stillwater to Lansingburgh 54
Hudson River–Mohawk River Confluence 61
Upper Hudson Tributaries
Cedar River
Cedar River Flow 63
Indian Lake Village to Hudson River 66

Miami River 70
Cheney Pond and Boreas River
    Cheney Pond and Lester Flow 72
Schroon River
    Schroon Falls to Schroon Lake Village 75
    Starbuckville to Riverbank 78
    Riverbank to Warrensburg 81
Sacandaga River, Middle Branch
    Christine Falls to Auger Falls 84
    Kunjamuk River (tributary)
        Lake Pleasant to Elm Lake 88
Sacandaga River, West Branch
    Route 10 Bridge to Shaker Place 90
    Whitehouse to Pumpkin Hollow 95
    Fall Stream (tributary)
        Piseco Lake to Vly Lake 99
Sacandaga River, Main
    Wells to Hope 101
    Stewarts Bridge Reservoir 105
    Stewarts Dam to Hudson River 106
Moses Kill 112
Batten Kill
    Introduction 115
    Manchester, Vermont, to Arlington, Vermont . . 117
    Arlington, Vermont, to
        New York State Rest Area 122
    New York State Rest Area to Shushan 123
    Shushan to NY 22 Bridge 124
    NY 22 Bridge to Battenville 126

Kayaderosseras Creek
    Rock City Falls to Ballston Spa 127
    Ballston Spa to Saratoga Lake 131
Fish Creek
    Saratoga Lake to Grangerville 134
    Grangerville to Victory Mills 137
Hoosic River
    Introduction 140
    North Pownal, Vermont,
       to Hoosick Falls, New York 141
    Hoosick Junction to Johnsonville Dam 144
    Johnsonville Dam to Valley Falls 149
Round Lake and Anthony Kill 151
Grafton Lakes
    Long Pond, Second Pond, Mill Pond,
    Shaver Pond, and Martin-Dunham Reservoir . . 153

LOWER HUDSON WATERSHED 156
Lower Hudson Tributaries
    Kinderhook Creek
       Introduction 157
       Stephentown to West Lebanon 160
       East Nassau to Chatham Center 162
    Normans Kill
       Watervliet Reservoir to New Scotland Avenue . 166
    Catskill Creek
       Cooksburg to East Durham 169
    Esopus Creek
       Allaben to Boiceville 172

LAKE CHAMPLAIN DRAINAGE 178

Lake George

Northwest Bay Brook 179

Poultney River

West Haven, Vermont, to Whitehall, New York . 182

Champlain Canal

Introduction 185

Whitehall to Fort Ann 186

Fort Ann to Fort Edward 189

Glens Falls Feeder Canal

Feeder Dam to Martindale Avenue 192

MOHAWK RIVER WATERSHED 196

Mohawk River Tributaries

West Canada Creek

Introduction 197

Trenton Falls to Poland 198

Poland to Middleville 201

Middleville to Kast Bridge 203

East Canada Creek

Stratford to Dolgeville 206

Schoharie Creek

Introduction 210

North Blenheim to Middleburgh 211

Middleburgh to Esperance 214

Esperance to Power House Road 218

Power House Road to the Mohawk River 220

Cobleskill Creek (tributary)

Cobleskill to Sagendorf Road 224

Alplaus Kill

    Introduction 228

    Charlton Road to Van Vorst Road 229

    Kristel Falls to the Mohawk River 230

LOWER CONNECTICUT AND HOUSATONIC WATERSHEDS . . . 234

Deerfield River, Massachusetts

    Fife Brook to Charlemont 235

Housatonic River, Connecticut

    Introduction 239

    Falls Village to West Cornwall 239

    West Cornwall to Kent 242

APPENDICES

    Appendix A: Whitewater Trips 247

    Appendix B: Flatwater and Quickwater Trips 251

    Appendix C: Safety Code of American Whitewater . 253

    Appendix D: River Level and Flow Information 264

    Appendix E: Glossary 266

    Appendix F: Resources 270

    Appendix G: Hudson River PCB

        Dredging Information 272

ABOUT THE AUTHORS 273

INDEX 278

Introduction

The waterways included in this guide were selected by the paddlers who use them. These contributors volunteered their time and expertise to provide detailed accounts of the rivers and lakes which they consider to be the best paddling opportunities in the region. They range from exciting whitewater to tranquil lakes. All of the trips, with the possible exception of the most northern section of the Hudson River, are one-day excursions for those living in the vicinity of the Capital Region of New York State.

The region covered in this book extends from Newcomb in the north to Kingston in the south, and from Herkimer in the west to Charlemont, Massachusetts, in the east. The map on the back cover of the guide provides an outline of the area. Since paddlers follow waterways that cross state boundaries, and because our region lies close to Vermont, Massachusetts, and Connecticut, we have included sections of rivers and in some cases entire trips that are located in an adjacent state. The criterion for selection was the frequency of use by the paddlers, which in turn is determined by the qualities of the rivers and lakes themselves.

It is important for those who use this guide to realize that, although every effort was made to provide accurate information about each waterway at medium water level, conditions change. There are wide variations in water levels and river conditions from year to year and season to season. The paddler must be able to assess the specific conditions of a particular waterway on a particular day. For example, a river which is relatively benign at medium level may be exceedingly dangerous at high water. Every paddler should study the section on Paddling Safely.

Seasonal factors that affect water levels include snow depth, temperature, rainfall, and absorption of water by vegetation. March is the beginning of the paddling season on many rivers in New York and New England. As snow and ice melt, rivers rise; when the ground is frozen, runoff is swift. As the earth thaws and begins to absorb water, rivers that were initially too high to negotiate become runnable. When leaves appear, trees and other plants begin to use water, causing levels in rivers and lakes to drop rapidly. Summer months see a drastic reduction in water flow in many rivers; only a sustained rain can bring these waterways back to runnable levels. Come fall, when deciduous plants lose their leaves and rains usually increase, rivers rise and are again paddleable.

Rivers which are only runnable in spring and fall often flow through steep terrain and have significant rapids. Rivers and lakes that flow through relatively flat land may be paddled all summer. The larger the body of water, the less it is affected by seasonal changes.

Some rivers and lakes are controlled by dams. Water releases from dams can extend the paddling season on rivers which would normally be too low during all but a few weeks of the year. Releases may be used to generate power, to draw down lakes and reservoirs, or, in some instances, to provide recreational whitewater paddling on a regular schedule.

Because of the wide variation in water levels, many rivers have gauges which the paddler can access before deciding where and when to paddle. Gauge readings and water release data are available by phone and on the Internet. Appendix D provides information on obtaining daily gauge readings and water release schedules. Individual river descriptions explain how to interpret gauge levels and release volumes.

Paddling Safely

Although this guidebook can help you evaluate a waterway, it cannot keep you safe. You must be able to assess your own abilities and choose a waterway that is appropriate to your skill level.

Since all boating has inherent risks, it is important to minimize them with proper training and equipment. A major cause of problems is lack of experience, which leads to inappropriate choices. There are paddling groups that offer courses and run trips for individuals of all levels of ability. These groups are glad to have new members and will help you paddle safely. In addition there are paddling schools which offer professional lessons. Consult Appendix F for a list of local clubs and schools.

You must choose a boat and other equipment that are appropriate for your trip. A whitewater canoe or kayak will not track easily across a windy lake; conversely, a narrow beam tracking boat will not maneuver readily around rocks in a whitewater stream. You will need a lifejacket wherever you paddle, but you will not need a boat packed with flotation on a flatwater trip.

Even the best precautions cannot eliminate unexpected obstacles or permanent changes in waterways that have occurred since this writing. Changes occur frequently and vary from downed trees to broken dams or floods that can alter the course of rivers. Water levels can change dramatically in a matter of hours, due to rain or water releases. Expect the unexpected.

The Safety Code of American Whitewater is provided in Appendix C. We urge you to read it. Some sections will be useful to flat and quickwater paddlers as well as whitewater enthusiasts. Below is a list of the main topics covered by the Safety Code. Comments in parentheses are ours; they emphasize subtopics of particular importance.

I **Personal Preparedness and Responsibility** (Be sure you have proper protective gear; study dangers of high water, cold, strainers, dams, ledges, holes, hydraulics, and broaching; train in rescue techniques for you and others.)

II **Boat and Equipment Preparedness** (Read how to outfit your boat for safety and do it!)

III **Group Preparedness and Responsibility** (Learn how to organize groups for different river conditions, what equipment to bring, and how to keep the group compact.)

IV **Guidelines for River Rescue** (Learn techniques for coping with an upset.)

V **Universal River Signals** (Learn and practice these signals; make sure all members of your party know them.)

VI **International Scale of River Difficulty** (Study the six classes of difficulty; discuss them with others, and practice classifying rapids by difficulty.)

Although the Safety Code, outlined above and printed in its entirety in Appendix C, gives complete coverage of topics relating to safe paddling, there are a few situations which we believe need extra emphasis.

The *strainer*, or sweeper as it is sometimes called, presents a particular hazard to the unwary or inexperienced river paddler. Obstacles such as fallen trees, branches, brush, or undercut banks allow current to pass through, but "strain out" large objects like canoes and kayaks. The force of the flow pins the boat broadside against the sweeper and rolls the boat upstream. Once the gunwale dips below the water, the boat submerges and paddlers may be pinned in the branches either above or under water. Rescue may be difficult or impossible. Sweepers on the outside bends of the river, where the water is deep and the current fast, are particularly dangerous. Paddlers must know the strokes and ferrying techniques to avoid being swept into these obstacles.

Another situation for serious consideration is high water. The speed and power of a river increases dramatically as the water rises. In most cases, the difficulty of rapids becomes progressively harder. At high water, floating debris, strainers, waves, and holes become difficult to negotiate. It is essential to check river gauges and understand the significance of levels and flow rates before launching. If there is no gauge, check the river at various places. A wide section may be quite navigable whereas a narrow, rocky shoot may be extremely turbulent and beyond your skills. Never paddle any river in flood (over the banks)!

A third condition that warrants discussion is the danger presented by cold. A general rule followed by many paddlers says that if the air and water temperature add up to less than 100 degrees F, wear a wet or dry suit. Anyone who capsizes without appropriate protective clothing can develop hypothermia, which, if left untreated, can lead to death. Signs of hypothermia (lowering of normal body temperature) are uncontrollable shivering followed by slurred speech and inability to coordinate body movements. Treatment involves changing to dry clothes, warming with hot drinks, putting the individual into a sleeping bag, and getting help to transport the victim to a medical facility. Always carry a change of clothing in a waterproof bag.

Respecting Landowners

Although most of the trips in this guide provide information that enables paddlers to park, launch, and take out boats on public property, occasionally you may encounter a situation where you need to cross private land. Unfortunately, many landowners whose properties border popular waterways have posted their land against trespass. To prevent future postings and to instill and maintain goodwill it is imperative to ask permission to carry boats and equipment across private property. Most people respond positively to a courteous request. If you are given permission, be sure to move quickly. Don't hang around or have a picnic! Pick up any litter; take care not to disturb vegetation along the banks. Always park off the pavement on public roads or in specified parking areas. Your behavior will affect those who come after you.

Using This Guide

Organization

This guide groups waterways by watersheds or drainages. A map at the beginning of each watershed or drainage shows the particular rivers and lakes selected for paddling. Within each watershed, the main waterway is presented first, starting at its source and working downstream in segments that are no longer than a one-day trip. The tributaries follow and are discussed in the order in which they enter the main waterway, starting with the one farthest upstream. This system integrates whitewater and flatwater/quickwater segments in each waterway. For the convenience of paddlers who want to distinguish easily between these two categories, there are separate listings of whitewater and flatwater/quickwater trips, organized by watershed or drainage (see Appendices A and B). The whitewater list provides the difficulty classifications at medium water levels.

Format

Rivers with several segments are usually prefaced with an introduction. Each river, lake, or segment of a waterway is organized according to the same format, beginning with a summary of the most important information:

Name of waterway

Segment:	the geographic beginning and end points of the trip
Counties:	location of the segment
Length:	miles and kilometers from launch to takeout
Drop:	feet and meters of drop from launch to takeout
Difficulty:	at medium water; flatwater, quickwater, or a rating based on the American Whitewater Scale
Problems:	special difficulties the paddler may encounter
Maps:	topographic quadrants covering the segment; pages in the DeLorme Mapping Company's *New York State Atlas & Gazetteer; Vermont Atlas & Gazetteer; Connecticut/Rhode Island Atlas & Gazetteer;* and *Massachusetts Atlas & Gazetteer.*
Contributor:	person(s) who contributed the description

Length. Each segment represents a trip that can be completed in one day or less. Distances (in miles) are the best approximation available from maps, which tend not to show every bend.

Drop. The *drop* or gradient (feet of drop divided by length in miles) is useful, but must be interpreted in that it can be spread out in small increments over the length of the trip or can be concentrated in a short distance, such as a waterfall or dam. This information is available in the detailed trip description and can be determined using the topographic maps (see Maps below).

Difficulty. This rating represents the most difficult rapids found on the segment at medium water level. The rating is based on the American Whitewater Scale included in Appendix C, as interpreted by the contributor. As the water level increases, so does the difficulty of many rapids. Difficulty of rapids depends on the combined effects of gradient, volume of flow, and the nature of the bottom.

Problems. These may include any obstacles or conditions the writer deems important to note (a dam, particularly difficult rapids, etc.).

Maps. Topographic maps can be very helpful in understanding details of waterways and surroundings. They provide contour intervals which indicate the location and severity of drops as well as the type of terrain through which a waterway flows. Although most waterway descriptions refer to topographic quadrants in the 7.5-minute series, some maps are 7.5 x 15 minute and a few are 30 x 60 minute. Some of the maps referenced are DOT (New York State Department of Transportation) and others are USGS (United States Geological Survey). Although DOT maps are often more recent, both offer approximately the same information. Topographic maps may be obtained from the New York State Office for Technology, 74 North Pearl Street, 2nd Floor, Albany, NY 12207; telephone 518-443-2042. Order forms are available for download at www.nygis.state.ny.us and mail orders should be sent to New York State Office for Technology Center for Geographic Information, State Capitol ESP, P.O. Box 2062, Albany, NY 12220.

The DeLorme Mapping Company publishes an atlas for every state. These maps are very detailed and offer much more information than most road maps; DeLorme maps are particularly helpful for finding routes to waterways located in remote places. In addition, they show campgrounds and historic features.

Following the table, the trip description is divided into sections: **Launch** provides directions to the beginning of the trip, where to park, and conditions at the put-in. **Description** gives details of the trip, including rapids, scenery, possible problems, and experiences of paddlers. **Takeout** describes the highway, where to park, and where to take boats out of the water. Some descriptions include *Notes* or **Cautions** of particular importance.

Each description is accompanied by a page map that gives an overview of the waterway. We use the term launch to designate the beginning or put-in of a particular segment. Access points refer to other places along the route where paddlers can start or end their trip. Takeouts are also indicated. The following map legend illustrates the various symbols used on the page maps.

Map Legend

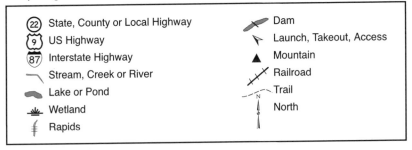

(22)	State, County or Local Highway		Dam
(9)	US Highway		Launch, Takeout, Access
(87)	Interstate Highway	▲	Mountain
	Stream, Creek or River		Railroad
	Lake or Pond		Trail
	Wetland		North
	Rapids		

Paddlers with Physical Disabilities

Today, as with many sports, paddling is available to persons with physical disabilities. Disabled persons who have never paddled, as well as persons who were paddlers before their disability, can experience the pleasures of traveling across water in a canoe. They may need some help from friends, some adaptive equipment, and some training. To obtain information on this subject contact the American Canoe Association, Disabled Paddlers Committee, P.O. Box 1190, Newington, VA 22122-1190; www.acanet.org or 703-451-0141.

Acknowledgments

Much of the work on this guide was done by the volunteers who ran the rivers and wrote the reports, which are the heart of the book. These paddlers know and love the rivers they describe. Each description reflects the special knowledge and experiences of the contributor(s). Their names accompany each entry. We thank them for their enthusiastic efforts.

We are especially grateful to Mary Bruno, who not only paddled most of the flat and quickwater rivers, but also coordinated the writing of the descriptions of these waterways. In addition, we wish to thank Mark Freeman, whose previous work provided a baseline for some of the introductory material and flatwater descriptions.

The inspiration for writing this book came from the staff of the Adirondack Mountain Club who recognized the need for regional guides to the best waterways of New York State. Special thanks are due to John Kettlewell, publications director, Andrea Masters, editor; their patient encouragement and expertise turned a concept into a reality. Karen Brooks provided the technical skill behind the beautifully constructed maps which accompany each description. Michele Phillips, an independent contractor who worked with ADK for several years, contributed layout, design, and typography. Allison Bell is responsible for the set design of the series.

Finally, we want to thank Neil Woodworth, our friend and whitewater paddling companion, who persuaded us to take the job of coordinating and editing this book. It has been a tremendously challenging and rewarding experience.

Upper Hudson River near Blue Ledge   Chet Harvey

Upper Hudson Watershed

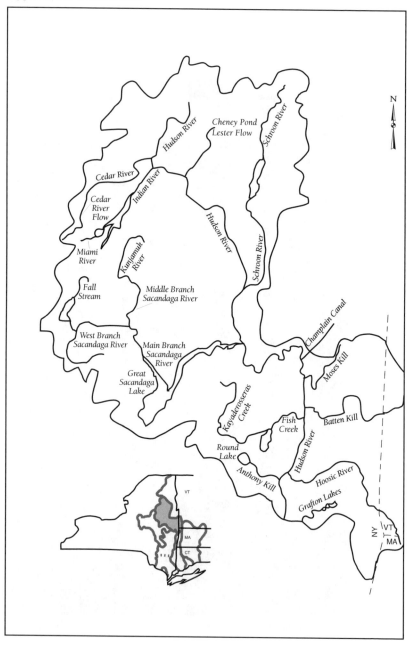

Hudson River

Introduction

The Hudson River's waters rise from some of the world's most ancient rocks and gather in a small lake high on the flanks of Mount Marcy, the Adirondacks' highest peak. The little lake is newer than the rocks but older than the human species. From its outlet, Feldspar Brook flows to the Opalescent River, which joins waters of lower origin to form the modest beginnings of the mighty Hudson. In its 300-mile course, the Hudson descends 4322 feet from the lake outlet to the sea at New York City, with almost all of the drop occurring in the first seventy miles. In 1872, when naturalist Verplanck Colden bushwhacked through dense stands of spruce, balsam, and cedar to reach the lake, it bore the name Summit Water. He described it in his report to the New York State Legislature as "a minute unpretending tear of the clouds." Although not his intent, the source of the Hudson became officially known as Lake Tear of the Clouds.

The magnificent Hudson, so important to our heritage, remained largely unreported in the journals of the early explorers of the New World until 1524 when Giovanni Verrazano, sailing under the flag of France, entered New York Harbor. But it was Captain Henry Hudson, an Englishman sailing for The Dutch East India Co., who first explored the river in 1609. He anchored the *Half Moon* at Overslaugh Bar and sent a small party 20 miles further upstream to the mouth of the Mohawk River. Captain Hudson knew he was sailing a mighty river but he could not have envisioned its future contribution to the political, economic, and cultural development of a great nation. The Hudson provided a waterway for the earliest settlers and a highway for the American and British armies who battled for the control of the region during the Revolutionary War. With the completion of the Champlain Canal in 1822 and the Erie Canal in 1825, the Hudson became the major trade route connecting New York harbor with the Saint Lawrence River in the north and Buffalo in the west. The commerce which traveled these waterways transformed New York City into the largest and wealthiest urban center of the United States. In addition, New York City became the "open door" for two centuries of immigrants who helped make America great.

Prior to the 1950s, the major activities on the upper regions of the river were the great log drives supplying wood to the lumber and pulp mills in the

Glens Falls area. Evidence of the old log drives can still be found where remnants of cables and chains remain attached to rocks in the riverbanks.

Today the major activities of the upper Hudson center on tourism. The world famous Hudson Gorge runs from the confluence of the Indian and Hudson Rivers to the town of North River. Rafting companies guide thrillseekers through this remote area of raging rapids and rugged beauty. Those who brave the rapids discover a land of steep banks overhung by hemlocks and towering cliffs which rise 400 to 500 feet above the swirling waters of a great river. Until the 1950s the Gorge was considered uncanoeable; today experienced kayakers and canoeists come from all over the world to paddle these waters and experience the beauty of this unique region.

Canoeists and kayakers also come to paddle other parts of the Hudson. The Hudson River Whitewater Derby, one of the most popular whitewater racing events in the northeast, takes place annually between North River and Riparius. The many spectators and paddlers in all types of craft give the event a carnival atmosphere.

The Champlain Canal carries commercial and recreational craft between Lake Champlain and Fort Edward on the Hudson River. The canal continues down the Hudson from Fort Edward, dropping through a series of locks and flatwater sections to the Port of Albany. Along the way, the river passes the site of the Battle of Saratoga where, in 1777, British general "Gentleman Johnny" Burgoyne surrendered to American general Horatio Gates. Many historians consider this the turning point of the Revolutionary War.

Oceangoing ships ride the tide upriver from New York City to Albany. From Albany to New York City the Hudson flows quietly through constantly changing urban and rural surroundings with spectacular views of the Catskill Mountains. The beauty of the surrounding countryside attracted nineteenth-century artists who formed the much admired Hudson River School. Among the most notable of these landscape painters was Frederick Edwin Church who, in 1872, built a dramatic home overlooking the river in the town of Hudson. He named the 35-room mansion Olana, which means "our castle on high." The river flows by many other historical sites, including the Schuyler House in Schuylerville, the home of Franklin D. Roosevelt at Hyde Park, and the U.S. Military Academy at West Point, as it descends to the sea at New York City.

As we view the natural beauty of the landscape it is easy to forget how we have abused the river for two centuries. It wasn't until the 1960s that a significant number of people realized that the river ecosystem was systematically being destroyed by all kinds of pollutants, ranging from raw sewage to heavy metals and other wastes, that were purposely discharged into the water by companies and communities along the banks. The first organization to mobilize against pollution was Scenic Hudson, which successfully fought off the Storm King Pumped Storage project. Many other groups followed, such as the Hudson River Sloop Clearwater, Riverkeepers, and the Hudson River Foundation for Science. Thanks to the efforts of organizations and individuals, laws are now in place to prosecute polluters.

Today, treatment plants prevent industrial wastes and sewage from reaching the river. Over the past 40 years the water has become measurably cleaner; many species of fish and shellfish have returned to their natural habitats. In spite of great improvements, some contaminants remain. PCBs, long-lasting hazardous chemicals that were discharged into the water at Fort Edward over a thirty-year period, remain buried in the sediments. Although scheduled for cleanup by a ruling under the Environmental Protection Act, it will be many years before this task can be accomplished. In addition, constant pressure for development from a burgeoning population is creating demands for new homes, more energy, and clean water. The river remains under siege.

Throughout history, river valleys have been the origins of great civilizations. To experience Manhattan is to know that one is in the heart of a great intellectual and cultural center which grew up around the mighty Hudson River. Traveling north up the river past the homes of famous Americans and the sites of famous events is to relive much of the early history of a great nation. Arriving in the upper reaches of the river, one finds a countryside with many parts that are much the same as when early settlers lived here. It is these upper waters of the Hudson and its tributaries which provide the fine river experiences to which this book is dedicated.

—Chet Harvey and Kathie Armstrong

Hudson River: Newcomb Bridge to Indian River Confluence

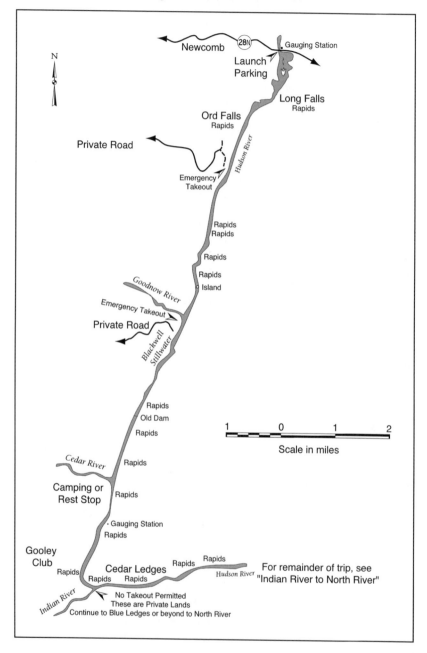

Newcomb 28N Gauging Station

Launch Parking

Long Falls
Rapids

Ord Falls
Rapids

Private Road

Emergency Takeout

Hudson River

Rapids
Rapids

Rapids

Rapids
Island

Goodnow River

Emergency Takeout

Private Road

Blackwell Stillwater

Rapids
Old Dam
Rapids

1   0   1   2
Scale in miles

Cedar River   Rapids

Camping or Rest Stop   Rapids

Gauging Station
Rapids

Gooley Club

Rapids   Rapids

Cedar Ledges   Rapids   Rapids

Rapids   Rapids   Hudson River   For remainder of trip, see "Indian River to North River"

Indian River

No Takeout Permitted
These are Private Lands
Continue to Blue Ledges or beyond to North River

Hudson River

↕ **Segment:**:	Newcomb Bridge to Indian River Confluence
☆ **County:**	Essex
↔ **Length:**	12.0 mi (19.3 km)
↘ **Drop:**	131 ft (40 m)
♦ **Difficulty:**	Class II with two Class III drops; medium level between 4.0 and 5.0 ft at North Creek gauge (see Appendix D, entries 1–4 to access water level information)
✳ **Problems:**	Remote setting; possible rapid rise in level due to large drainage area; lack of permission from Gooley Club to take out on private property at the Indian (See discussion of alternatives under "Takeout")
♠ **Maps:**	Page 14; USGS Newcomb, Dutton Mountain; DeLorme page 87
✐ **Contributor:**	Paul Lozier

Background Notes:

This description is based on notes from a series of paddling adventures from Newcomb to North River. Trips were traditionally held on Father's Day and many were run before commercial rafting began from the Indian. The usual trip began with a late afternoon meeting at Basil and Wicks Tavern on NY 28 at North Creek before driving to Newcomb. Setting up tents in the dark at the town dump elicited many bear jokes; in those days, bears were frequent visitors. The group would start downriver at 6 A.M., hoping to see early morning wildlife. Often we saw deer wading in the river to escape the black flies and otters swimming through the mist on the Blackwell Stillwater. Additional paddlers usually joined the group at the mouth of the Indian at 10 A.M. for the trip through the gorge to North River. At normal water levels the paddlers arrived at North River at approximately 3 P.M.

Records indicate that the lowest level at which these trips were run was 3.1 ft at the North Creek gauge. The highest level resulted from a storm bubble which caught the group between Newcomb and Ord Falls, recorded later that day as greater than 8 ft. The river was out of its banks at the Blue Ledges. Only half of the canoes and kayaks made it to North River. One person with a leg injury was taken out through the Goodnow Flow roads. A kayaker who dislocated his shoulder was able to hike out to Huntley Pond where some fishermen drove him to North Creek.

At least one of the trips continued 18.0 mi beyond North River to the Glen. On one occasion two kayakers from the Father's Day group made a remarkable run, leaving Newcomb at 6 A.M. with the river at 6.4 ft and arriving at North River at 10 A.M. and Hadley/Luzerne at 3 P.M.

⏚ Launch:

There are two routes to Newcomb, both on NY 28N. From the west, drive through Long Lake and travel east approximately 15.0 mi to the bridge over the Hudson at Newcomb. From North Creek, drive approximately 25.0 mi north and west to the bridge. This route is part of the Marcy–Roosevelt trail traveled by Teddy Roosevelt after McKinley's assassination. Teddy did it in a hurry by horse-drawn wagon. Some ride!

A little over 2.0 mi north of Minerva, the North Woods Club road enters on the left leading from Huntley Pond, the trailhead to the spectacular Blue Ledges in the Hudson Gorge. After another 6.0 mi, NY 28N crosses the Boreas River, which flows south into the Hudson just downstream of the railroad bridge above North River. Two miles north of the Boreas, NY 28N crosses the railroad tracks that run from North Creek to Tahawus. NY 28N turns west toward Newcomb and passes the town rest stop where there is a panorama topographic map identifying the High Peaks. This is a good place to stop and organize for the trip. Two miles farther west NY 28N crosses the Hudson.

Immediately after crossing the bridge, turn 120 degrees left onto the Town of Newcomb Land Fill Road. Park on the right after making the turn. Make sure your tires are fully off the paved road or the local safety officer will remind you of the law with a ticket. This is a relatively safe place to park since it is across the road from a contractor's house and is in full view of NY 28N.

A right-of-way between the contractor's house and NY 28N leads to the launch site at a gauge station on the riverbank downstream of the bridge. A registration book is provided.

✍ Description:

The Hudson from Newcomb to the Indian is an easy day trip with plenty of rest time. There are two Class III rapids that require attention: Long Falls and Ord

Falls. Both rapids can be scouted easily from either bank and both can be portaged.

At low water it is difficult to avoid the small cobble rocks at the launch. However, less than 20 yds downstream there is sufficient depth to clear the bottom. Here the river widens to form a small shallow lake. Downstream, take the right channel past a group of three islands. Beyond the islands the river narrows and a marsh on the right (west) bank juts to a point. Opposite the marsh is a solid rock point on the left bank. These points pinch the river, forming the entrance to Long Falls Rapids. As the flow accelerates past a small island on the right, look downstream to see a point on the left that identifies the entrance to the full flow of the rapids. Enter left of center, on the outside of a gentle right turn.

Approximately two-thirds of the way through the rapids there is a short flatwater section. Stay left and then go far left near a rock outcropping protruding from the left bank that directs the flow to the right. Paddle hard to the right to pick up the right hand passage and avoid a shallow rock strainer extending from the left bank. Follow the flow to the left below the rock strainer. Here a large marsh opens on the right.

The river is smooth for about a mile, but stay alert for the sound of Ord Falls Rapids as the river narrows. Ord starts out easy. Enter right of center and slide to center as the river bends slightly to the left. There is a prominent boulder bar on the right which directs all flow toward the left bank. Slide left of center and stay in the best-flow channels. There is a large white boulder in the bar marking the right edge of the channel as the river turns right. Remain centered in the flow and exit into calm water. Try to spin around and look upstream to appreciate the route you have just paddled.

Fifty to 75 yds up the west bank at the 1575 ft contour line is a snowmobile trail that leads back along the river to the Newcomb landfill and downstream to the Goodnow Flow area. This trail can serve as an escape route. Approximately one-third of a mile below Ord Falls signs of civilization appear on the right. There is a private road from Newcomb which also can serve as an exit if needed.

There are four sets of very mild riffles in the next mile. The second set is particularly scenic as it flows around a right turn. The fourth set has a small island which identifies the beginning of Blackwell Stillwater, a long flat section of the river which is somewhat impounded by the remnants of a boulder dam about 3.0 mi downstream. About 0.5 mi into the Blackwell Stillwater the

Goodnow River enters on the right, draining water from the Goodnow Flow. At the confluence of the Hudson and Goodnow some cabins have been built, mostly along the left bank. If time permits, a trip up the Goodnow for three-quarters of a mile will add interest to an already memorable trip. Roads at the Goodnow Flow provide an exit leading back to Newcomb. Two miles downstream from the Goodnow River is the old boulder dam with low water passage on the right. This is a good place to stop and stretch and scout the drop before continuing downriver.

To run the dam, paddle a short distance upriver to orient the boat for the drop on river right. The flow turns left after the drop and may get a bit scratchy, depending on the water level. A mile and a half farther a gentle rapids leads to the entrance of the Cedar River on the right. Just past the confluence is an open area where one can camp or rest and enjoy the river environment. A small rapids at the mouth of the Cedar prevents exploration of the river by canoe.

The Cedar enters the Hudson just 2.0 mi above the Gooley Club, a private hunting and fishing club. Three-quarters of a mile downstream of the Cedar is a mild rapid followed by a short stretch of flatwater where there is a gauging station with an elevated cable across the river. A third of a mile below the gauging station, a small rapids identifies a place to look up and right to see the Gooley Club on a bluff. Continue left around a 90-degree turn; the Indian joins the Hudson one-quarter mile down on the right.

Takeout:

Although there is a trail leading from the point of land between the Hudson and the Indian to a road, this is private land owned by the Gooley Club. Using the land or road as an access point is not permitted. Paddlers must continue 3.5 mi down the Hudson through the Gorge as far as the Blue Ledges, where there is a two-mile trail on river left to the road at Huntley Pond. Alternatively, paddlers can continue 9.5 additional miles to NY 28 at North River, a total of 13.0 mi from the Indian. Another option is to camp either at the junction of the Cedar or at the Blue Ledges, continuing on to North River the next day. See the next segment for a description of the Hudson Gorge.

Hudson River

↕ **Segment:**	Hudson Gorge: Indian River to North River	
☆ **Counties:**	Hamilton, Essex	
↔ **Length:**	14.0 mi (22.5 km)	
↘ **Drop:**	490 ft (149 m)	
◆ **Difficulty:**	Class III–IV; medium level, 3.5 to 4.5 ft at North Creek gauge (see Appendix D, entries 1–4 to access water level information); water releases from Abanakee Dam into the Indian River are scheduled regularly during the spring, summer, and fall months; for information on release schedule, call Wild Waters Outdoor Center (518-494-4984)	
✳ **Problems:**	Long rapids; remote setting	
▲ **Maps:**	Page 20; USGS Dutton Mountain, Thirteenth Lake; DeLorme pages 87, 88	
✏ **Contributor:**	Andy Beers	

⛟ Launch:

The Hudson Gorge trip begins on the Indian River. Approaching the hamlet of Indian Lake from the south, the launch on the Indian is reached by turning north from NY 28 just after it crosses Lake Abanakee. Follow the Lake Abanakee Road, a well-maintained gravel road, north for approximately 1.3 mi. Several hundred yards after passing the small dam at the outlet of the lake, look for a large town-maintained parking lot on the left. From the lot, it is an easy 50-yard carry to the put-in on the Indian.

✐ Description:

The Hudson Gorge is one of the classic Adirondack river trips, combining challenging whitewater, a true wilderness setting, and scenery straight from a Winslow Homer painting.

! Caution:

The Gorge is also a serious matter: long rapids, cold spring runoff, and lack of access in an emergency dictate that this is a place for competent paddlers only.

Hudson Gorge: Indian River to North River

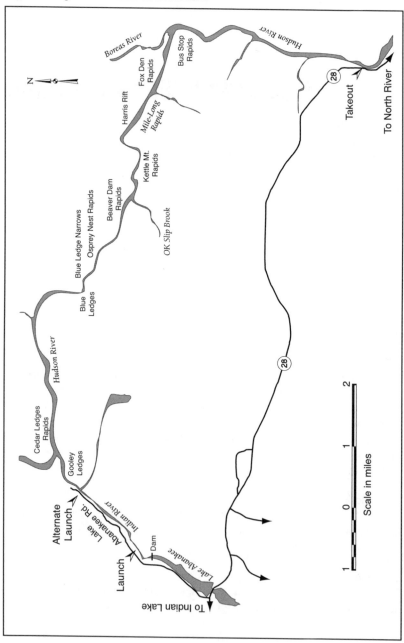

Once the Gorge is reached, there is no road access. With the exception of several lengthy trails leading to isolated parking lots, the only way out is down the river.

Before reaching the Hudson, the paddler must first navigate a difficult 2.5-mile stretch down the Indian River. The Indian typically is runnable only when water is released from the small dam at the outlet to Lake Abanakee. The Town of Indian Lake releases water for several hours on weekend mornings, and recently on some weekdays as well, during the paddling season. At levels below 4.0 ft, most paddlers will want to stay with this "bubble" for the entire trip.

!Caution:

When the release is running, the Indian is quite a ride. This relatively small river is filled bank to bank and becomes a tumultuous jumble of choppy, irregular waves. The pace is fast and furious. Long Class III and III+ rapids are the rule, with pourovers and small holes next to the banks often forcing the paddler out into the middle of the channel. When the Hudson is flowing below 4.5 ft, the Indian can be the most difficult portion of the run, particularly for open boaters. Strong self-rescue skills are required; it is difficult for others to assist a swimmer. For this reason, some boaters drive another two miles past the main parking lot before putting in, thereby avoiding the most difficult rapids on the Indian. Even at this access, the Gooley Ledges present a challenge to open boats.

Once the confluence with the Hudson is reached, the character of the rapids changes: the river is wider, the waves more regular, and although the paddler must navigate large standing waves, small ledges, and big hydraulics, there are multiple paths through each rapid. Many of the rapids are long, however, with several exceeding 0.5 mi in length. A swim from the top of one of these rapids can be a memorable event. For the first 3.0 mi, the Hudson is largely Class II, presenting the paddler with some terrific scenery. Steep wooded banks with graceful overhanging cedars rise from the river.

The fun begins when the river turns right, narrows, and begins to pick up gradient. Following the Class III entrance rapid (avoid the large hole on river left at the bottom), a large pool and the 200-foot high Blue Ledges cliff face signal the beginning of the Narrows. Paddlers often collect in an eddy on river right that is formed by a trailer-size boulder;an excellent surfing wave forms here. After exiting this eddy, the paddler enters a 200-yard Class IV rapid. The top of this rapid can be paddled anywhere. However, roughly two-thirds into it, the paddler must avoid a large hydraulic on river left. The tail end of the Narrows features a large but friendly wave train.

After several hundred yards of Class II, the paddler reaches Surprise Rapid, a short 40-yard Class IV that ends in a very large pool. From here, the Hudson provides roughly 3.0 mi of challenging but fun water, punctuated with a number of Class III rapids that provide endless opportunities for practice and play.

A stream flowing in from the right marks the entrance to the final major Class IV rapid, a 150-yard constricted boulder field known both as Soup Strainer and Harris Rift. At low to medium water, this rapid is generally paddled on river left, with several routes available. An easier sneak route appears on the far river right at levels above 4.5 ft. However, a large hydraulic that forms right of center—the Soup Strainer—must be avoided.

Below Harris Rift is Mile-Long Rapid, a continuous Class III that extends for 0.8 mi (but feels longer). From here, the river slowly winds down, becoming largely Class II.

After passing below the abandoned railroad bridge that marks the entrance of the Boreas River, the paddler encounters Bus Stop, a ledge rapid extending across much of the channel from river right. At levels below 5.0 ft, the ledge forms a challenging but safe surfing wave/hydraulic. Swimmers are easily collected in the large pool below.

The remaining 3.0 mi to the takeout are Class I, providing a chance to reflect on the day's events before reaching the takeout on river right, about 0.5 mi below the Barton Garnet Mine processing facility.

As indicated previously, an accurate reading of the gauge at North Creek is available by phone or Internet: see Appendix D. A hand-painted gauge also exists on one of the Route 28 bridge abutments in the hamlet of The Glen. The gauge can be viewed from the west bank of the river. The reading here is approximately six inches higher than the gauge at North Creek.

At levels below 3.8 ft, the Hudson is a Class III+ river, but remember the long rapids and remote setting! The river can still be descended at 3.0 ft, but this level is extremely scratchy, suited to those who want to explore the gorge in summer months. At 4.5 ft the Hudson Gorge becomes Class IV. Open boaters are rarely seen above 5.5 ft, but expert closed boaters routinely paddle the gorge up to 7.5 ft (and even higher). At this level, approaching 10,000 cfs, the river becomes Class IV+, with powerful currents that tend to funnel boats into very large waves and holes. Commercial rafting has become a big business on the

Hudson; dodging rafts on the Indian can be as much of a challenge as dodging rocks. However, paddlers who put in at the end of the two-hour release, and stop to play once they reach the Hudson, will soon find that they have the river all to themselves. The Gorge remains one of the great whitewater wilderness trips in the Adirondacks.

🛶 Takeout:

The Hudson Gorge takeout is located on NY 28 about 0.5 mi north of the hamlet of North River. Park well off the roadway's shoulder at the last point where the railroad tracks cross NY 28, just before the highway climbs up and to the left, away from the river.

Hudson River

↕ **Segment:**	North River to North Creek
☆ **County:**	Warren
↔ **Length:**	4.6 mi (7.4 km)
↘ **Drop:**	60 ft (18 m)
♦ **Difficulty:**	Class I and II; medium level, 4.0 to 5.0 ft at the North Creek gauge (see Appendix D, entries 1–4 to access water level information)
✳ **Problems:**	None
🔼 **Maps:**	Page 24; DOT North River, North Creek; DeLorme page 88
✍ **Contributor:**	Tom Gibbs

🛶 Launch:

From I-87 Exit 23 drive north on US 9 through Warrensburg to NY 28. Follow NY 28 23.0 mi to the State rest area at the junction of Thirteenth Lake Road and NY 28 in North River. There is adequate parking at this area for most canoe groups.

📝 Description:

This is a lovely Class I–II section of the Hudson. The river parallels NY 28 and the old abandoned railroad tracks most of the way to Barton Mines. Except for

Hudson River: North River to North Creek

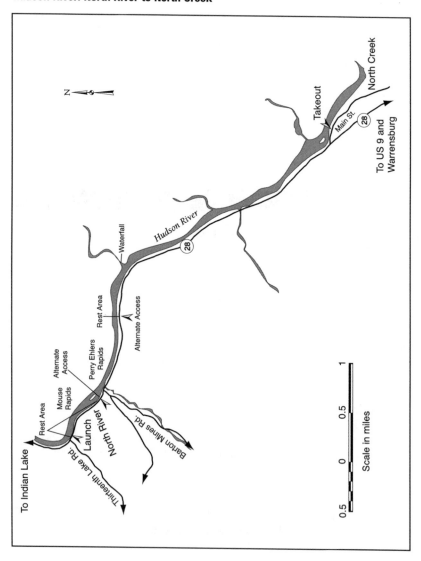

two easy Class II rapids near the put-in, the water is flat and fast moving.

Mouse Rapids is encountered immediately after launching at the State rest area and followed closely by Perry Ehlers Rapids. These are short Class II drops which, at medium to high levels, are best run slightly left of center. Both rapids can be scouted easily from the NY 28 side of the river. Perry Ehlers Rapids is the site of the slalom course for the Hudson River Whitewater Derby that has been held on the first weekend in May since 1957. Following Perry Ehlers, there are three Class I rapids spaced about 0.5 mi apart. The remainder of the run to North Creek is flatwater. Upstream of the takeout is a small island on river right which can be passed on either side.

About 3.0 mi from the launch site at North River there is a beautiful waterfall close to the Hudson in a tributary on river left. The waterfall is difficult to spot and visible only for a minute or two in the spring and fall when the leaves are off the surrounding trees. If you are persistent you can probably find the waterfall at any time of year by exploring tributaries on the left shore.

⬆ Takeout:
Leave cars in a small parking area off Main Street at the north edge of the town of North Creek. This area is just upstream of the old North Creek railroad station and about one-quarter mile north of the Copperfield Inn. Paddlers take out on river right.

Hudson River

↕ **Segment:**	North Creek to The Glen	
☆ **County:**	Warren	
↔ **Length:**	14.0 mi (22.5 km)	
↘ **Drop:**	269 ft (82 m)	
◆ **Difficulty:**	Class I, II, III+; medium level, 5.0 ft at North Creek gauge (see Appendix D, entries 1–4 to access water level information)	
✳ **Problems:**	Several long rapids; sometimes windy	
🚶 **Maps:**	Page 27; USGS North Creek; DeLorme page 88	
✍ **Contributor:**	Will Holt	

🛶 Launch:

From I-87 Exit 23 follow US 9 north through Warrensburg to NY 28. Continue 5.3 mi along NY 28 to the bridge that crosses the Hudson at The Glen. From the bridge look upriver for a view of the last rapids before the takeout. To leave a shuttle car at the currently proposed county access takeout, turn L on Glen-Athol Rd., immediately after crossing the bridge. The proposed access will be clearly marked on the L, 0.3 mi S of the bridge. Continue 11.8 mi to North Creek. There are several roads from NY 28 turning right into North Creek; the most direct route is the road to the right just past the Senior Citizens Center. This road leads down to the north end of town and intersects the main street. Turn L on Main St., and after about 100 yd turn R into a small parking area by the river, just upstream of the old North Creek RR station. It's an easy carry over the railroad tracks to the river.

✏ Description:

This segment of the Hudson River is one of the best known whitewater runs in the northeast. It is a mix of fast, smooth water and Class I, II, and III rapids of various lengths. The river flows through very attractive hilly and forested country with few signs of habitation.

The North Creek to Riparius section is the site of the annual Hudson River Whitewater Derby downriver race which has been held here in May for more than 40 years.

! Caution:

Here the Hudson is a big river, wide enough for wind to be a problem for solo boats and wide enough to make self-rescue from midstream difficult.

This segment of the river can be run at a wide range of levels. It is best between 4.0 and 6.0 ft on the North Creek gauge, but can be run a little below this (maybe as low as a scratchy 3.0 ft), and (with considerable caution) somewhat above this. At lower levels the rapids have many rocks and few passages, but the current is light. At high levels, the current is powerful and there are large holes and waves capable of sinking canoes. Open canoes increasingly take on water at levels above 5.5 ft and need frequent bailing or dumping. At 6.0 ft and above, the current is very strong and rescue or salvage is difficult. An upset at these levels may result in a long swim. At 7.0 ft the river is up among the trees on the shore and the size of waves and strength of current in the middle

Hudson River: North Creek to The Glen

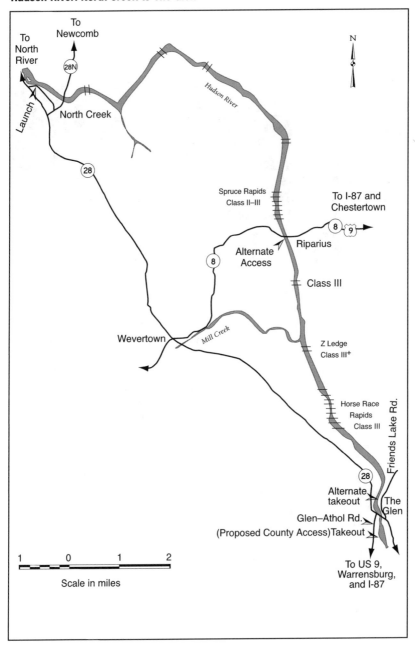

Scale in miles

Foot of Horse Race Rapids   Unidentified

are such that canoes, if out at all, should be hugging the shore. The river usually goes briefly above 7.0 ft in the early spring. It can be run at such levels only by experts in closed boats as the river is in flood and rescue is questionable.

This segment of the river can be conveniently divided into two sections, which can be run separately or in sequence. The first section, North Creek to Riparius, is about 8.0 mi; the second section, Riparius to The Glen, is about 6.0 mi. This part is somewhat more challenging, but both sections have good white-water and are very scenic. At low water many paddlers choose to run only the second section, as there is more water for maneuvering. A railroad follows the river on the right bank most of the way, but road access is available only at the start, middle, and end.

North Creek to Riparius: Starting from North Creek, the river alternates between fast smooth water and short Class II rapids. Most rapids are at bends in the river. About halfway there is a 0.3-mile long Class II–III rapid at a bend to the right. This can be identified (after the rapid begins) by an automobile-sized boulder on the right bank at the foot of the rapid. The end of this rapid is quite steep and there are only a few passages between large boulders. At lowest water the best route is right of center, angling out to center at the end. At high water a route along the left bank avoids the largest waves.

Below this spot there are two Class II–III rapids that are more challenging, but suitable routes are usually visible. About 1.0 mi above Riparius is the start of Spruce Mountain Rapid, which is about 0.8 mi long and Class III most of the way.

It is the most challenging rapid in this section. The beginning is difficult to identify from upstream since it starts steeply down at a right bend where the river is relatively narrow. There is a low island on the right side just above the start, which at low and moderate levels can be used to identify the spot. At high river levels the island may be covered, but the sound ahead will get the paddler's attention.

The main current at the start of the Spruce Mountain Rapid is in the left half of the river and waves are large at high water. A route just to the right of the main current and working to the right is best at moderate levels. At 6.0 ft and above, a route along the right bank avoids the largest waves.

After the first drop of Spruce, the next 0.5 mi is less steep and has several passages. The last 0.3 mi (the Riparius bridge comes into view) steepens and has significant holes and waves at high levels. A route along the left bank can be used at 6 ft and above to avoid the largest waves. A route along the right bank is also possible. At low and moderate levels, several passages can be found near the center. At the foot of the rapid, 0.3 mile of fast water leads to the takeout, just beyond the Riparius bridge on the right shore.

The mowed bank makes a pleasant and convenient lunch spot. In recent years a snack shop has opened near the railroad station, which has been restored and offers restrooms to travelers. There is ample parking for canoeists who wish to takeout or access the river at this point. To reach the Riparius access, drive 4.3 mi east on NY 8 from the intersection with NY 28 at Wevertown.

Riparius to The Glen: The second section, Riparius to The Glen, starts as a mix of fast smooth water and Class II rapids. At about 1.3 mi, a 0.3-mile Class III rapid occurs where the river turns slightly left and then right. Waves here can be large at high water. The main current is about midriver and the usual route is to the left of this current; more to the left as levels get higher.

! Caution:

About 1.0 mi farther there is a Class III steep drop followed by 0.5 mi of rapids. This is the most challenging part of the run and deserves considerable respect. The steep drop occurs over a river-wide ledge that is difficult to see from upstream. The location is about 0.1 mi below Mill Creek, which flows in from the right under a railroad bridge. There is an automobile-sized rock and a drop near the left shore about one hundred yards above the ledge. Anyone not familiar with this ledge should pull out well above and scout it before running.

At most levels the preferred (maybe only) route over the ledge enters at a point about one-third of the total distance from the left bank to the right shore. Take a sharp left at the top of the ledge followed by a sharp right and continue down a fast-moving chute. A boat missing this route will probably go over the ledge with a good chance of sinking and some chance of being caught in the back flow. At levels above 6.5 to 7.0 ft a route along the right shore is possible, avoiding the large waves. This drop is sometimes called the Z ledge because of the zigzag passage.

Except for a short respite immediately below the ledge, the next 0.5 mi is a continuous Class III to III+ rapid in which the river narrows and runs steeply between rocky shores. This rapid was known as The Horserace by the river drivers. Although there are several paths through the middle, there are large waves and holes at high water levels. A route along the left shore is the most conservative; at high levels canoes can pass within touching distance of the rocky cliffs on the left bank for the last, and steepest, one hundred yards. At the foot of this rapid is the Washburn Eddy, a stillwater where one can bail and collect lost equipment if necessary. The stillwater is one of the most scenic spots on the river with its view upstream of The Horserace flowing between rocky banks and evergreen trees on both shores. The railroad is close on the right shore and there is a nearby road if one should need to exit the river.

The remaining 2.5 mi below the stillwater are nearly continuous Class II rapids. About 0.5 mi into this stretch is a rocky island near the right shore. The ledge between the island and the shore offers good surfing. About 2.0 mi further downstream there is another surfing wave on river L. The trip ends near the NY 28 bridge at The Glen. Currently there is no officially designated takeout. Two possible access sites are described below.

🏠 Takeout:

Because most of the property along the Hudson at The Glen is privately owned, Warren County must contract with landowners for canoe access sites. Negotiations are currently in progress for an access on river R 0.3 mi downstream of the NY 28 bridge on Glen-Athol Rd.

If this site is not available, it is currently possible to takeout from one of two eddies on river L just upstream of the NY 28 bridge. A brushy path leads up

Hudson River: The Glen to Thurman Station

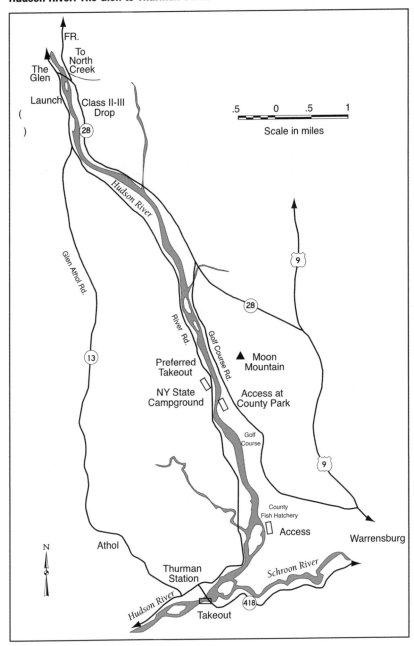

the bank to a parking area on Friends Lake Rd., which branches N from NY 28 just S of the bridge. The present owner allows public use of this property.

Paddlers must locate an appropriate takeout before launching.

Hudson River

↕ **Segment:**	The Glen to Thurman Station
☆ **County:**	Warren
↔ **Length:**	8.5 mi (13.7 km)
↘ **Drop:**	120 ft (37 m)
♦ **Difficulty:**	Class I and II with one Class II–III drop; medium level, 4.6 at the North Creek gauge (see Appendix D, entries 1–4 to access water level information)
✳ **Problems:**	Low water may require walking the canoe in some sections of the last few miles
⚲ **Maps:**	Page 31; DOT The Glen, Warrensburg; DeLorme pages 80, 88
✐ **Contributor:**	Tom Gibbs

⛟ Launch:

From I-87 Exit 23 drive north on US 9 through Warrensburg to NY 28. Follow NY 28 about 5.3 mi to the bridge which crosses the Hudson at The Glen. Because most of the property along the Hudson at The Glen is privately owned, Warren County must contract with landowners for canoe access sites. Negotiations are currently in progress for an access on river R 0.3 mi downstream of the NY 28 bridge on Glen-Athol Rd.

If this site is not available, it is currently possible to launch from a large eddy on river L just upstream of the NY 28 bridge. Leave cars in a parking area on the L side of Friends Lake Rd., a short distance from where it branches N from NY 28 just S of the bridge. A brushy path leads down the bank from the parking area to the eddy. The present owner allows public use of this property.

✐ Description:

This section of the Hudson is less hilly and more spread out than the upstream landscape. The river valley is broader and the surrounding hills are lower in elevation.

There is an informal river gauge painted on the NY 28 bridge pier which reads about six inches higher than the official gauge at North Creek. A river level of 3.5 ft on the North Creek gauge is probably a minimum for running.

If launching from the proposed county access on river R, ferry across the current to the moderately-sized island located on the L side of the river. If launching from the eddy upstream of the bridge, stay on river L and paddle down either side of the island. Several hundred yards downstream of the island a large boulder near midstream signals the approach to the Class II-III drop. The degree of difficulty of this rapid increases through its approximately 150-yard length. It terminates in a ledge which creates a powerful hydraulic starting near the right bank and extending most of the way across the river. This rapid is best scouted from the left bank. Put ashore on the left below the island and walk down the shore. The drop can also be scouted from the right on Glen Athol Road.

If passing to the right of the island, stay to the left of the large boulder and enter the rapid just left of center. Work the canoe left where there is a passage missing the hydraulic and ending in an eddy below the ledge.

For the next 4.5 mi the river is generally flat with short swiftwater sections at 0.3- to 0.5-mile intervals. At this point there is good access on river right from nearby River Road. This takeout is opposite the sheer rock face of Moon Mountain on the left, and can be identified by two houses on river left and a large boulder on river right. The boulder forms an upstream bay providing a good place to put ashore. This is Forest Preserve land, with a large camping area west of River Road. The shore is marked with yellow Forest Preserve signs. This is the preferred takeout.

The remaining 3.5 mi to the takeout at Thurman Station is flat with many shallow places at low water, so be prepared to walk the canoe occasionally. Even at medium levels, follow the channel carefully to avoid running aground.

There is another takeout at a Warren County park on river left. This park is designated a canoe access site, but it involves a 0.3-mile carry from the river to the parking lot.

Soon, golf balls on the river bottom indicate Cronin's Golf Course on the left. Along this stretch, Hickory Hill Ski Area looks down from Three Sisters Mountain to the south. At about 7.0 mi from the launch site at the Glen there is a large island where the main channel flows to the right. At medium water level it is worthwhile to take the left channel, which passes the Warren County fish hatchery where there are picnic tables, good parking, and easy access to the river. The hatchery is easily reached by car via Golf Course Road in Warrensburg. The Schroon River enters the Hudson on the left about 0.5 mi downstream of the fish hatchery. After another 0.3 mi the NY 418 bridge is just above the takeout.

🛖 Takeout:

The preferred takeout is 6.0 mi south of The Glen on River Road (see map). Park cars at the New York State campground on the west side of the road. From the river, yellow Forest Preserve signs on the right shore mark the takeout across the road from the campground.

The takeout at Thurman Station is on the right, just downstream of the NY 418 steel bridge. The shuttle back to The Glen is 8.0 mi via River Road. One can also return to The Glen by driving 8.0 mi over Bowen Hill Road and The Glen Athol Road.

Hudson River

↕ **Segment:**	Lake Luzerne to Corinth
☆ **Counties:**	Warren, Saratoga
↔ **Length:**	5.5 mi (8.9 km)
↘ **Drop:**	Negligible
◆ **Difficulty:**	Flatwater
✳ **Problems:**	None
♠ **Maps:**	Page 35; USGS Lake Luzerne, Corinth; DeLorme page 80
✍ **Contributor:**	Mark Freeman

🛖 Launch:

There is a convenient, well-maintained public access area at the confluence of the Sacandaga River and the Hudson River in the town of Hadley. This site is part of the Sacandaga River White Water Recreation Area, owned by the power company.

To reach the launch site via NY 9N, drive north from Corinth 4.7 mi, or south from I-87 Exit 21 10.0 mi, to the town of Lake Luzerne. At the first traffic light turn west on Bay Road (County Route 44). Follow Bay Road about 0.5 mi to the intersection of Bridge Street entering on the left. Turn left and drive another 0.5 mi across the bridge to Hadley. In the center of town turn left and

Hudson River: Lake Luzerne to Corinth

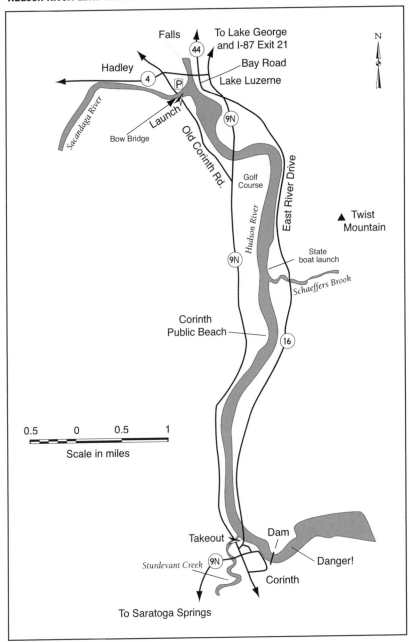

drive 0.2 mi on Old Corinth Road, ending at the historic Bow Bridge which crosses the Sacandaga at this point.

The original 1813 covered bridge burned in 1885 and was replaced by the uniquely designed Bow Bridge. Placed on the National Register in 1977, this historic structure was closed in 1983 as unsafe and slated for dismantling. Saved by the efforts of a group of preservationists, the bridge is scheduled for restoration. A nearby sign recording this history was erected in 1999 by the Town of Hadley.

A short gravel road to the left leads to a parking area with a building maintained by the Sacandaga Outdoor Center. The Outdoor Center operates a shuttle to Stewarts Dam for paddlers running this whitewater section of the Sacandaga. A ramp leads to the launch site at the confluence of the Hudson and Sacandaga Rivers.

A quarter of a mile upstream from the launch site on the Hudson are the powerful falls created as the Hudson flows through the Hadley-Luzerne gorge. These falls have claimed more lives than any other locale on the entire Hudson. Most of the fatalities are teenagers who jump into the river to float over the falls; almost every year someone drowns.

Description:

The Hudson is the largest river in New York State and the most important commercially, historically, and recreationally. There are fairly definite divisions in the river. Above the falls at Hadley-Luzerne, except for a few brief stretches, it is the province of whitewater enthusiasts.

The Hudson between Hadley-Luzerne and Fort Edward consists mostly of short stretches of wide flatwater ending in dams. Much of the region is remarkably wild, in spite of its proximity to the city of Glens Falls and surrounding farmland and suburbia.

About 1.0 mi from the launch, the river flows under NY 9N, which for the remainder of the trip closely parallels the river on the right. County Route 16 (East River Drive) parallels the left bank. One mile from the launch, the river bends sharply south and flows by the Bend in the River Golf Course and a nearby cemetery. Twist Mountain rises steeply on the left to over 1100 ft above sea level, and a short distance downstream Schaeffers Brook enters on the left. There is a New York State boat launch on the Hudson, just upstream of the mouth of the brook.

Most of the way from the golf course to the takeout in Corinth, the scenery alternates between evergreen forest and small summer camps, with an occasional year-round home. Ducks and other aquatic birds abound, and fishing is said to be good.

About 3.5 mi from the launch, the river flows past the public beach in the town of Corinth on the right. After paddling another 2.0 mi, the trip ends in Corinth at the bridge that connects NY 9N with County Route 16 (East River Drive). The takeout is just upstream of the bridge on the right.

! Caution:

There is a dam just beyond the bridge. When the bridge first comes into view, paddlers are advised to follow the right bank closely to the takeout.

Takeout:

Immediately above the bridge on river right is a paved ramp leading to a parking lot owned by the First National Bank and Corinth Post Office. Signs announce that the lot is for the exclusive use of customers, but there are two or three parking spots right at the ramp to which this does not apply, and there is ample parking in the general vicinity.

! Caution:

Below the Corinth dam the river travels for a short distance through an inaccessible gorge, leading to the International Paper Company dam. Canoeing this stretch is not considered feasible.

Hudson River

↕ **Segment:**	Corinth Dam to Spier Falls Dam
☆ **Counties:**	Warren, Saratoga
↔ **Length:**	10.0 mi (16 km) round-trip
↘ **Drop:**	Negligible
◆ **Difficulty:**	Flatwater
✳ **Problems:**	None; but avoid going too close to dams
⛰ **Maps:**	Page 38; USGS Corinth, Lake Luzerne; DeLorme page 80
✍ **Contributor:**	Mark Freeman

Hudson River: Corinth Dam to Spier Falls Dam

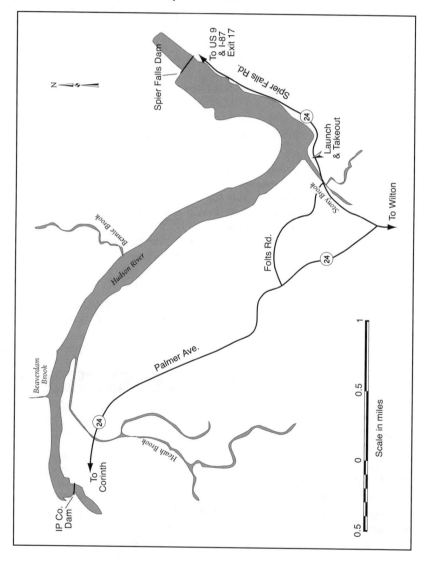

⚓ Launch:

The pool between the International Paper Company dam at Corinth and Spier Falls Dam downstream is accessible from a boat launch maintained for the benefit of the public by the power company. The launch is at a small bay where Stony Brook enters the Hudson. Access is easy and there is adequate parking.

From I-87 Exit 17 take US 9 northeast about 0.7 mi to Spier Falls Road. Turn left and drive about 4.2 mi to the launch, which is off Spier Falls Road on the right and marked with a sign.

Note: The power company maintains two launch sites, one above and one below Spier Falls Dam. The first launch you see, on Spier Falls Road about 3.0 mi from US 9, is the one below Spier Falls Dam. Continue another 1.8 mi to the correct launch for this trip. This site is on the right shore where the Hudson makes a 90-degree bend to the left.

✎ Description:

This lake-like segment of the Hudson offers the canoeist surprisingly unspoiled wilderness, not often seen this close to towns and factories. Shores are steep and mostly forested, particularly on river left. Deer, otter, beaver, and waterfowl are commonly seen. The area is popular with fishermen in slow-moving boats; large powerboats are seldom a problem.

From the launch, paddlers can start this round trip either downstream towards Spier Falls Dam, or upstream toward the International Paper Company dam as described in this segment. About 1.5 mi upstream Bennie Brook enters on river left and at 3.0 mi Beaverdam Brook enters on the same side. Except at low water, most of the brooks that enter this section of the Hudson, including Stony Brook at launch, can be paddled upstream for a short distance into the forest.

! Caution:

Water at the base of the huge International Paper Company dam may look tranquil, but a dam can be dangerous at the foot as well as at the top. For this reason, paddlers are cautioned to keep a safe distance from the foot of the dam.

After the turnaround, Heath Brook enters on river right, about 1.0 mi below the dam. From here, it is about 2.5 mi to the launch site and the completion of the upstream leg of the trip.

The downstream leg takes the paddler about 1.5 mi toward the top of Spier Falls Dam.

! Caution:

This dam also is dangerous if approached too closely. The return trip upstream is 1.5 mi to the takeout.

🛖 Takeout:

The takeout is at the launch site where the trip began.

Hudson River

↕ **Segment:**	Spier Falls Dam to Sherman Island Dam
☆ **Counties:**	Warren, Saratoga
↔ **Length:**	7.0 mi (11.3 km) round-trip
↘ **Drop:**	Negligible
♦ **Difficulty:**	Flatwater
✳ **Problems:**	None; but avoid going too close to dams
🛉 **Maps:**	Page 41; USG Saratoga, Schuylerville, Glens Falls; DeLorme page 80
✍ **Contributor:**	Mark Freeman

🛶 Launch:

The pool between Spier Falls Dam in the town of Moreau and Sherman Island Dam is accessible from a boat launch maintained for the benefit of the public by the power company. From I-87 Exit 17 drive northeast on US 9 about 0.7 mi and turn left on Spier Falls Road. Follow Spier Falls Road west about 3.0 mi to the boat launch.

✎ Description:

This is a round-trip starting and ending more than 0.5 mi below Spier Falls Dam. The turnaround point is somewhat less than 3.0 mi downstream of the launch site, at a safe distance above the Sherman Island Dam.

Hudson River: Spier Falls Dam to Sherman Island Dam

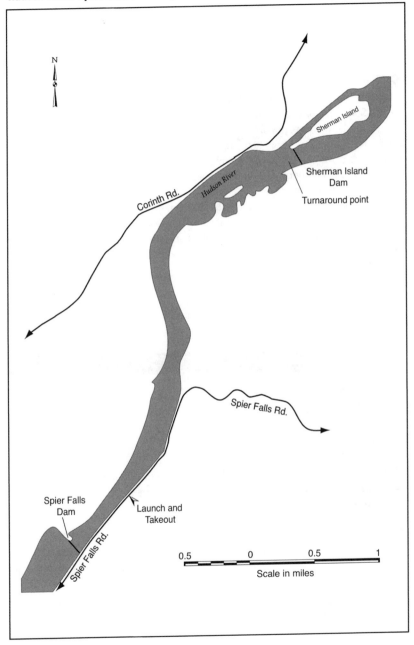

! Caution:

It is dangerous to approach any dam too closely, either from above or from below. Stay clear of both dams.

From launch it is possible to paddle upstream 0.5 mi to a point well below Spier Falls Dam. The shores here are steep and for the most part, heavily forested. After returning to the launch point, continue downstream almost 3.0 mi to within sight of the Sherman Island Dam and power plant. Keep a safe distance above the lip of the dam.

On both sides, there are alternate flat shores and steep wooded areas; at the turnaround point there are low marshy islands and small coves on river right. On the opposite side, just above the dam, Corinth Road runs close to the river and the shore is steep and wooded with several cottages. There is no legal access from Corinth Road.

☖ Takeout:

Paddlers must return to the launch site for takeout.

Hudson River

↕ **Segment:**	Sherman Island to Big Boom Road	
☆ **Counties:**	Warren, Saratoga	
↔ **Length:**	6.0 mi (9.7 km) round-trip	
↘ **Drop:**	Negligible	
♦ **Difficulty:**	Flatwater	
✳ **Problems:**	Large waves if windy; motor boats in season	
♟ **Maps:**	Page 44; USGS Glens Falls; DeLorme pages 80, 81	
✍ **Contributor:**	Mark Freeman	

☵ Launch:

Take I-87 to Exit 18; drive east on Main Street about 0.1 mi and turn right on Big Boom Road in West Glens Falls. Follow Big Boom Road south about 2.6 mi to the end. A park with recreational facilities and a boat launch provides ample parking. The park is located on the north shore of the Hudson, just downstream of the I-87 bridge, and can be seen from the northbound lanes.

Description:

As you paddle upstream from the launch, the north (right) shore is dotted with seasonal cottages. On the south shore, close to the I-87 bridge, is a cluster of houses that extends about a half mile to an interesting bay on river left. Take time to explore the bay. For the remainder of the trip the south side remains wild and uninhabited.

The river widens considerably about 1.7 mi upstream of the launch; this area can become very windy. This is a popular area for powerboats, so be prepared to deal with both wind and boat wakes.

About 2.5 mi upstream from the launch site is the Hudson Point Preserve on the north shore. This nature preserve, a property of The Open Space Institute, is a lovely place to stop for lunch. The Preserve has 2.0 mi of hiking trails as well as a boardwalk leading through a wetland. (The Preserve can also be reached by driving 1.5 mi west on Corinth Road from I–87 Exit 18 and turning left through the Hudson Point subdivision.)

About 3.0 mi from launch the paddler reaches the turnaround point at the lower end of Sherman Island; the Sherman Island Power Plant is on river right. The Sherman Island dam is within sight at the far end of the island, beyond an uncanoeable rock garden.

Takeout:

Return to the launch site.

Hudson River

↕ **Segment:**	Big Boom Road to Feeder Dam	
☆ **Counties:**	Warren, Saratoga	
↔ **Length:**	3.0 mi (4.8 km) one way, or 6.0 mi (9.6 km) round-trip	
↘ **Drop:**	Negligible	
◆ **Difficulty:**	Flatwater	
✳ **Problems:**	None	
♠ **Maps:**	Page 44; USGS Glens Falls; DeLorme page 81	
✑ **Contributors:**	Mark Freeman, James Young	

Hudson River: Sherman Island to Feeder Dam

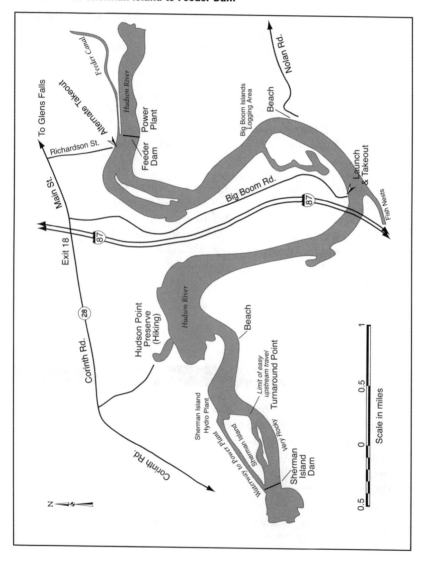

🦫 Launch:

Take I-87 Exit 18 and drive east on Main Street about 0.1 mi, then turn right on Big Boom Road. Follow Big Boom Road south about 2.6 mi to its end where there is a pleasant park with recreational facilities and a boat launch with plenty of parking. This launch site is also used for the upstream round-trip described in the Sherman Island to Big Boom Road segment.

✐ Description:

Though not far from the urban scene, this trip provides the attractive river scenery and diverse wildlife experienced by wilderness enthusiasts in more remote places. In addition, the river passes through an area rich in history.

Three similar names are attached to this area: Big Bay, Big Bend, and Big Boom. The first two describe geographical features. The river makes a huge bend from south-southeast to northwest, creating a very large backwater just upstream from the bend. The Big Boom, however, was a man-made feature. In the log-driving days from the 1850s into the twentieth century, a huge log boom was chained across the river. The many logging companies upstream would brand their logs before sending them downriver where they were held by the big boom. Here they were sorted by brand, like cattle in the old West, and guided to the mills. The remains of the big boom are clearly visible in a series of square man-made islands that extend across the river about one mile downstream of the launch. Opposite the square islands an attractive stream enters on the left, inviting the paddler to take time out for a 1.0-mile round-trip exploration.

The trip past the big-boom islands is easy paddling and the surroundings are pleasant, with low shores, few buildings, and only occasional glimpses of the tall buildings in Glens Falls. Fish and waterfowl are common, and a sharp-eyed paddler may glimpse an otter or beaver.

After about 3.0 mi the river bends to the east and approaches the Feeder Dam. This dam was built to divert water from the Hudson to the Champlain Canal (see Champlain Canal Introduction). There is a power plant on the right bank, not far from the Feeder Dam. The conservative approach to the Feeder Dam is to stay to the left of a series of low islands which lie near the left bank as the river starts its bend. A takeout is immediately left, above the Feeder Dam.

The trip can end here if a shuttle car has been left, or the paddler can return to the launch at Big Boom Road. The current is slight and presents no problem for paddling back upstream. Another option is to carry around the

Feeder Dam and launch immediately into the Feeder Canal. (See Glens Falls Feeder Canal, page 192.)

🛖 Takeout:

To reach the takeout at the Feeder Dam from I-87 Exit 18, travel east on Main Street 0.6 mi and turn right on Richardson Street. Continue 0.6 mi to the river. There is parking for one or two cars. The takeout is a few dozen feet upstream from the dam.

Hudson River

↕ **Segment:**	Fort Edward to Fort Miller
☆ **Counties:**	Washington, Saratoga
↔ **Length:**	5.5 mi (8.8 km); 6.5 mi (10.5 km) (depending on takeout point)
↘ **Drop:**	Negligible
♦ **Difficulty:**	Flatwater
✳ **Problems:**	Occasional dredging activities; dam
🛖 **Maps:**	Page 48; USGS Hudson Falls, Fort Miller; DeLorme page 81
✍ **Contributors:**	Mark Freeman; revised by Will Holt

From Fort Edward to the Federal Dam at Troy, the Hudson is a part of the Champlain Canal and carries light commercial traffic and pleasure boats. This stretch is easy, pleasant traveling, and brings a sense of history as one paddles through or carries around the locks. From Troy to the Atlantic the river is tidewater and carries ocean-going ships.

Note: Most of the 6.0 mi from the US 9 bridge at Glens Falls to Fort Edward is canoeable, but not recommended because of shallow rapids and heavy industry along the banks.

🛖 Launch:

The best launch site is on Rogers Island in Fort Edward on the upstream side of NY 197. Here NY 197 crosses the Hudson via Rogers Island and two bridges.

From I-87 Exit 17, drive 1.2 mi north on US 9, then right 4.3 mi on NY 197 to the first bridge. After crossing the bridge, turn left on Bradley Avenue to the boat launch. From US 4 drive west over the NY 197 bridge from Fort Edward to Rogers Island and turn right on Bradley Avenue to the boat launch.

! Caution:

During the spring runoff the current south of Fort Edward may be fast; canoeists must be prepared to move the boat from side to side to avoid obstacles. The only other problem occurs when the river is being dredged to deepen the channel. This is done every few years in the spring. The dredging rig and its accompanying pipes on floats can block most of the river. Since the current can be strong, paddlers must plan ahead to pass safely around the dredge.

The EPA decision to remove PCB sediments from the Hudson will result in increased dredging activity starting about 2005. See Appendix G for information on PCB dredging and phone contacts.

✐ Description:

For most of the year the river from Fort Edward south is deep, placid, and wide. The surroundings are mostly farmland with a few commercial installations, alternating with permanent homes and summer cottages. The few large commercial tugs and barges can be easily avoided by staying outside the buoyed channel; a strong southerly wind may be a greater nuisance.

Immediately after the launch, the river flows under the NY 197 bridge and under a railroad bridge where there are riffles and, at high water, eddies behind the piers. These are the only bridges in this segment, making the area seem relatively undeveloped even though US 4 parallels the river on the east and River Road (Route 29) follows closely on the west.

For the first 0.8 mi Rogers Island is on the paddler's left. This island was the site of an Indian encampment in precolonial times, and Fort Edward was an important military camp in both the French and Indian and Revolutionary Wars. One of the most important archaeological digs in New York is on Rogers Island.

At the foot of Rogers Island on the left is Lock 7 (518-747-4614), the entrance to the Champlain Canal. While all of the canalized parts of the river south of here are considered part of the Champlain Canal, at this point boaters headed for Lake Champlain and points north, such as Montreal, leave the Hudson River. Canoeists should keep away from the lock gate, which could

Hudson River: Fort Edward to Fort Miller

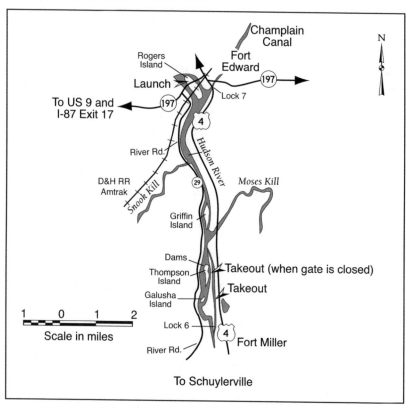

open and create currents and eddies that might swamp a small boat.

Here the river, which has been flowing generally east and then south since leaving Corinth, turns south-southwest. It continues to flow, with only minor bends, generally south to New York Harbor. For the rest of this trip, residences and farms line the banks.

About 2.0 mi from Lock 7, Snook Kill enters on river right. It is possible to paddle a short way up this stream. Griffin Island is 4.5 mi from the launch on river right. The island can be circumnavigated only at flood time. During most of the season there is a causeway which connects to the mainland enabling farmers to plant and harvest crops. Griffin Island is 0.8 mi long and about 0.3 mi at its widest.

About 1.0 mi below the head of Griffin Island, Moses Kill enters on the left. A quarter mile farther, a stone jetty with a day mark on it projects upstream from the left bank. This is the entrance to a 2.5-mile long canal, which avoids several dams and rapids and leads to Lock 6. (Lock Operator: 518-695-3751.)

! Caution:

It is essential to move left of the upstream end of the jetty in order to enter the canal. A short distance downstream, the river flows over a good-sized dam.

🏠 Takeout:

Just inside the entrance to the canal is a huge guillotine-like gate. This gate is open only during the canal operating season and closed during the off-season and during emergencies, such as floods. If this gate is closed, boats can be taken out on the left up a steep slope over protective riprap. There is good parking at the top. When the gate is open paddlers can continue about 1.6 mi farther to an easier takeout on the canal just opposite a rest area on US 4. Both takeouts are on the west side of US 4; the first is 5.7 mi south of the traffic light in Fort Edward (at the intersection of US 4 and NY 197); the second is 1.6 miles farther. There is no good takeout at Lock 6.

Hudson River

↕ **Segment:**	Fort Miller to Stillwater	
☆ **Counties:**	Washington, Saratoga, and Rensselaer	
↔ **Length:**	19.0 mi (30.6 km)	
↘ **Drop:**	25 ft (8 m), all at locks	
◆ **Difficulty:**	Flatwater	
✳ **Problems:**	Occasional dredging activities; dams to avoid	
♠ **Maps:**	Page 51; DOT Fort Miller, Schuylerville, Schaghticoke, Mechanicville; DeLorme pages 81, 67	
✏ **Contributors:**	Mark Freeman, Warren Broderick	

Note: The EPA decision to remove PCB sediments from the Hudson will result in dredging starting about 2005. See Appendix G for information on PCB dredging and phone contacts.

⚓ Launch:

Launch at the takeout point for the Fort Edward to Fort Miller segment, in the canal above Lock 6, at the highway rest area on US 4. (See page 49.)

✐ Description:

Paddlers will navigate Locks 6 (518-695-3751), 5 (518-695-3919), and probably 4 (518-664-5261) depending on the chosen takeout. This stretch is similar to the adjacent segments; the river runs wide, deep, and placid. The banks are farmland dotted with summer cottages interspersed with year-round residences. There is very little commercial development, even though there are several large cities less than an hour's drive away.

Paddlers should expect to see canal boats in the channel between the buoys that mark the Champlain Canal. Every few years, dredging operations occur, usually in the spring, and canoeists may encounter difficulty in passing the dredging rigs, which sometimes extend nearly the width of the river. Currents can be strong as the river sluices between the rig and the shore and paddlers must be prepared to maneuver around the dredging apparatus.

Paddlers should plan to "lock through." This procedure is often much safer than carrying around a lock. Generally speaking, lock operators are happy to provide this service to all boaters, between the hours of 7:00 A.M. and 10:00 P.M., during the canal operating season, usually from early May until mid-November. The turbulence to be encountered during the locking procedure is not excessive. There are few restrictions: each person must be wearing an approved personal flotation device or have one close at hand and one paddler must hold a mooring rope and keep the boat close to a lock wall while the water level is raised or lowered. Lock operators appreciate being notified in advance of an expected time of arrival, and they will pass the word to their colleagues along the route. Permits are not required for nonmotorized boats.

Note: Although it is theoretically possible and technically legal to canoe the Hudson outside of the navigation season, it is strongly discouraged by the state because it is unsafe. During this portion of the year the water level is drawn

Hudson River: Fort Miller to Stillwater

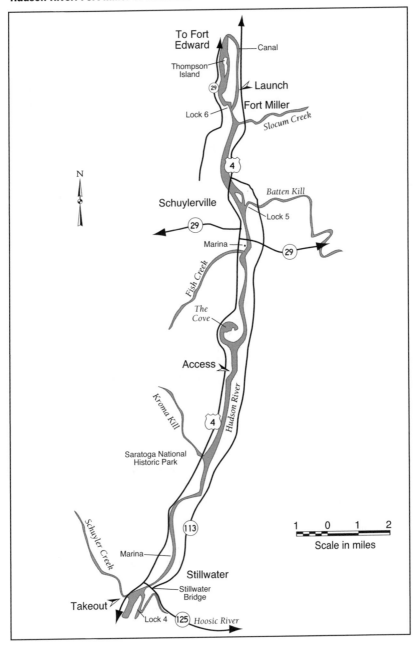

To Fort Edward

Canal

Thompson Island

29

Launch

Lock 6

Fort Miller

Slocum Creek

4

Batten Kill

Schuylerville

Lock 5

29

Marina

29

Fish Creek

The Cove

Access

Hudson River

4

Kroma Kill

Saratoga National Historic Park

N

113

Schuyler Creek

Marina

Stillwater

Stillwater Bridge

Takeout

Lock 4

125

Hoosic River

1   0   1   2
Scale in miles

down, exposing some rocks and rapids and creating strong currents near dams and hydroelectric plants. Finally, launch and takeout sites for portaging around locks may be nonexistent, difficult, and/or dangerous.

Just after launching, the route passes through Lock 6. It is advisable to notify the lockkeeper before launching.

Slocum Creek enters on the left about 0.6 mi downstream of the lock. US 4 follows the river closely on the east side for 2.5 mi before crossing to the west side at Northumberland. From here to the takeout, US 4 follows the Hudson on the west side, and County Route 113 runs near the river on the east side. County Route 113 in Washington County becomes County Route 120 in Rensselaer County.

Lock 5 and the dam above it are about 1.3 mi downstream of the US 4 bridge. Paddlers should move toward the right bank well upstream of the dam. The entrance to the short canal which leads to Lock 5 is at the extreme right, and not difficult to find provided canoeists stay within the buoys and keep to the far right side of the river well above the dam. Don't confuse a small factory canal on the left side of the river with the barge canal.

This is historic country. The improvised bridge over which General Burgoyne led his British troops across the Hudson to the place that became Saratoga Battlefield was located close to the site of Lock 5, in Schuylerville. For several miles downstream, the paddler passes the Saratoga Battlefield on river right, the site of possibly the most important battle in the history of this country. Occasionally the tall monument that marks the spot of Burgoyne's surrender is visible.

Just below Lock 5 the Batten Kill enters on the left; NY 29 crosses the Hudson at an island in Schuylerville, 1.0 mi below the lock. The buoyed channel of the Champlain Canal passes east of the island, but canoes can pass easily on the west side. There is a marina just below the bridge on river right, and 1.0 mi farther downstream is another fair-sized island.

A private boat launch site and aircraft landing strip are located on river right, about 6.5 mi downstream of Lock 6. Two miles farther is the large river backwater known as The Cove. This marshy area can be explored for about a mile, to a small marina.

About 9.0 mi from Lock 6, just over half a mile below The Cove, is an unmarked access on river right with a partially paved ramp and room to park several cars. Access is from US 4 about 0.4 mi north of the River Road turnoff. Paddlers may prefer this takeout rather than the one below Lock 4 that is described below.

A mile or so past The Cove, US 4 moves farther west from the river. A secondary road called River Road connects to US 4 at this point and runs close to the Hudson near the right bank for about 2.0 mi. River Road is lined with attractive summer cottages and older permanent homes.

Here the remains of the old Champlain Canal lie west of the river for miles. About 12.0 mi downstream of Lock 6, Kroma Kill enters on river right. Paddlers can explore the stream as far as US 4, where a short uphill scramble will reveal the remains of the old canal. The US 4 entrance to the Saratoga National Historical Park is nearby.

At 13.5 mi from Lock 6, the Hudson turns southwest for about 1.5 mi and then turns back toward the south. A corner of the Washington County–Rensselaer County line is in midriver 17.0 mi below Lock 6. Here the Hudson bends gradually westward, and there is a marina on river right. The Stillwater Bridge (Route 125) is visible a short distance downstream and it is 2.0 mi to the takeout. At the first glimpse of this bridge, the paddler should move left, following the buoys, to enter the canal that leads to Lock 4. The canal entrance is the channel nearest the left end of the bridge span. To reach the takeout, canoeists must pass through the lock, ferry across the Hudson to the west bank and then paddle a short distance upstream against the current below the dam.

🏠 Takeout:

The takeout is on the west (right) side of the Hudson, 0.1 mi below the Lock 4 dam and just above the mouth of Schuyler Creek. Drive south on US 4 about 0.2 mi from the village of Stillwater to reach this access point. There is a small park and a parking area.

Hudson River

↕ Segment: Stillwater to Lansingburgh
☆ Counties: Rensselaer, Saratoga, Albany
↔ Length: 12.0 mi (19.3 km)
↘ Drop: 52 ft (16 m), all at locks
◆ Difficulty: Flatwater
✳ Problems: Dams; wind waves; commercial and other powerboat traffic
⚑ Maps: Pages 56–57; USGS Mechanicville, Troy North; DeLorme page 67
✐ Contributor: Warren Broderick

Note: The EPA decision to remove PCB sediments from the Hudson will result in dredging starting about 2005. See Appendix G for information on PCB dredging and phone contacts.

Launch:

Launch at the takeout point for the Hudson River segment, Fort Miller to Stillwater, described on page 53. This site is on the west side of the Hudson just above the mouth of Schuyler Creek, about 0.1 mi below the Lock 4 dam. Drive south on US 4 about 0.2 mi from the village of Stillwater. There is a small park and a parking area.

Description:

In this stretch of the river canoeists will navigate Lock 3 (518-664-5171), Lock 2 (518-664-4961), and Lock 1 (518-237-8566). Be sure to read the discussion of "locking through" given in the Fort Miller to Stillwater segment before embarking. Read also the note explaining why paddlers should only travel during the navigation season. (See page 50) This description applies only during the season when the locks are in operation.

The river is large and frequently used by pleasure boats, which can cause troublesome waves. In addition, headwinds from the south can be a problem. In spite of these considerations, the trip has many fascinating aspects, both historical and scenic.

About 0.5 mi below launch, the river passes Green Island on the left. The island is owned by Donovan Tree Service of Mechanicville, which will usually give permission for canoeists to land and observe the magnificent old growth oak forest, and the shale cliffs on the west side.

At about 1.5 mi from launch, the B&M railroad trestle crosses overhead, and at 1.8 mi Lock 3 appears on the east side of the river. The recently reconstructed New York State Electric & Gas Corporation (NYSEG) hydroelectric dam at Lock 3 is well marked with buoys, and paddlers should move toward the left side of the river well in advance of reaching the lock.

About 0.6 mi below Lock 3, the NY 67 (Howland Avenue) bridge connects Mechanicville on the west to the Hemstreet Park area on the east side of the river. A short distance below the bridge, on the west bank, there is a fairly good alternate access point just upstream from a large, conspicuous boulder on the paddler's left. The river is shallow outside the marked canal channel. This access is located at the north end of a public parking lot at the foot of Terminal Street. Drive here by turning east from Main Street at City Hall.

Just below is a long, low island called First and Second Island that is owned by the state. This island is frequently flooded and swampy, providing wetland habitat to a variety of wildlife. In this respect, it is quite different from Green Island upstream and Quack Island downstream which are high, with shale cliffs. The area seems quite remote.

State-owned Quack Island is 4.0 mi from launch. Choose the shallow east channel because it is away from activity in the shipping lane. In addition to steep banks and shale cliffs, Quack has an oak forest with an understory of huckleberry, blueberry, and sheep laurel. These islands are seldom visited and worth exploring.

! Caution:

Lock 2 is just downstream of Quack Island. This is the most hazardous part of the trip because the lock is between an unmarked dam on river left and the hydro plant on river right. Canoes must keep right. The opening to the lock is between two jetties and is well marked.

Between Lock 2 and Lock 1 the river is fairly straight for about 4.0 mi; the scenery is quite attractive with a feeling of remoteness. Just below Lock 2 there is an alternate access point on river right. About 3.0 mi farther, a small creek enters through a cove on the left and can be explored for a short distance. Deer Kill enters on the left about 0.4 mi downstream. Paddle up this kill for about 0.3 mi to look for birds and other wildlife.

Hudson River: Stillwater to Lansingburgh

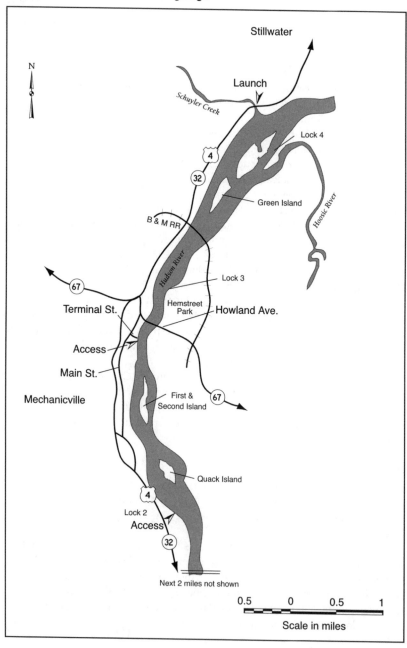

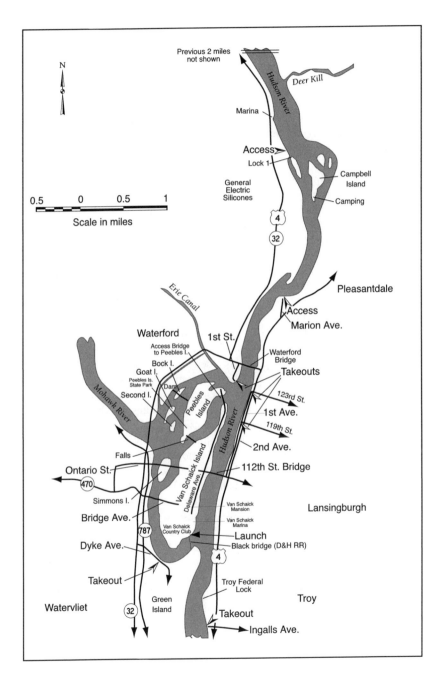

Lock 1 Marina is 0.2 mi below the mouth of Deer Kill, on the opposite (west) side of the river. Although there is no public boat launch at this marina, canoeists can patronize the snack bar. Paddlers on a long voyage might wish to use the overnight accommodations, but since marina policies change, it is wise to inquire in advance. Lock 1 is 0.4 mi downstream, also on the west side of the river. The Lock 1 dam has a superstructure that is easily visible from upstream. On river right, just upstream of the dam, there is an access point for canoes at the north side of a small park, easily accessible from Route 4. Lock 1 is about 8.0 mi from launch.

Below Lock 1 the route is separated from the main river by a long, narrow strip of land. Just below this strip, state-owned Campbell Island appears on the left with five, low, small islands north and east of it. All of these islands can be reached and explored by paddling upstream against the current. The passages between the islands are shallow but canoeable at most water levels. Most of these islands are owned by the state, and there is a dock and crude camping/picnic area near the southern tip of Campbell, on the east side. Campbell is rich in Native American history and was farmed in years past, but the open fields have given way to cottonwoods, maples, box elders, shrubs, and vines.

For the next 2.0 mi commercial and industrial development, including the General Electric silicone plant, line the west bank. On the opposite (Schaghticoke) side, steep clay banks are gradually sliding into the river, and the bank has reverted to a more natural state. This condition continues to the town of Pleasantdale, where a conical rocky hill juts into the river. There is a good access point in Pleasantdale, at the end of Marion Avenue, just before this conical landmark. It is just past the Riverbend Marina, which is private and does not cater to paddlers. This is the site of Halfmoon or Lansings Ferry, where on January 4, 1776, Colonel Henry Knox transported some of the cannon captured at Ticonderoga across the ice, on the way to Boston. After one of the cannon fell through the ice, he altered his route.

The landscape is urban as one paddles past Waterford on river right and Lansingburgh on river left. One mile from the rocky cone, the canoeist passes under the US 4 bridge, constructed on the abutments of the original 1804 bridge. Approximately 0.3 mi below this bridge, the Mohawk River and the Erie Division of the State Barge Canal enter from the right, creating turbulence and greatly increasing the volume of flow in the Hudson. Downstream from this point, powerboat traffic increases considerably.

⌂ Takeouts:

There are three good takeouts in this area. The first is at the southernmost tip of the village of Waterford where there is a state boat launch in Canal Park at the end of First Street, where the North Branch of the Mohawk joins the Hudson. On the opposite (east) side of the Hudson, there are two other takeout points, both in Lansingburgh; the better one is at the end of 123rd Street, and the other is at 119th Street. Between these two is the private Troy Motor Boat and Canoe Club. Limited on-street parking is possible at all of these points. Lansingburgh is just north of Troy on US 4, and Waterford is across the river on the same highway.

Hudson River near Lansings Ferry   Gene Baxter

🏛 Alternate Takeouts:

Canoeists who choose to continue past the three takeout points must either paddle back to one of the upstream takeouts, "lock through" to the takeout on the Hudson below the Federal Lock at Troy (phone: 518-272-6442) or paddle a short distance up the South Branch of the Mohawk River to a takeout at Dyke Avenue.

Continuing past the 119 Street takeout the paddler passes under the concrete arch of the NY 470 bridge (Ontario Street). The Van Schaick mansion, built in 1735, is visible on river right, about 0.2 mi below the bridge. The mansion served briefly as the capitol building of New York during the Revolution. Approximately 0.3 mi farther, on river right (west), is the Van Schaick Island Marina, which offers no canoe or kayak access. Just beyond the marina on the same side is an abandoned railroad bridge and the mouth of the South Branch of the Mohawk. Some turbulence may be encountered here.

Paddlers who wish to avoid the Federal Lock can paddle back upstream to 119 Street (which may be difficult) or 0.5 mi up the South Branch of the Mohawk to Dyke Avenue. To reach this point by car from Cohoes, take NY 787 north to the traffic light at the intersection where Dyke Avenue is a sharp right turn or south to the same intersection where Dyke Avenue is a shallow left turn. The takeout is about 0.2 mi on the left.

The Federal Dam and Lock at Troy are about 0.5 mi farther. The procedure for passing through this Federal Lock is similar to that at state-run locks, but somewhat more formal. The lock is open from May through November, 24 hours a day. Signaling the lock tender with an air horn is advisable, and phoning ahead is definitely recommended. Paddling near the lock, both upstream and downstream, can be hazardous due to turbulence resulting from lock-gate operation.

The takeout is at Ingalls Avenue, about a quarter of a mile below the lock on river left.

Hudson River

↕ **Segment:**	Hudson River–Mohawk River Confluence
☆ **Counties:**	Rensselaer, Saratoga, Albany
↔ **Length:**	North Branch, 1.6-2.0 mi (2.6-3.2 km); Middle Branch, 1.2-2.6 mi (1.9-4.2 km)
↘ **Drop:**	Negligible (except for the dam and lock at Ingalls Avenue takeout)
◆ **Difficulty:**	Flatwater
✳ **Problems:**	Commercial traffic; power boats
▲ **Maps:**	Page 57; USGS Mechanicville, Troy North; DeLorme page 66–67
✍ **Contributors:**	Warren Broderick; revised by Kathie Armstrong and Chet Harvey

Note: The EPA decision to remove PCB sediments from the Hudson will result in dredging starting about 2005. See Appendix G for information on PCB dredging and phone contacts.

The Mohawk empties into the Hudson in three places: the North and Middle Branches around Peebles Island, and the South Branch around the lower end of Van Schaick Island. The present route of the Erie Canal enters the Hudson via the North Branch. Each of these waterways provides an interesting canoe trip, requiring a few hours at most. All are round-trips unless the canoeists wish to enter the Erie Canal, negotiate the locks, and wind up in Buffalo some months later! These short trips offer a near wilderness environment within a few miles of three large cities.

⚓ Launch:
The launch sites for the three Mohawk branches can be any of the takeouts described for the prior Hudson River segment, Stillwater to Lansingburgh.

✎ Description:
Canoeists and kayakers can paddle up the North Branch for about 0.8 mi. From the Hudson at Waterford, the route passes under an abandoned D&H Railroad

bridge. At 0.2 mi the Erie Canal enters on the right. Another half mile brings the paddler to a low island on the right. Keep to the left channel. The Mohawk Paper Mill can be seen beyond this island, to the right. A short distance farther is a small island of solid rock in midstream. The left channel is shallow and rocky, but the right channel can be paddled another 0.2 mi to the base of the paper mill dam. This interesting dam is divided in the middle by small, rocky Bock Island. The Mohawk below the dam is shallow, rocky, and quite turbulent. This is the turnaround for the trip back to the Hudson.

The Middle Branch enters the Hudson at almost the same point as the North Branch, separated by the northeast tip of Peebles Island, the location of a historic New York State park. Open daily from 7:30 A.M. to dusk, this lovely island has hiking and interpretive trails, picnic facilities, and fascinating remains of Revolutionary War fortifications. The fortifications were built as a second line of defense in the event that British forces were able to advance down the river following the Battle of Saratoga. Boaters can access Peebles Island at a dock located on the north end across from the Waterford launch site on First Street. For more information on Peebles Island, call New York State Parks Division for Historic Preservation: 518-237-8643.

Shortly after leaving the Hudson, the route passes under another abandoned railroad bridge on the old D&H Railroad line. The bridge and the railroad bed leading to it have been converted for vehicular traffic to Peebles Island. After paddling upstream under the bridge, the route turns to the left and the abandoned Arrow Shirt bleachery appears to the right, on Peebles Island.

Continuing upstream, the surroundings become less urban, with wooded Peebles Island on the right and Van Schaick Island on the left. About 0.8 mi from the Hudson, near the southern end of Peebles Island, there is a short steep falls which creates a large downstream eddy where swimmers and fishermen enjoy the river. One of the more famous "fishers of the eddy" was Herman Melville, who grew up in Lansingburgh on the east side of the Hudson. Melville's activities in the area are described in Hershel Parker's book, *Herman Melville: A Biography*, published in 1996. Included in Parker's book are letters by Melville referring to the falls as Little Falls. Another book, *A History of Waterford*, by Sydney Hammersley, published in 1957, contains a copy of an 1844 map that designates the steep drop as Little Cohoes Falls. Even today, the surroundings are amazingly wild for an area so close to Troy, Albany, and Schenectady. The turnaround point is at the foot of the rapids.

The South branch is paddleable for a mile or so at medium or high water levels, but for far less distance at low water because of shallow, rocky ledges. The route starts at the foot of Van Schaick Island and immediately passes under the "black bridge" of the D&H Railroad. The route bends right as you paddle upstream and passes the Van Schaick Island Golf Club on the right shore. At 0.5 mi there is a fairly good access point on the left along Dyke Avenue at the Cohoes/Green Island town line. (See Alternate Takeouts for Stillwater to Lansingburgh segment.) Slightly over a mile farther the river flows under Bridge Avenue, the usual limit of this trip. At high water, strong paddlers may be able to continue another 0.3 mi to the southern tip of Simmonds Island. The channels on either side of this island are too shallow to paddle except at very high water, when currents would probably be too strong for upsteam paddling.

🏠 Takeouts:

Takeout at the chosen launch or, if paddlers decide to "lock through," below the Federal Dam and Lock at Ingalls Avenue.

Upper Hudson Tributaries

Cedar River

↕ **Segment:**	Cedar River Flow
☆ **County:**	Hamilton
↔ **Length:**	7.0 mi (11.8 km)
↘ **Drop:**	Negligible
♦ **Difficulty:**	Flatwater
✳ **Problems:**	Downed trees; beaver dams
🏕 **Maps:**	Page 64; DOT Lewey Mountain, Cedar River Flow; DeLorme page 87
✏️ **Contributor:**	Ed Miller

The Cedar River Flow is typical of many Adirondack Lakes lying in a northeast-southwest trending fault valley. It is, however, a manmade lake, having been dammed in the logging days to hold timber harvested during the winter. During

Cedar River Flow

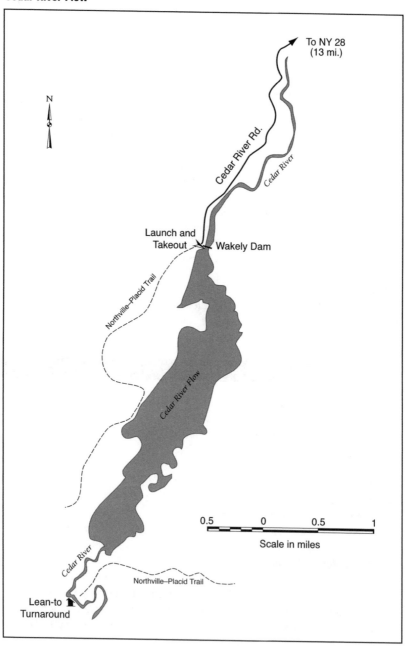

To NY 28
(13 mi.)

Cedar River Rd.

Cedar River

Launch and
Takeout

Wakely Dam

Northville–Placid Trail

N

Cedar River Flow

Cedar River

0.5   0   0.5   1

Scale in miles

Cedar River

Northville–Placid Trail

Lean-to
Turnaround

the spring runoff the logs were washed down to Glens Falls, a process accomplished by opening the gates on the dam and other "flows" in the watershed. In 1946 the old wooden structure was leaking badly and only a remnant of lake remained. The present concrete structure, Wakely Dam, replaces that earlier dam.

⚓ Launch:

The access to the Cedar River Flow is by a 15-mile dirt road that leaves NY 28 3.0 mi west of Indian Lake Village. There is a good launching and takeout area just above Wakely Dam. The suggested trip includes passage up the meandering Cedar River to a lean-to on the Northville-Placid Trail.

✐ Description:

There is a ranger station at Wakely Dam along with some campsites, picnic facilities, and a trailhead for accessing the Cedar Lakes and West Canada Lakes areas via the Northville-Placid Trail. There is no boat ramp for big motor boats, although small motors are not prohibited.

From Wakely Dam the dirt road continues over the mountain to the Moose River plains and on to Limekiln Lake and the Fulton Chain of Lakes. One of the ranger's jobs is to make sure that those continuing past the dam understand and follow the special usage rules of the area. Gould Paper Company insisted that the area remain accessible to vehicles when the land was sold to the state in the 1950s, so it does not have wilderness status.

The wind (if present) will probably be in your face as you are going southwest on the lake. The shore is completely wooded and there are several sandy beaches on the southeast side. The water is the usual tea color of most Adirondack Lakes. You will probably see loons. Be careful not to disturb them. If they give their tremolo call or appear agitated, you are too close to their nests. Back off!

You may hear bitterns; you may even see one. More common, or at least more visible, are the great blue herons, geese, mergansers, and other ducks. In the late summer swallows gather in flocks and migrate before Labor Day. Bless them (and the bats) for the mosquitoes they eat!

The entrance to Cedar River from the Flow is not in the grassy area at the head of the lake. Instead, look for it about 0.5 mi up the eastern shore. When you find the entrance, look carefully for the channel that has the most current. This is indicated by the direction that the eelgrass is streaming along the bottom.

Don't be misled by the grassy strands floating on the surface that might be affected more by wind than water. In June 1998 the main channel was a quick turn right immediately after leaving the lake. In other years, flood debris or beaver dams or both may create a new main channel. Be prepared to check out several routes.

Once in the channel there are several nice spots to stop for lunch. There is one on a bluff which is particularly attractive. Continuing up the river about a mile brings you to Cedar River lean-to. This is also a nice spot for lunch. If your legs need a stretch, you might like to explore a stretch of the Northville-Placid Trail that passes nearby. I remember finding some purple fringed orchids somewhere along this trail, probably in early July. Later there should be cardinal flowers and joe-pye weed along the river and lakeshore. Return by the same route, perhaps on the other shore to fully explore the lake.

🛖 Takeout:

Same as launch.

Upper Hudson Tributaries

Cedar River

↕ **Segment:**	Indian Lake Village to Hudson River
☆ **Counties:**	Hamilton, Essex
↔ **Length:**	13.0 mi (20.9 km)
↘ **Drop:**	255 ft (78 m)
◆ **Difficulty:**	Class I–III+; medium level, 4 to 5 ft at the Hudson River gauge at North Creek (see Appendix D, entries 1–4 to access water level information)
✳ **Problems:**	Long flatwater sections; probable strainers at some drops; land at confluence of the Hudson and Indian is private Gooley Club property; no takeout is permitted (see discussion of alternatives under Takeout)
⛰ **Maps:**	Page 69; USGS Blue Mountain Lake, Dutton Mountain; DeLorme page 87
✎ **Contributors:**	Bob and Linda Cooley

🦫 Launch:

The Cedar River launch site is in the village of Indian Lake. Going northwest on combined NY 28 and 30 turn right (north) on Pelon Road in Indian Lake village (almost directly across the street from the Central School). Turn left at the fork in 0.3 mi and go to the end of the road where there is a swimming hole and a parking lot with space for 4–6 cars. Launch at the swimming hole.

🖋 Description:

The Cedar flows through beautiful wooded land. Few people see this unspoiled wilderness as much of it is on private land inaccessible to the public. Canoeists can paddle here only by continuing downstream to a public access point.

At a medium level of 4.6 ft on the Hudson gauge at North Creek, it took 4 hours to paddle to the Indian River. At a somewhat higher level and with prior knowledge of the river, the time could be reduced to 2–3 hours. At high water (above 5.5 ft) the river will be difficult (Class IV) and all the drops must be scouted. Portages will be difficult. Below 4 ft the river will be scratchy and slow. Levels between 4 and 5 ft are ideal.

The swimming hole is the beginning of 1.7 mi of flatwater which flows in nearly a straight line. The river then enters a 0.5 mile-long gorge with a 1.5 ft entrance drop. The rest of the gorge is Class I and II. After 1.8 mi of flatwater, there is a short Class II drop of 50–100 yds. The river turns 90 degrees to the left and the outlet from Corner Pond comes in from the right. There are two sandy, treeless areas (Elm Island), followed by more flatwater and one or two small, short Class II sections.

The river then makes a hard U-turn to the right and enters a tight gorge. You can boat scout at low water, but it pays to look at this drop, especially the center constriction where the river narrows to less than 20 ft. The entrance drop of 1–2 ft is run on the left. The constriction is no challenge at 4.6 ft, but it could easily hold strainers. As the constriction opens up there is another ledge drop of 1–2 ft. At high water this gorge will have some nasty waves and holes. Scout it from the left shore.

After about a half mile of flatwater, Pine Lake outlet enters from the right. The river curves to the left, where Rock River Rapids drops about 10 ft over 150 yds. There are two ledges to run. At low water, the chutes are on the left side. Rock River enters on the left and forms a pool. The best island for swimming, lunch, or camping is here. The water is deeper on the left side of the island. After the island is a mile-long straight flatwater section that is shallow and sandy. The river crosses into Essex County, putting the paddler on Gooley Club lease. The roads on both banks are private property. A 100-yard Class II rapid is followed by another mile of flatwater after which the descent to the Hudson River begins.

The first rapid is Class II+, about 300 yds long. It empties into a big round pool, and the river goes right. You'll see a good size white pine on an island (at high water there is a second island on the right) just as you leave the pool. The far right channel is dry except at very high levels. This is Two Island Rapids. Scout this rapid (Class III+) from the right shore; logs frequently block parts of the drop. The far left channel has a 3-foot ledge, but can be run. The main center channel has a chute that hugs the island that is runnable at 4.6 ft. Stay on the right side of the chute aiming for the center of the drop at the bottom.

There are several other Class II and III rapids that can all be boat scouted. About 0.1 mi above the confluence with the Hudson is a 3-foot ledge drop (Class III+). Scout this drop from the right shore. At 4.6 ft, avoid the far left hole, and run center or right. You are then at the Hudson. There is a nice campsite on New York State land on the right shore just at the junction.

There are two or three Class II–II+ rapids on the Hudson. After passing a gauge station and cable, the river bends left and the Gooley camp is on the right. You may not take out at the Gooley camp or at the confluence with the Indian River, which is about 0.3 mi farther down stream. This is all Gooley Club lease and is posted. You must continue down the Hudson River through at least part of the Hudson Gorge to a public access point.

🛖 Takeout:

Paddlers must continue down the Hudson through the Gorge at least as far as the Blue Ledges where there is a 2.0-mile trail on river left to the road at Huntley Pond. Since this is a long carry, paddlers may choose to continue to NY 28 at North River. The distance from the Indian to North River is 13.0 mi, which means the entire trip from the put-in is a little over 26 mi. Another option is to camp overnight at the Rock River confluence, at the junction of the Cedar and Hudson, or at the Blue Ledges. See the segment describing the Hudson Gorge.

Cedar River: Indian Lake Village to Hudson River

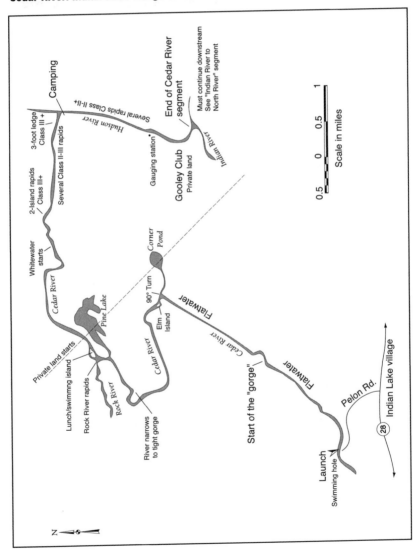

Upper Hudson Tributaries

Miami River

↕ **Segment:**	All that is navigable
☆ **County:**	Hamilton
↔ **Length:**	7.0 mi (11.3 km) round-trip (approximately 1.5 mi on Lewey Lake and 2.0 mi on Miami River)
↘ **Drop:**	Negligible
♦ **Difficulty:**	Flatwater or slight current
✳ **Problems:**	Beaver dams and occasional log jams
▲ **Maps:**	Page 71; DOT Lewey Mountain, Page Mountain; DeLorme page 87
✍ **Contributor:**	Will Holt

🚣 Launch:

The usual launching spot is the Lewey Lake state campground boat launch. There may be a day-use charge in season. The campground is on NY 30 about midway between Indian Lake village to the north and Speculator to the south. Lewey Lake joins and flows into Indian Lake.

✎ Description:

The Lewey Lake campground is at the northeast corner of the lake and the mouth of the Miami River is at the southern end. Although there are a few houses on Lewey Lake, the river is isolated and wild. The best route to the river depends on wind direction. Crossing and following the west shore of the lake is best with a northwest wind. The east shore may give some protection from a south wind, but probably not much. The mouth of the river is closer to the west shore of the lake and can easily be found in spite of the weedy surroundings. The riverbanks become higher and firmer as one enters the river.

This is an upstream-and-back trip extending to where the river becomes too shallow and steep. The Miami River is a typical meandering Adirondack stream, ranging in width from 15.0 to 30.0 ft. It wanders back and forth through an attractive valley. The banks are mostly low and soft, sometimes sandy, and sometimes, when near the sides of the valley, forested and rising well

Miami River

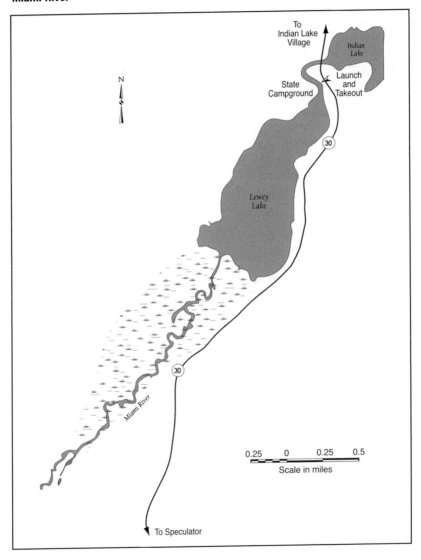

To
Indian Lake
Village

Indian
Lake

State
Campground

Launch
and
Takeout

30

Lewcy
Lake

Miami River

30

0.25   0   0.25   0.5
Scale in miles

To Speculator

above the water. The current is hardly noticeable. In places there is more than one apparent channel and one has to look closely at the flow direction of the plants and grasses growing on the bottom to find the channel with the main current.

Most of the paddleable length of the river has adequate water all summer. At low water there are occasional shoals. Usually the paddler encounters several beaver dams that require stepping out and dragging. There may also be downed trees to negotiate. Wading shoes are a prerequisite. The upstream trip ends where the river becomes too shallow and steep for paddling.

The paddler will see a variety of interesting plants, birds, and signs of animals. Common plants include pickerelweed, water lilies, and underwater grasses. One is likely to see great blue herons, red-winged blackbirds, warblers, and various species of ducks. Signs of deer, beaver, and muskrats are evident along the banks. Allow 5 or 6 hours to enjoy the tranquil environment of this trip.

⛺ Takeout:
Same as launch.

Upper Hudson Tributaries

Cheney Pond and Boreas River

↕ **Segment:**	Cheney Pond and Lester Flow	
☆ **County:**	Essex	
↔ **Length:**	6.0 to 8.5 mi (9.7–13.7 km) round-trip, depending on side trips	
↘ **Drop:**	Negligible	
◆ **Difficulty:**	Flatwater or slight current	
✳ **Problems:**	Beaver dams; a few rocks	
⚑ **Maps:**	Page 73; USGS Blue Ridge (7.5' x 15' series); DeLorme page 88	
✍ **Contributor:**	Tom Gibbs	

Cheney Pond and Lester Flow

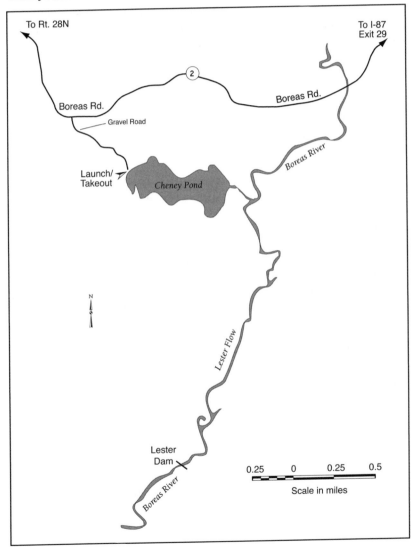

🦆 Launch:

Take I-87 to Exit 29 and drive west 13.5 mi on County Route 2 (Blue Ridge Road, which becomes Boreas Road). Turn left on a gravel road leading to the launch. There is a DEC trail marker at the turn. From North Creek take NY 28N north 22.0 mi to the junction with County Route 2; turn right and follow County Route 2 (Boreas Road) east 5.0 mi to the gravel road. Follow the gravel road south about 0.5 mi to the launch on the northwest corner of Cheney Pond. The gravel road is rutted and can be difficult in wet weather. There are a few places to park at the launch and some before the launch if you decide the road is too rough for your vehicle.

There are two points of interest on the way from I-87 to the launch. Look for the large balanced rock on the north side of Boreas Road about 6.0 mi west of Elk Lake Road. On the same side of the road is a bison ranch where one may sometimes catch a glimpse of these imposing animals.

📝 Description:

This is an interesting trip at almost any time of year. The pond and river usually retain enough water for paddling all summer. From the launch at the northwest corner, paddle east across the pond to the outlet leading to the Boreas River. A lovely sand beach borders the right side of the outlet. Take a few minutes to explore and swim in the tea-colored water, darkened by tannin from the surrounding trees.

In years of average water levels the August shoreline on Cheney Pond blooms with hundreds of lady tress orchids. Periodically beavers build dams across the outlet of the pond, raising the shoreline a foot or so and covering the sites of the flowers. If the beavers are present it may be necessary to lift canoes over the dams to access the Boreas; the population of these energetic creatures varies from year to year.

Years ago loggers built a dam on the Boreas about 2.0 mi downstream from the pond outlet, creating a large lake of which Cheney Pond was a part. The flooded area was known as Lester Flow, a name still found on many maps. Today the old Lester Dam is partially washed out. All that is left of Lester Flow is Cheney Pond and the gently flowing Boreas extending 0.5 mi upstream from the outlet and downstream to the broken dam.

Paddle downstream and climb out on the rock ledge on the east side of the dam. The reward is a spectacular view of the High Peaks.

On the return trip it is possible to paddle upstream on the Boreas about a half-mile beyond the pond outlet to a point where the stream becomes too rocky to continue. On the way back across the pond one may explore the inlet located on the south shore about midway between the launch and the outlet. Although downed trees are common, the inlet may have enough water to paddle 0.5 mi upstream.

The minimum distance from the put-in to Lester Dam and back is 6.0 mi. With excursions one can add another 2.5 mi.

⛺ Takeout:
Same as launch.

Upper Hudson Tributaries

Schroon River

↕ **Segment:**	Schroon Falls to Schroon Lake Village
☆ **County:**	Essex
↔ **Length:**	8.0 mi (12.9 km)
↘ **Drop:**	40 ft (12 m)
♦ **Difficulty:**	Class I; medium high water, usually runnable until Memorial Day, or later after a heavy rain
✳ **Problems:**	Possibility of fallen trees or strainers
♠ **Maps:**	Page 77, USGS Paradox Lake, Blue Ridge, Schroon Lake; DeLorme page 88
✍ **Contributor:**	Al Fairbanks

⛺ Launch:
Schroon Falls is located on US 9, 4.5 mi north of Schroon Lake village. Take I-87 to Exit 28 and drive 2 mi north on US 9. Parking is available on the right side of the road just north of the bridge over the Schroon River. There is good access to the river on the downstream side of the bridge.

The Alder Meadow bridge provides access for a shorter trip (4.0 mi). Drive

1.8 mi north from Schroon Lake village on US 9 to Alder Meadow Road, entering on the right. The bridge is 0.2 mi east of US 9, and river access is at the east end of the bridge. From I-87 take Exit 28, drive 0.7 mi south on US 9 and turn left on Alder Meadow Road.

Description:

This section of the Schroon passes through flat, partially wooded country. Many species of birds nest in the vegetation along the shores during the spring months and the sandy banks are home to cliff swallows.

The trip starts at Schroon Falls with nicely flowing current which gradually diminishes as the trip progresses. There is always the possibility of a strainer, but the river is generally clear. At 2.0 mi the river flows under the NY 74 bridge and passes a campground on the left bank. From here to Schroon Lake the current slows and the river takes a more meandering course.

At 4.0 mi the river flows under the Alder Meadow Road bridge, the alternate access point described above. Alder Creek enters on the left at 6.5 mi. You can paddle up the outlet and, depending on the water level, make a loop or explore farther up the creek.

At 7.0 mi the river enters Schroon Lake. There is a 1.0-mile paddle across the lake to Schroon Lake village. The paddle on the lake is pleasant, but can become windy. For those who would rather not paddle the lake, there is a marina at the northwest end which can be reached by paddling west from the river mouth.

Takeout:

The takeout at Schroon Lake village is a public boat launch site one block west of the center of town. There is a town park with an excellent public bathing beach.

Schroon River: Schroon Falls to Schroon Lake Village

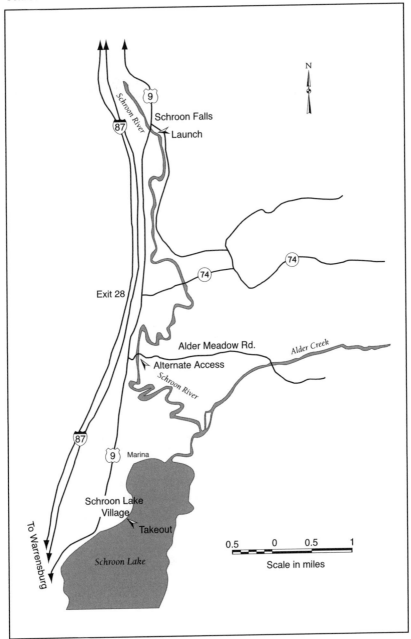

Upper Hudson Tributaries

Schroon River

↕ **Segment:**	Starbuckville to Riverbank
☆ **County:**	Warren
↔ **Length:**	6.5 mi (10.5 km)
↘ **Drop:**	110 ft (34 m)
◆ **Difficulty:**	Class II–III; medium level is 3.0–4.0 ft on Riverbank gauge (see Appendix D, entries 1 or 3 to access water level data); informal riverside gauge described in text; runnable till Memorial Day or later after a heavy rain.
✳ **Problems:**	One steep (Class III–IV) drop
♠ **Maps:**	Page 79; USGS Chestertown, Brant Lake, Bolton Landing; DeLorme page 88
✍ **Contributor:**	Al Fairbanks

⏛ Launch:

Access is via I-87 to Exit 25. Drive east 0.1 mi on NY 8 toward Brant Lake and turn left onto Schroon River Road. Proceed on Schroon River Road 0.5 mi to a one-lane bridge which crosses the river parallel to the top of a low-head dam. Access to the river is just before the bridge on the right, downstream of the dam. Parking is available for a few cars at the launch site; there is more parking at the other end of the bridge on the right.

Caution: Stay away from the low-head dam; persons caught in the hydraulic created by the flow over the dam are unlikely to escape from the recirculating current. A number of drownings have occurred at this site.

✐ Description:

This section of the Schroon is woods interspersed with private camps, especially on the upper part where there are stretches of flatwater for docks and swimming. There are many wildflowers such as trout lily, trillium, and lady slippers blooming in the spring months.

The paddle from Starbuckville to Riverbank is a challenging and exhilarat-

Schroon River: Starbuckville to Riverbank

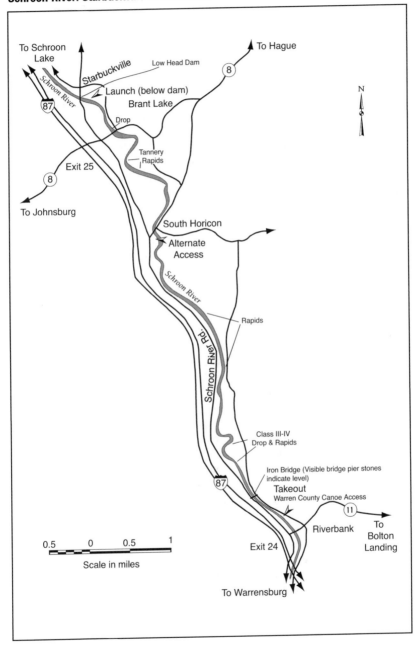

To Schroon Lake

Schroon River

87

Starbuckville

Low Head Dam

8

Launch (below dam)

Brant Lake

Drop

Tannery Rapids

Exit 25

8

To Johnsburg

To Hague

N

South Horicon

Alternate Access

Schroon River

Rapids

Schroon River Rd.

Class III-IV Drop & Rapids

Iron Bridge (Visible bridge pier stones indicate level)

Takeout

Warren County Canoe Access

87

Riverbank

11

To Bolton Landing

Exit 24

To Warrensburg

0.5   0   0.5   1

Scale in miles

ing experience. It should be attempted only by competent whitewater paddlers experienced in reading rapids. This portion of the river is generally runnable when the gate on the dam at Starbuckville is open. Water levels usually remain high enough for paddling until Memorial Day. Paddlers have found that counting the stones above water on the upstream east side of the iron bridge just above the takeout serves as an informal gauge of water levels. The greater the number of stones showing, the lower the river. Eleven or twelve stones above the river level indicate good paddling; 13 is low; 10 is high, and less than 10 is flood stage.

When launching, remember to keep boats well downstream of the base of the dam. At 0.6 mi one reaches the NY 8 bridge. Directly under the bridge is a drop with partially concealed rocks. This drop may be scouted on the drive to the launch or by getting out on river left just before the bridge and observing from the shore and the bridge. Most paddlers run the drop somewhere left of center. Just above the bridge is an island on river right. At high water it is possible to paddle a narrow section of water flowing to the right of the island, thus avoiding the rocks under the bridge.

From the bridge 1.3 mi of flatwater leads to Tannery rapids. These rapids run for about half a mile and end in a large pool. The drop is steep but straightforward, a series of big waves. After less than a mile of flatwater, the river passes under the Horicon bridge where access is available just downstream on the right.

At 3.4 mi, a long series of rapids begins. The first is short with large standing waves ending in a pool. This drop may be scouted from river right. After a short stretch, the river enters the next rapid which continues for 0.7 mi, diminishing to minor riffs at a right bend in the river. At 4.8 mi the river enters a short rapid followed by a pool and another short rapid.

At 5.3 mi the river makes a sharp bend to the right, continues flat for a short distance, and then turns left as it approaches the major rapid of the trip known as "the Flume." This rapid starts with a sharp drop, followed by a bend to the left and then a bend to the right. It should be scouted from the left after putting ashore, well upstream.

The easier route, having the least abrupt drop, is near the bank on river right. This passage requires precise maneuvering to the right just at the top of the drop and then left toward the center immediately below the drop to avoid large, partially covered rocks. The more challenging route is through a narrow, center passage between two large, nearly convergent waves formed by the water pouring over two rocks, one on each side. At medium to high levels, the location of these midstream rocks and the river below the brink of the drop cannot be seen from upstream. Paddlers must scout this passage carefully from shore.

After the drop, rapids continue for a short distance, gradually decreasing as the river flows right around a bend. There is an iron bridge at 6.1 mi. Riffs are encountered from this bridge to the takeout at 6.5 mi.

🏠 Takeout:

Take I-87 to Exit 24. Drive toward Bolton Landing a short distance to Schroon River Road, east of I-87. Turn left on Schroon River Road and drive 0.5 mi to a dirt road entering on the right. Turn right, cross the river, and turn right again at the east end of the iron bridge. Drive 0.4 mi on a gravel road along the river to the Warren County Canoe Access on the right.

Upper Hudson Tributaries

Schroon River

↕ **Segment:**	Riverbank to Warrensburg
☆ **County:**	Warren
↔ **Length:**	13.0 mi (20.9 km) to Warrensburg; 10.0 mi (16.1 km) to County Farm Bridge
↘ **Drop:**	40 ft (12 m)
♦ **Difficulty:**	Class I at medium high water; usually runnable until Memorial Day, or later after a heavy rain
✳ **Problems:**	Critical takeout point 0.2 mi upstream of dangerous rapids in Warrensburg
↟ **Maps:**	Page 82; USGS Bolton Landing, The Glen, Warrensburg; DeLorme pages 80, 88
✍ **Contributor:**	Al Fairbanks

Schroon River: Riverbank to Warrensburg

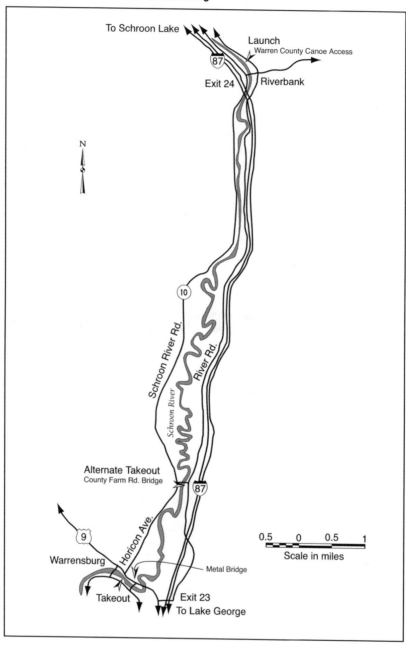

Launch:

Take I-87 to Exit 24. Turn right (east of I-87) toward Bolton Landing and drive a short distance to Schroon River Road. Turn left on Schroon River Road and drive 0.5 mi to a dirt road entering on the right. Turn right, cross the river, and turn right again at the east end of the bridge. Drive 0.4 mi on a gravel road along the river to the Warren County Canoe Access on the right.

Description:

This section of the Schroon River is wooded, with some fields and occasional camps. The water is clear with a sand bottom and banks where cliff swallows often nest. Naturalists can enjoy a leisurely paddle with opportunities to see a variety of birds and wildflowers.

The paddle starts with light riffs, followed by a short stretch of fastwater. At 0.2 mi, the river passes under the bridge at Riverbank and at 0.6 mi flows under I-87. After 1.0 mi the paddler passes a campground on the right; the river turns left and then right. At 4.8 mi, the course becomes meandering and continues in this pattern for most of the way to Warrensburg.

At 10.0 mi the river passes under the bridge at County Farm Road. This access is a good place to end the trip for those who have had enough paddling and wish to avoid the more populated area near Warrensburg. Taking out here also avoids any possibility of involvement with the dangerous whitewater just downstream of the takeout in town.

Approaching Warrensburg, the paddler passes several campgrounds. At 12.6 mi, the river flows under the US 9 bridge, where there is a slight drop. After another 0.2 mi, one passes under a second bridge. The takeout is on the left 0.2 mi downstream.

!Caution:

Concentrate on locating the takeout, because 0.2 mi downstream, the river enters very heavy whitewater with dangerous drops.

Takeout:

To end the trip in Warrensburg take I-87 to Exit 23 and turn west a short distance to US 9. Turn right on US 9, drive 0.4 mi north, and turn left across a metal bridge. Immediately after crossing the bridge turn right on River Road. The canoe access site is 0.2 mi on the right.

To takeout at the County Farm bridge, use the above directions to US 9. Follow US 9 to the first traffic light in Warrensburg and turn right on Horicon Avenue. Follow Horicon Avenue 1.8 mi north to the bridge on your right. The Warren County Canoe Access site is just downstream of the bridge on the east side (river left).

Upper Hudson Tributaries

Sacandaga River, Middle Branch

↕ **Segment:**	Christine Falls to Auger Falls	
☆ **County:**	Hamilton	
↔ **Length:**	7.0 mi (11.3 km)	
↘ **Drop:**	Approximately 550 ft (168 m)	
◆ **Difficulty:**	Class III–VI; medium water level with a gauge reading of 3.5 ft (1800 cfs) at Hope, usually runnable only in spring (see Appendix D, entries 1–4 to access water level information)	
✳ **Problems:**	Christine Falls (Class V); Austin Falls (Class V+); Auger Falls (Class VI). You must know the location of Auger Falls and where to takeout for the portage before you get on the river!	
↥ **Maps:**	Page 85; DOT Kunjamuk Creek, Wells; DeLorme pages 79, 87	
✍ **Contributor:**	Sally Dewes	

⛟ Launch:

The put-in is off NY 30 on the west side of the river 6 or 7 miles north of the junction of NY 30 and NY 8. It is marked as a place where snowplows turn around. The launch requires a short steep climb down the riverbank

✐ Description:

Since the gauge at Hope is located on the main Sacandaga, it reflects the combined flow of the middle, east, and west branches. Consequently, the gauge is not necessarily an accurate indicator of water level on the Middle Branch. However, it can help the paddler decide whether a trip to check out the river is worthwhile. The supposed rule of thumb for the Middle Branch is that roughly

Sacandaga River, Middle Branch: Christine Falls to Auger Falls

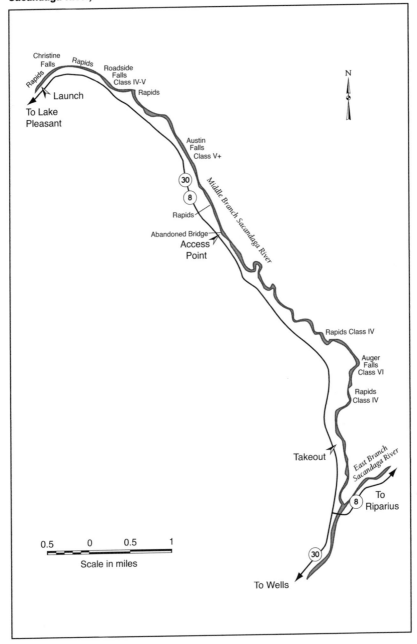

half the flow of the Hope gauge comes from the Middle Branch, except right after a rainstorm when the East Branch flashes and contributes to the flow measured at the gauge.

The Middle Branch is an exciting Class III–VI run. It starts with a few hundred yards of Class III rapids which end in a pool above a dam. You must walk around the dam; just below is Christine Falls. You may choose to run part or all of this Class V rapid. It can be scouted from the right or the left. If you decide not to run it, portage the dam and the rapid on river left.

Below the dam are more Class III–IV rapids before the river flattens out for about half a mile; here the river narrows and runs parallel to the road. The next drop is Class IV–V; we call it Roadside Falls. It is a small 10-foot waterfall that can be scouted from the left or right and portaged on river right. Although the hole below the drop may look bad, it is not a keeper. Since this spot is close to NY 30 it can be scouted before you run the river. Park on NY 30 and walk in.

Immediately after Roadside Falls is a Class IV rapid; stay right to avoid ledges on river left. The Class IV water continues for about half a mile. Watch out for wood, holes, and shallow rocks. At one point the river bends to the right and there is a rock island in the middle; be careful as there is often wood piled to the left of the island. After this exciting ride, the river temporarily flattens out for about half a mile before reaching Austin Falls.

Austin Falls can be seen from an old road that parallels river left. The falls is not one drop but a cascading series where the water moves fast and the holes are treacherous. As you approach Austin Falls, the river narrows and the rocks on river left slope up at a 45-degree angle. Make sure you don't miss the portage on river left. It is an easy portage; just hop the guardrail with your boat and walk along the road. The meat of this Class V+ rapid ends where most of the water hits a massive rock in the middle of the narrow corridor and is forced upward to create a huge impressive rooster tail! Very few people run this section. You can put in just below the rooster tail for a short stretch of Class IV fun, or a little farther down where the river calms down.

For the next mile or so there are great Class III sections of river. You can boat scout to avoid the holes, rocks, and occasional strainer, zigzagging back and forth across the river. Now the flow slows to Class I for a few hundred yards. You can takeout at an old abandoned bridge off NY 30 on river right, or continue into the lower section.

The Class VI drop at Auger Falls is located in the lower section. After the abandoned bridge there is at least a mile and a half of meandering flatwater. Things begin picking up, increasing to Class III and then Class IV. This long section of rapids, at least half a mile, leads you to Auger Falls.

! Caution:

It is imperative that you know exactly where the falls are before getting on the river, so that you don't accidentally go over them. It is highly recommended that you hike in and look carefully both at the falls and the terrain upstream of the falls so that you know where to takeout. You must get out well above Auger Falls and portage river right. There are plenty of side eddies for the takeout in the upstream area where the falls cannot yet be seen. You must takeout here. Auger Falls appears after the river takes a sharp bend to the right. If you wait until you see the horizon line, it will be too late. The water moves fast and you don't want to miss the last eddy!

Once you know where to takeout, it is easy to get your boat out of the water, but the carry around the falls is somewhat difficult. Getting back down to the river can be a Class IV–V job if there is snow or ice. Climb down the steep slope and put in below Auger Falls in the middle of some Class IV rapids. The river slows and gets progressively less steep. After a half mile or so, takeout on river right about a mile above the junction of NY 30 and NY 8.

⌂ Takeout:

There is a pullout on the east side of NY 30 about a mile above the junction of NY 30 and NY 8. Several cars may be parked there for the takeout.

Upper Hudson Tributaries

Kunjamuk River (Tributary of Sacandaga River, Middle Branch)

↕ **Segment:**   Lake Pleasant to Elm Lake
☆ **County:**   Hamilton
↔ **Length:**   10.4 mi (16.7 km) round-trip
↘ **Drop:**   Negligible
♦ **Difficulty:**   Flatwater
✳ **Problems:**   Beaver dams and sharp turns
🗻 **Maps:**   Page 89; DOT Wells, Kunjamuk Creek; DeLorme page 87
✍ **Contributor:** Norm Dibelius

🛶 Launch:

The put-in and takeout are on the Sacandaga River at Lake Pleasant in the village of Speculator. Canoe access is at the parking lot on the northeast side of NY 30 and NY 8 where the highway crosses the river. Paddle down the meandering Sacandaga for 1.5 mi (about 30 minutes at a leisurely pace) through an attractive wetland meadow to the junction of the Sacandaga and Kunjamuk Rivers. The slow moving Kunjamuk comes in from the north whereas the Sacandaga continues in an easterly direction. There is a gray house on the left side of the Sacandaga, just beyond the junction of the two rivers.

✏ Description:

The Kunjamuk has many sharp turns and a few dozen beaver dams, and is one of the prettiest flatwater rivers in the Adirondacks. The bow paddler must be able to do all or most of the steering strokes (draw, cross-draw, sweep, bow rudder, and back) in order to get around the sharp turns of the narrow river without difficulty.

Depending on the water level, some of the beaver dams may be low enough to canoe over without exiting the canoe. A few dams will be too high to run. Both paddlers will get their feet wet dragging the canoe over the higher dams.

About 3.0 mi after the put-in there is the first of two logging road bridges. The Kunjamuk Cave is near the first bridge. There is a short trail that leads to the cave, starting near the northeast corner of the bridge. There is a second

Kunjamuk River

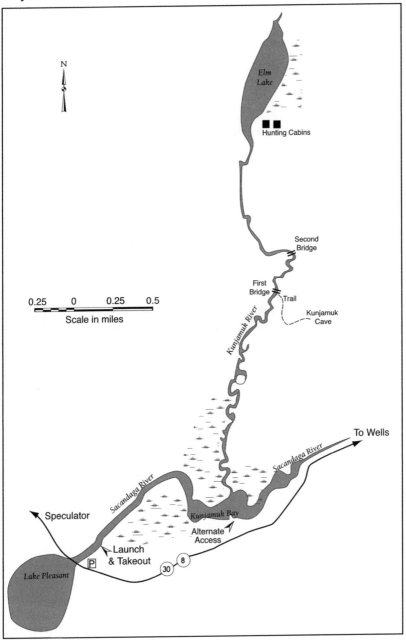

bridge about another 0.5 mi farther on. Either bridge is good for a lunch stop.

The entrance to Elm Lake is about 1.0 mi beyond the second bridge. Elm Lake is 0.7 mi across, with two hunting cabins on the shore. The total one-way distance from the put-in to the far end of Elm Lake is about 5.2 mi, 10.4 mi round-trip.

An alternate access point is on the northwest side of the highway where the highway runs close to the junction of the Sacandaga and Kunjamuk Rivers. There is a combined sign, near the parking spot on the right hand side of the road heading toward Speculator, that reads, "Adopt a Highway Program Next 10 Miles–Speculator-Lake Pleasant-Piseco Chamber of Commerce."

🛖 Takeout:
Same as launch.

Upper Hudson Tributaries

Sacandaga River, West Branch

↕ **Segment:**	Route 10 Bridge to Shaker Place
☆ **County:**	Hamilton
↔ **Length:**	8.0 mi (12.9 km)
↘ **Drop:**	Negligible
♦ **Difficulty:**	Flatwater
✳ **Problems:**	Logjams and beaver dams
♠ **Maps:**	Page 91; DOT Sherman Mountain; DeLorme page 79
✐ **Contributor:**	Ed Miller

The drive north to the West Branch of the Sacandaga River passes Nick Stoner's Golf Course and, farther north, Stoner Lakes. Stoner was a trapper in this region before it was settled. He discovered Stoner Lakes around 1800 and called them Stink Ponds in honor of the dead fish which gave a very distinct aroma to the place. That name lasted until people started to buy land for summer camps. You can imagine the difficulty of selling land on Stink Pond!

Sacandaga River, West Branch: Route 10 Bridge to Shaker Place

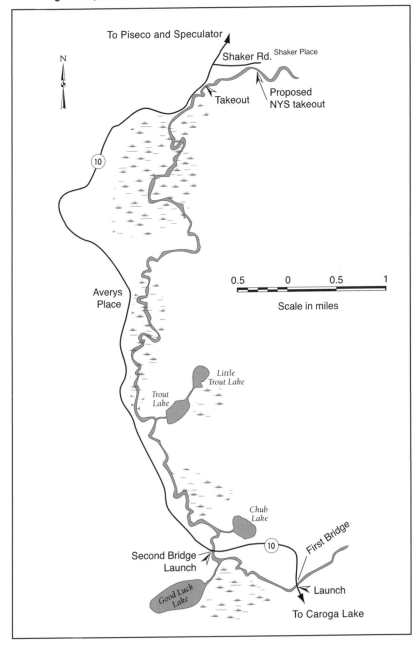

🛶 Launch:

Drive north from Caroga Lake on NY 10 approximately 9.0 mi. Just beyond the Arietta Hotel cross the first of two bridges over the West Branch. If you are willing to drag your canoe a short distance you can start the trip here. The better put-in is two miles north at the second bridge, where there is good parking on both sides and deep water for launching.

✐ Description:

This stretch of the West Branch of the Sacandaga offers some of the most beautiful flatwater paddling in the Adirondacks. The river meanders through a broad valley of fields and marshes lined by mountains. There are a variety of different paddling possibilities: round-trips of approximately 4, 6, 8, and 10 mi or a one-way trip of 8 or 9 mi. Round-trips can begin at the first or second bridge and go as far as Trout Lake or Averys and back. Distances will vary according to the number and length of side trips into Chub and Trout Lakes. The one-way route begins at the first or second bridge and ends at a steep bank where NY 10 comes close to the stream. About 0.2 mi farther is an old Civil Conservation Corp camp dating from the 1930s known as Shaker Place. At present there is a locked chain-link fence blocking Shaker Road, so canoeists can no longer use this area to exit the river.

If you choose to launch from the second bridge, an interesting side trip is to paddle upstream for about 0.5 mi to a side channel on the right leading to Good Luck Pond (another place name attributed to Nick Stoner). A fisherman's trail follows the north shore and there are a number of pleasant picnic and camping spots. Swimming is mucky, but the shores are interesting with the normal complement of wetland plants. If you continue up-river you will find beaver dams and logjams that will probably be more of a problem than the current. If you persist you can paddle to within sight of the first bridge.

Downstream from the launch at the second bridge the river is wider, but not so wide as to discourage beavers. A five-minute paddle down the meandering stream brings you to the outlet of Chub Lake entering on the right. Around the Fourth of July, rose begonias and grass pinks add their color to the boggy perimeter of this pond. Later, pickerelweed adds its blue. At high water you can paddle across the lake to a lovely picnic spot atop a high rock.

Back on the river and downstream another hour, you come to the outlet of

Trout Lake, on the right 2.0 mi below the second bridge. In June 1998 the beavers abandoned their dams on the main stream, dropping the water level so that it was very difficult to enter the lake. In other years the dams will be restored and paddling will be easier. At low water you will likely be pushing against the bottom. Bring a spare paddle just in case. In the fall of 1999 the water was so high it was possible to paddle up the outlet and across Trout Lake into Little Trout Lake. Peering down, we saw cranberry bushes with ripening berries fully a foot under water. Colonies of the insectivorous pitcher plant grew among the other bog vegetation. A pair of sleek northern harriers circled and swooped close to the surface of the pond searching for prey.

For those making a round-trip, the paddle back up river to the launch should go quickly as the current is slow and wind is rarely a factor. Strong paddlers may wish to go 2.0 mi further downstream to Averys before paddling back

Trout Lake, Sacandaga River, West Branch   Chet Harvey

to the car. Averys was a famous hunting camp in the old days and some say it was a busy place during prohibition. Until recently it was a restaurant and bar catering to the summer, hunting, and snowmobiling crowds, but also welcoming cross-country skiers. In September of 1999 the building looked cared for, but there was a closed notice nailed across the door.

Paddlers who choose the delightful 8.0-mile one-way trip from the second bridge will continue past Averys another 3.6 mi. Below Averys the river moves east away from NY 10 to pass by the base of Pine Mountain. Beyond this lovely wooded area, marshland reasserts itself and the river continues its meandering course to the takeout.

🏠 Takeout:

Depending on the trip you choose, the takeout will be either at the launch site or at a steep bank on river left where the stream comes close to NY 10. There is a rough trail up the bank where others have lifted their canoes to the road. A few cars can be parked beside the road in a narrow pullout area. The cars can be seen easily from the river. By car it is 6.0 mi on NY 10 from the second bridge to the takeout.

As of 2005 New York State is proposing a new canoe access. About 0.25 mi beyond the steep takeout described above, a dirt road leads 0.4 mi down to the river. This area is known as Shaker Place. In recent years the road has been blocked by a chain fence. From the river this spot is 0.5 mi farther downstream on the left. If the state opens the road and constructs a new canoe access, this takeout would be easier and more convenient than the steep banks by NY 10.

Upper Hudson Tributaries

Sacandaga River, West Branch

↕ **Segment:**	Whitehouse to Pumpkin Hollow
☆ **County:**	Hamilton
↔ **Length:**	8.0 mi (12.9 km) from Whitehouse to junction with the Main Branch; 10.0 mi (16.1 km) from Whitehouse to Pumpkin Hollow
↘ **Drop:**	341 ft (104 m) to junction; 406 ft (124 m) to Pumpkin Hollow
◆ **Difficulty:**	Class II to III, but may be Class IV when the Hope gauge reads higher than 5.5 ft flatwater; gauge is located approximately 1.5 mi downstream of the junction so it reports the total flow of the main Sacandaga, including the West Branch; West Branch is usually runnable above 3.5 ft on the gauge (see Appendix D, entries 1–4 to access water level at Hope gauge)
✳ **Problems:**	Continuous rapids; long stretches with small eddies; many large, irregular waves at high water levels; may have scratchy sections at low water levels
⚑ **Maps:**	Page 97; USGS Three Ponds Mountain 7.5' series; DeLorme page 79

✍ **Contributor:** Charles Beach

⛵ Launch:

Take NY 30 to the town of Wells and turn west over the bridge below the Lake Algonquin dam. Continue about 0.5 mi, then turn left onto West River Road. It is about 9.0 mi from Wells to the launch site at Whitehouse, near the end of West River Road.

! Caution:

About 2.0 mi out of Wells, West River Road comes close to the river and is joined by Blackbridge Road entering from a bridge on the left. Stop and scout the river from the bridge. These rapids are among the largest on the river. If the water appears too turbulent, don't attempt the run.

At 4.0 mi the road again comes close to the river and crosses a bridge over the mouth of Jimmy Creek. This is an alternative access site and a scenic spot for lunch. Take a look at the river for characteristics which will enable you to recognize the lunch spot from the river.

Four miles beyond Jimmy Creek is the launch site at Whitehouse. Here the road is separated from the water by about 20 ft of brush and tall grass. The river is flat but fast flowing as it hurries to the start of the rapids some 300 yd downstream. No rapids can be seen upstream of Whitehouse. There is no defined parking area, so cars must be parked along the shoulder of the dirt road.

The last 1.8 mi of the gravel road to Whitehouse goes through New York State land and may be blocked to vehicular traffic during winter and spring, into May. Determined paddlers can carry canoes and gear 0.3 mi beyond the blockade to a low spot in the dirt road, and then 0.1 mi down to the river. This launch point is about 1.4 mi downriver from Whitehouse.

✐ Description:

Whitehouse was once a community of camps. An old cemetery, some open areas, and a couple of chimneys are all that remain.

The West Branch is one of the most isolated and beautiful whitewater runs in New York. Throughout the trip, high hills and wild forest bound the river valley, especially upstream of Blackbridge. An occasional tributary pours over a falls to enter the river. Patches of snow can be seen under the trees along the riverbanks well into May.

Except for one short, calm stretch at about 0.5 mi, the river is continuous Class II, III, and III+ whitewater from the initial drop to the takeouts at the junction with the main Sacandaga and at Pumpkin Hollow.

At Whitehouse the boats are carried thorough the brush to launch in the flatwater above the rapids. About 20 ft offshore is a rounded rock which serves as a gauge of the water level. If the rock is covered, the river level is near the practical limit for open canoes. At average water levels the rock forms an eddy where boats can wait until the group is ready to start downriver.

A few hundred feet below the launch the main flow of the river is deflected to the right by exposed rocks extending from the left bank. Most of the water flows over a short steep drop on river right with large waves at the bottom. By staying on the left edge of the drop the paddler can avoid the biggest waves and pull left into an eddy below the rocks.

Sacandaga River, West Branch: Whitehouse to Pumpkin Hollow

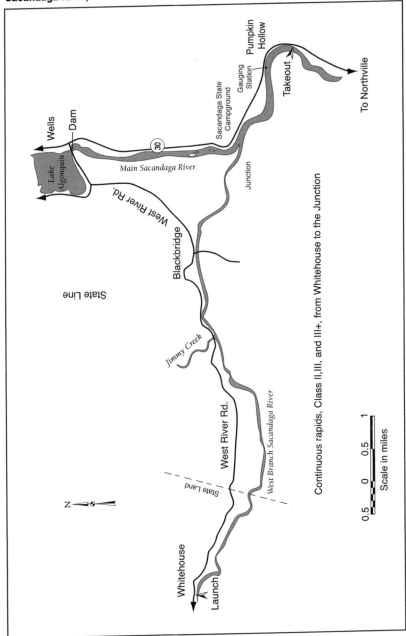

A stony zigzag course brings one to a short calm area in 0.3 mi. Enjoy the beauty of the pool and the woods because you'll be concentrating on the antics of the river for the rest of the trip!

At about 2.0 mi an island appears on the right and the river spreads out. Keep to the left of the island and gradually work from right to left through the shallow rock garden.

After 4.2 mi of continuous whitewater, most paddlers are ready for a lunch break at Jimmy Creek. The current is swift here and paddlers should prepare early to catch the eddy on the left bank just upstream of the creek mouth. A small beach provides a comfortable place to eat and enjoy the scenery. At Jimmy Creek the river passes over the remnants of an old log dam.

The 1.6 mi of rapids between Jimmy Creek and Blackbridge are the most difficult of the run; the first section can be scouted from the road. The difficult passage beneath Blackbridge must be approached with caution and run carefully, according to the route chosen when scouting from the bridge on the way to the launch.

The junction with the main Sacandaga is reached after paddling about 2.2 mi of continuous Class II rapids below Blackbridge.

Paddlers who continue 2.0 mi beyond the junction down the main Sacandaga to the alternate takeout at Pumpkin Hollow will experience additional Class II rapids. (See description under Wells to Hope, page 101.)

⛺ Takeout:

The first takeout is at the State campground, opposite the confluence of the West Branch and the Main Sacandaga. The campground is on the river side of NY 30, about 12.5 mi north of Northville, and 2.5 mi south of Wells. Car access is via the campground road leading from NY 30. Early in the season the campground may be closed, but there is room outside the gate for parking. Boaters must ferry across the main Sacandaga from the confluence to reach the campground on the east bank. Boats must be portaged along the campground road if the gates are closed.

Road access to the takeout at Pumpkin Hollow is a small parking area on NY 30, 10.0 mi north of the bridge to Northville. This pullout is next to the river, about 0.8 mi downstream of the gauging station. From the river you will see the small gauging station house on river left. Less than a mile downstream there is a parking area on NY 30. Several fishing camps are located here and there is a small eddy where boats may be lifted out one at a time. Since the current is swift and the eddy hard to spot, it is wise for first time paddlers to walk down to the shore from the parking area to find landmarks that can be identified from the river. If the camps are occupied, ask permission to drive vehicles down the dirt road in order to load the boats.

Upper Hudson Tributaries

Fall Stream (Tributary of Sacandaga River, West Branch)

↕ **Segment:** Piseco Lake to Vly Lake
☆ **County:** Hamilton
↔ **Length:** About 10.0 mi (16.1 km) round-trip
↘ **Drop:** Meandering with only a slight drop
♦ **Difficulty:** Flatwater or slight current
✳ **Problems:** Beaver dams and occasional downed trees
⚲ **Maps:** Page 100; USGS Piseco, Lake Pleasant; DeLorme page 79
✍ **Contributor:** Will Holt

🛶 Launch:

Take NY 8 west from Speculator about 9.0 mi and turn north on Old Piseco Road. Continue 2.0 mi to the bridge over Fall Stream, which enters Piseco Lake at the north end. The well-used launch site is in quiet water a few yards upstream of the bridge. This access avoids the rapidly dropping water under the bridge. The put-in is purportedly on private land, so it is important to maintain access to the area by parking cars close to Old Piseco Road. Do not use the site for any activities besides launching.

✐ Description:

Fall Stream is a small, meandering Adirondack river which flows into Piseco Lake. It ranges in width from about ten to thirty feet. While much of the stream flows quietly through marshy terrain, occasionally it borders higher ground with rocky shores and forest. Even in summer there is usually light current and adequate water. The occasional beaver dam usually requires getting out of the canoe

Fall Stream

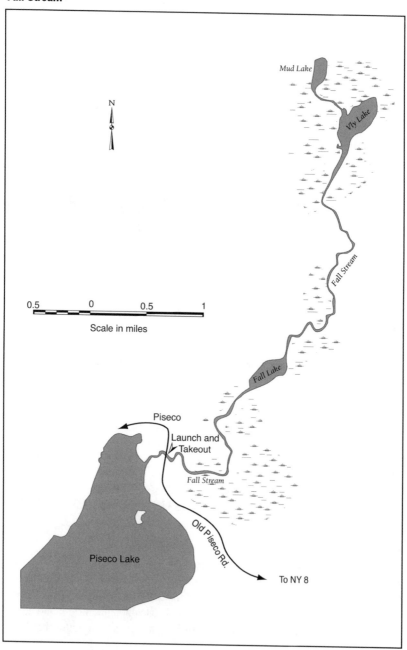

and dragging. Wear shoes for wading! The deeper water upstream of the beaver dams makes paddling easier, and at low water, this may be the factor that makes the upper end of the trip possible.

About 2.0 mi from the launch the stream widens into a pond with marshy shores known as Fall Lake. Another 3.0 mi brings the paddler to Vly Lake, a pond with rocky, forested shores and some attractive lunch spots. Vly Lake is often the limit of canoeing, although it is sometimes possible to push on another half-mile from the west side to a smaller pond called Mud Lake.

This is a very attractive stream. The forest is never far away and in some places hangs over the water. Herons, ducks, and red-winged blackbirds are common and white-throated sparrows may be heard in the surrounding woods. Water lilies, pickerelweed, and underwater grasses characterize the slow moving water. There may be campers on Vly Lake, but otherwise there is no sign of habitation. This trip is similar to the Miami River and Kunjamuk River described elsewhere in this book; for some paddlers Fall Stream may be the most attractive of the three.

🛖 Takeout:
Same as launch.

Upper Hudson Tributaries

Sacandaga River, Main

↕ **Segment:**	Wells to Hope
☆ **County:**	Hamilton
↔ **Length:**	8.6 mi (13.8 km)
↘ **Drop:**	187 ft (57 m)
◆ **Difficulty:**	Class I, II at medium water level; 4 to 5 ft on the Hope gauge (see Appendix D, entries 1–4 to access water level data)
✳ **Problems:**	During low water: dam at state campground; gravel bars in lower section; during high water: large waves in section below confluence with West Branch
🏕 **Maps:**	Page 103; USGS Wells, Three Ponds Mountain; DOT Hope Falls; DeLorme page 79
✍ **Contributor:**	Ken Robbins

⚓ Launch:

Take NY 30 to Wells, about 17.0 mi north of Northville. At Wells, take Algonquin Road west across the river to a parking area on the right side of the road near the Lake Algonquin dam. Put-in is just below the dam on public property. There is ample parking.

✏ Description:

This section of the Sacandaga River is canoeable in the spring during the runoff season. The large drainage area and the storage capacity of Lake Algonquin help the river to maintain its water level somewhat longer than some of the smaller streams. The automated gauging station at Hope is located 3.8 mi below Wells. Readings are recorded daily except weekends. This segment is runnable when the gauge reads 3.0 ft or higher. However, at the three-foot level it will be scratchy in the lower section. The level can reach 7.0 ft or higher after a heavy spring rain causing large waves below the dam and difficulty beyond Class II. The ideal level is around 5.0 ft.

For the first 0.4 mi below the put-in the river flows swiftly through a number of large rocks which are easy to avoid. At 0.4 mi the river turns right and enters a short, vigorous rapid. This rapid is best approached slightly to the left of center and requires maneuvering around the rocks and holes. The river widens below the rapids and flows at a moderate pace for the next mile through an area where scattered rocks are easily avoided. The river turns left and a New York State campground appears on river left. The campground may be used as an intermediate access point if the gates are open, but they are often closed in early spring. At the campground, a concrete dam crosses the river, forming a pool which is used for swimming in the warmer months. This is an ideal place to eat lunch and stretch your legs. Below the dam, the river is significantly influenced by water level; at high levels, you may want to scout by walking through the campground along a road which follows the left bank.

The dam is easily portaged, but most canoeists run it. Expect the stern to bump slightly, except at high water. The preferred route is straight ahead over the center. A footbridge and some rocks immediately below the dam require some maneuvering.

About a hundred yards below the bridge the West Branch of the Sacandaga joins the main river. The most exciting part of the trip begins below the river junction. There is an eddy on river right at the confluence where you can stop

Sacandaga River, Main: Wells to Hope

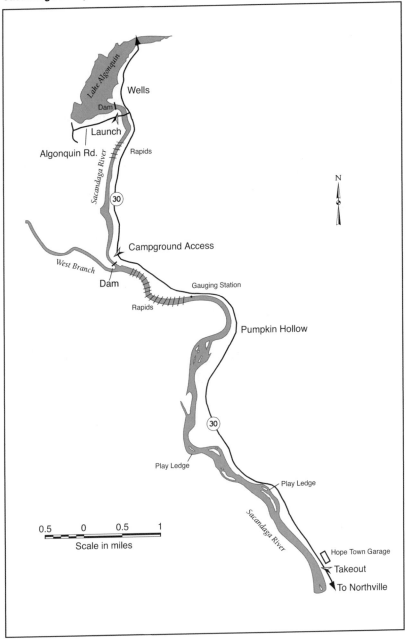

to plan your course.

For the next mile the river is wider and faster due to the steeper gradient and the added flow of the West Branch. Standing waves become progressively larger with increasing water levels and there are large rocks with heavy hydraulics behind them. Most of these rocks are visible, but it requires maneuvering to avoid them in the heavy current. Backpaddling may be necessary to prevent taking in water in an open canoe.

Just beyond the West Branch juncture the river turns right and then left. Stay to the center at the first turn to avoid large rocks close to the left shore. After the second turn the river widens and the current subsides. The rapids continue for about 0.5 mi to where the gauging station appears on river left. This is the Hope gauge and marks the end of the major rapids.

Downstream from the Hope gauge the river widens and the current diminishes. Rocks are easily avoided. At low water levels, the river becomes shallow, requiring careful channel picking. At several points the channel divides to create islands. Try to find the channel carrying the most water. For information on the takeout at Pumpkin Hollow, see page 98.

In this part of the river there are two ledges which create excellent play holes for practicing surfing and other maneuvers. If you dump the danger is minimal since there are pools downstream for easy rescue. These ledges are identified on the map on page 103. Be sure to take the correct channel around the islands to reach the play areas.

At 8.6 mi the river comes close to NY 30 and the highway garage of the Town of Hope is seen on river left. This is the takeout.

⌂ Takeout:

The Hope Town Garage is located on NY 30 about 8.0 mi south of Wells or 9.0 mi north of Northville. Parking is available for several cars. Canoes must be lifted up the bank, over the highway guardrail, and carried across the road to the cars. Be careful! NY 30 is a busy highway with fast traffic.

Sacandaga River, Main

↕ **Segment:**	Stewarts Bridge Reservoir
☆ **County:**	Saratoga
↔ **Length:**	6.0 mi (9.7 km) round-trip
↘ **Drop:**	None
♦ **Difficulty:**	Flatwater
✳ **Problems:**	Waves during windy periods; fast water near dams
⚑ **Maps:**	Page 107; DOT Conklingville; DeLorme page 81
✍ **Contributor:**	Tom Gibbs

🛶 Launch:

The launch is a power company site on the north side of the reservoir off County Route 4, about 4.0 mi west of Hadley. The town of Hadley also provides a launch on the south shore about 1.0 mile south of Conklingville Dam, off County Route 8.

The best place to launch is the Niagara Mohawk area on the north shore. There are two sites here, one on the left shortly after you enter the area, and the other at the end of the road. Camping is permitted at the end of the road. There is a cemetery nearby with graves of early settlers.

✎ Description:

This is a lovely flatwater trip, which maintains an adequate water level through the summer because of its location between two major dams; the Conklingville Dam upstream and the Stewarts Bridge Dam downstream. The shoreline is mostly forested and wild, with small mountains on all sides. The banks are steep in many places, and occasional streams flow in. Ferns and wildflowers are common along the shores and tall pines stand out among the many kinds of deciduous trees. Beaver are active in places and deer come to the shore to browse and drink. Eagles nest in the pines on the steep hillsides of the north shore near the Conklingville Dam.

A convenient way to paddle the reservoir is to turn right from the Niagara Mohawk area and paddle along the attractive north shore toward the Conklingville Dam, about 1.5 mi away. Watch for eagle nests high on the right as you approach the dam. The dam is an imposing sight from the downstream side.

! Caution:

It is important to keep a safe distance from the dam because currents may be strong.

Pass the dam and paddle along the south shore past a swampy area with typical wetland shrubs and flowers. Beyond the Hadley town launch and about a mile from the dam is a point of land where a stream enters; this is an attractive lunch spot. Two more miles along the south shore bring the paddler to Stewarts Bridge Dam. There are a few camps on the south shore near the dam, but the north shore is again unoccupied as you turn at the dam and head back towards the launch site.

⬆ Takeout:

Return to the launch site.

Upper Hudson Tributaries

Sacandaga River, Main

↕ **Segment:**	Stewarts Dam to Hudson River	
☆ **County:**	Saratoga	
↔ **Length:**	3.0 mi (4.8 km)	
↘ **Drop:**	60 ft (18.3 m)	
◆ **Difficulty:**	Class II–III; daily water releases June, July, and August; periodic releases in spring and fall; call Waterline, code 365122 (see Appendix D, entry 2) after 7 P.M. for next day data. Problems: Be aware of the large play hole on river right at the beginning and the large standing waves before the bridge at the bottom; paddlers who venture upstream on the Hudson after the confluence should know that the rocks below the falls at Hadley are severely undercut	
♟ **Maps:**	Page 109; USGS Lake Luzerne; DeLorme page 80	
✍ **Contributor:**	Chuck Wilkison	

Sacandaga River, Main: Stewarts Bridge Reservoir

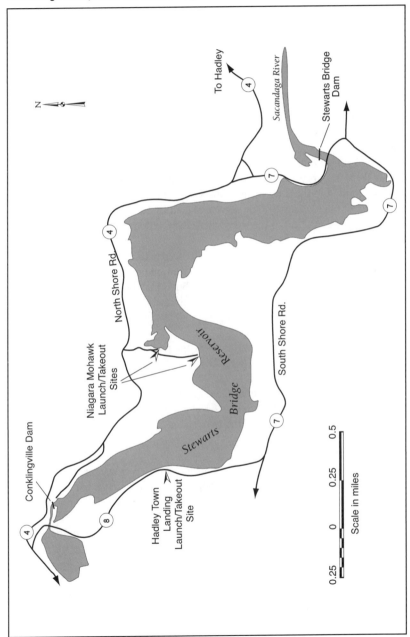

⚓ Launch:

This section of the Sacandaga is located near Lake Luzerne and Hadley in the northern part of Saratoga County, due west of Glens Falls. From the north or south, take NY 9N into the town of Lake Luzerne. Coming from the south, take a left onto Bay Road. Coming from the north, take a right on Main Street. Turn west on County Route 4 and pass over the bridge to Hadley. As you cross the bridge there is a great view of the falls on the Hudson. Continue 0.3 mi on County Route 4 to the intersection with Stony Creek Road. If you wish to take advantage of the low-cost shuttle service offered by Sacandaga Outdoor Center, take a left and go 0.3 mi to the river where the Outdoor Center is located. This is also the takeout; parking is available.

See map for the launch site for those who pay for the shuttle. Paddlers who wish to shuttle their own boats should continue on County Route 4 about 2.5 mi to a fork; bear left to a parking area. Boats may be unloaded slightly farther down the road, but cars must be left in the parking area. There is a trail leading down to the river. Both launch sites are a short distance below the dam.

Note: The "Sac" is a wonderful resource for the paddling community. Water releases are usually from 9 A.M. to 4 P.M.

In additional to shuttle service, Sacandaga Outdoor Center offers boat rentals and whitewater instruction (as do other commercial river outfitters). The phone for the Outdoor Center at the river site is 518-696-5710.

✐ Description:

The top section of the Sacandaga offers boaters a variety of routes. Far river left has the least difficult water with many opportunities to practice left eddy turns. There are several large rocks to the right of river left which provide powerful eddy lines and holes for boaters to practice big volume eddy entrances and exits. The middle of the river offers big, fast water with holes and drops to maneuver around.

River right leads quickly to the biggest hole and surf wave on the river. Here the most skilled paddlers wait their turn to either surf the top wave or to pop an ender in the hole directly below the wave. It is a great place to practice combat rolls necessary for all but the most skilled surfers. The eddy on the right river shore is quite large giving most paddlers plenty of time for their roll and

Sacandaga River, Main: Stewarts Dam to Hudson River

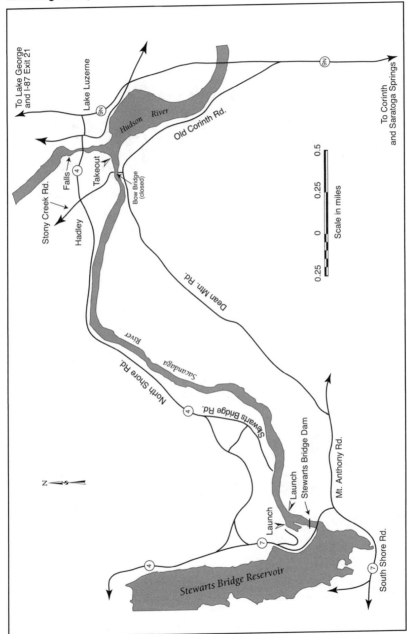

A low brace at the confluence of Hudson and Sacandaga Rivers   Barbara Brabetz the opportunity to get back into the eddy for another chance to hone their paddling skills. I know some adolescent brothers who used to bring their lunch to this spot, stash it on shore, and spend the day at " the hole" playing and practicing. They were fun to watch.

The top section does not end here; there are some mid-river holes and waves to play in before the whitewater ends shortly after passing some abandoned bridge abutments. The flatwater section is approximately one mile long and offers a chance to relax, eat a snack, drink some fluids, and converse with fellow paddlers

The pace of the river picks up as it bends to the right. The next 0.8 mi consists of easy Class II rapids with some gentle surf waves for play. Unfortunately most of these waves do not have a companion eddy next to them so they must be caught without this aid. The river narrows as it turns left and the holes and standing waves get much larger. The biggest waves are approximately three to four feet in height. They offer a thrill and an opportunity for open boaters to practice running large waves without taking much water into their boats.

After turning the corner and going under an abandoned bridge, there is a large eddy on river left. This eddy allows boaters to go into the hole directly above it for a wild side surf. Be careful of the rock causing the hole; miscalculations can lead to injury if paddlers land on the rock. It is also possible to go above this hole from a passage along the left bank leading to an eddy that provides access to a nice front surfing wave. There is one last drop before the end.

There are plans under consideration to enhance whitewater play opportunities by adding man-made ledges and rocks to this section of the Sacandaga.

🛶 Takeout:

The takeout is on river left at the confluence with the Hudson River and leads to the parking area by the Sacandaga Outdoor Center. It is possible to paddle upstream on the Hudson to the falls and, depending on the water level, there can be some waves to surf and enjoy. One should be aware that the section of the Hudson River immediately below the falls is severely undercut. The rocks below the falls and downstream of the bridge make a great place to enjoy lunch or take a swim.

Upper Hudson Tributaries

Moses Kill

↕ **Segment:**	All that is navigable	
☆ **County:**	Washington	
↔ **Length:**	5.0 mi (8 km) round-trip	
↘ **Drop:**	Slight	
♦ **Difficulty:**	Flatwater; occasional shallows; runnable only in spring or high water	
✳ **Problems:**	Ledges may require carrying	
☀ **Maps:**	Page 113; DOT Fort Miller; DeLorme page 81	
✍ **Contributor:**	Alan Cederstrom	

⛴ Launch:

From I-87 take Exit 17 and drive north 2.0 mi on US 9 to a right fork, which is NY 197. Follow NY 197 4.0 mi to Fort Edward, crossing Rogers Island via two bridges. Drive south on US 4 5.0 mi to a bridge over the Moses Kill. A break in the guardrail on the east side of US 4 just north of the Moses Kill leads to an overgrown road where several cars can be parked, one in front of the other. It is about a 450-foot carry down this road to the barricade at an old bridge site. A steep path on the right leads to the river.

An easier launch site is on river right on the upstream side of the US 4 bridge. Park cars temporarily on the shoulder by the bridge and lift boats and gear over the guardrail. Move cars to the overgrown road for parking. It is advisable to back in, as cars cannot be turned around; exiting by backing into traffic on US 4 can be dangerous.

A third launch possibility is off Richardson Lane. Turn east on Patterson Road just south of the US 4 bridge. Take an immediate left on Richardson Lane and drive to the barricade at the end. Launching involves carrying boats over private land, so permission from the owner is necessary.

✐ Description:

A round-trip on the Moses Kill takes about four hours. Although houses are visible near the launch, the stream banks soon take on the appearance of a dense wilderness and afford striking views of historical structures unreachable except

Moses Kill

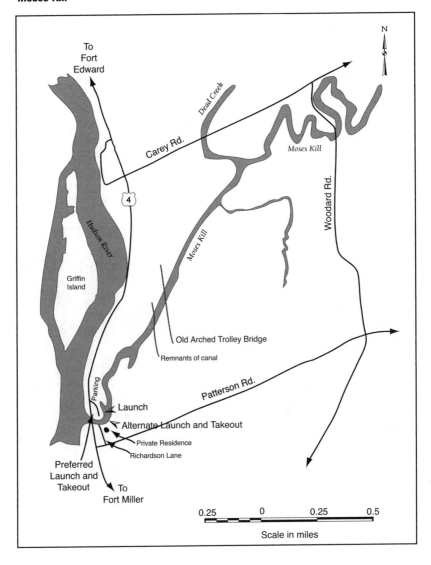

by canoe. The Kill may have been named for an early settler.

From the launch, take a moment to paddle a few hundred yards downstream to the mouth of the creek where it joins the Hudson River, passing under the highway bridge where dozens of birds nest. Upstream of the launch, the stream opens into a wide backwater with grasses, pond lilies, and other plants characteristic of shallow water. At about 0.5 mi the remnants of the old bridge that carried the original canal over the Moses Kill come into view. The remains of this early nineteenth century canal may be traced all along the Hudson from Troy to Fort Edward. A hundred yards farther upstream, the old trolley line bridge spans the Kill in a single, graceful 200-foot arch.

One mile from launch, the Kill flows through a wild and beautiful rock gorge where shale cliffs rise straight up as much as 20 feet. Striations on the rock give the illusion that the stream is ascending or descending. Although there are no real rapids, two shale ledges extend across the stream. At high water canoeists can paddle through breaks in these ledges; at low water it is necessary to lift the boats over.

Another half mile brings the paddler to Dead Creek, entering on the left.

Cement arch on the Moses Kill   Alan Cederstrom

This stream is only canoeable at flood level, when it provides a straight, fast, not very difficult run through farm fields from NY 197 to the Moses Kill. Where the two streams meet, there are interesting plants, including teasels, which early settlers used for carding wool.

For the next mile the stream steadily narrows as it winds through deciduous growth and pastureland. Several shallow places require maneuvering. The paddler will likely see a variety of birds including red-winged blackbirds, crows, robins, warblers, and ducks; tracks in the clay banks reveal the presence of deer and raccoons. In the spring, trillium is abundant and fern glades line the shores.

Just below the first bridge where Woodard Road crosses, the stream becomes impassable. The return trip to the launch site will probably take about a half hour less than the upstream paddle.

☂ Takeout:
Same as launch.

Upper Hudson Tributaries

Batten Kill

Introduction

The Batten Kill flows through a picturesque countryside that embodies the essence of rural New England. Rolling hills interspersed with farms, forest, and an occasional town create the intimate charm characteristic of Vermont and upstate New York. The stream rises near Ludlow, Vermont, and winds south and west, entering New York about eight miles below Arlington and emptying into the Hudson River ten and a half miles below Battenville.

The Kill moves at a lively pace, especially in spring when the upper sections challenge the novice paddler with a few Class II rapids. Although runnable all summer, the water level drops and by August some shallow areas may require the paddler to get out and walk the canoe. The stream is canoeable from Richville Road just downstream of Manchester, Vermont, to the town of Battenville, New York. Above Manchester water levels are usually too shallow. In late spring the section from Richville Road to Arlington may also become low. A gauge located in Battenville, accessible by Internet, measures river levels and flow (see discussions in individual river segments). Below Battenville dams requiring portages make canoeing difficult and land development is unattractive.

A gauging station accessible on the Internet measures water levels at Battenville. (See Appendix D, entries 1–3 to access Battenville gauge data.) There is also a visual gauge close to the bank on river left just downstream of the VT 313 bridge at Arlington. When the river is high, close to five feet on the visual gauge of the bridge at Arlington, the gauge at Battenville also measures about five feet. However, at lower water levels the depth measured by the visual gauge at Arlington drops faster than the depth measured at Battenville, due to the smaller volume of water carried by the narrowest upstream section of the river. For example, when the visual gauge at Arlington measures three feet, the gauge at Battenville is still at four and a half feet. This means that the Battenville gauge does not necessarily provide an accurate measure of water levels in sections of the river upstream of NY 22..

The Batten Kill is a premier trout stream. It's clear, cool waters make it an ideal home for trout. Certain stretches of shore are owned by exclusive fishing clubs. Orvis, the venerable and renowned fly-fishing company, is located in Manchester. Below Arlington the paddler will see occasional fish weirs, made of logs and stones, that extend out a short distance from the shore and create pools where fish hover and feed. During the fishing season many fly fishermen frequent the stream, standing in the water or on shore. Since we share these waters, canoeists are asked to avoid paddling before 9:30 A.M. and after 5:30 P.M. When encountering a fisherman, boaters should move as far to the side as possible and pass quietly, staying away from the fishing line.

The Battenkill Canoe, Ltd. is located on VT 7A at Hill Farm Road between Manchester and Arlington. This company rents canoes and equipment and can furnish guides for those who would like to learn the natural history of the area. They also have updated information on river conditions (800-421-5268). Twice a year Battenkill Canoe hosts a Clean-up and Guest Festival. Free canoes and garbage bags are provided for those who attend.

If you want to visit the Batten Kill by land, the Batten Kill Railroad runs scenic tours from Salem to Shushan. Fall is a particularly beautiful time as the maples, oaks, and birches are in full color. The tracks run beside the stream for most of the way, affording views from a vantage point above the water. In Shushan one can visit the old covered bridge museum, as described in the Shushan to NY 22 Bridge segment.

When you visit the Batten Kill, be prepared for a very special experience. Those of us who paddle here never tire of its beauty and peaceful presence.

Remember to bring binoculars as the area is filled with birds, including kingfishers, bank swallows, numerous species of warblers, ducks, herons, and an occasional osprey. In spring many species of wildflowers bloom along the banks. Paddling the Batten Kill is an experience worth reliving every year.

Contributor: Kathie Armstrong

Upper Hudson Tributaries

Batten Kill

↕ **Segment:**	Manchester, Vermont, to Arlington, Vermont
☆ **County:**	Bennington, Vermont
↔ **Length:**	7.0 mi (11.3 km)
↘ **Drop:**	50 ft (15.2 m)
◆ **Difficulty:**	Class I with one Class II drop; medium level, 2.5–3.5 ft on the visual gauge at the VT 313 bridge in Arlington are 840 cfs on Battenville gauge (below 257 cfs is too low).
✳ **Problems:**	Occasional strainers and logs
⛰ **Maps:**	Page 121; USGS Glens Falls (New York); DeLorme (Vermont) page 25
✍ **Contributor:**	Chet Harvey

!Caution:
When water levels are above 4.5 ft, the river is very high. Reduced clearance under the bridge at Arlington and bridges upstream make canoeing under them difficult and possibly dangerous.

〰 Launch:
Travel north on VT 7A from Arlington ,Vermont, 3.3 mi to Hill Farm Road, which enters on the right just before you see the Battenkill Canoe, Ltd. sign. Turn right, cross the Batten Kill, and continue 0.5 mi to the intersection with Sunderland Hill Road. Turn left and travel 3.0 mi to Richville Road, which enters on the right. The Batten Kill passes under Richville Road about 100 yds from the intersection. Put-in is from a meadow on the left after crossing the bridge. Limited parking space exists on the right side of the road opposite the put-in.

📖 Description:

The riverbanks are four to six feet high and quite steep for most of the trip, so the terrain next to the river is not always visible. However, the surrounding mountains provide beautiful views. Early in the trip, 3800-foot Mount Equinox dominates the skyline above the right bank, and a steep ridge called The Burning rises 1600 ft above the river close to the left bank.

After passing under the bridge at the launch site, the river runs flat for about 100 yds to a left bend where the first riffle is encountered. For the next two or three miles the river winds through a pastoral setting with cows and barn roofs occasionally visible. The paddling is easy but spiced with a lively swift here and there along the way. At medium-high level, the water in many of the upper sections of the trip is clear, about four to five feet deep, showing a gravel bottom where an occasional trout hovers.

At about 1.0 mi the river passes under an old wagon bridge followed shortly by a railroad bridge carrying the tracks of an old railroad which follows the river all the way from Manchester to Arlington. After the railroad bridge, the sur-

The Batten Kill   Alan Cederstrom

rounding countryside changes from pastoral to thickly wooded, and The Burning ridge on the left loses considerable elevation and comes closer to the river.

Two miles into the trip one paddles under the Sunderland bridge where Sunderland Hill Road crosses the river. There is a swimming hole with a rope swing 150 ft upstream of the bridge. The railroad crosses the river again about 100 yds downstream of the Sunderland bridge. There is a canoe access point on river left, just upstream of the railroad bridge.

At approximately 3.0 mi, Hill Farm Road crosses the river; the Battenkill Canoe launching site is upstream of the bridge on the right bank. This is a convenient place to eat lunch; walk up the bank to the Battenkill Canoe building to ask permission. The riverbanks in this section are all privately owned and canoeists should ask permission to stop.

In the next 3.0 mi, the river passes successively under the VT 7A and the old US 7 bridges. At 6.0 mi, there is a short Class II drop at a left bend where the outside bank is steep, perhaps 20 ft high, and Roaring Branch stream enters on the left near a camping area. This rapid, known as "The Rock," is about 200 ft long and follows a moderately curved arc. The large boulder for which the rapid is named sits in the stream about 5 ft off the right bank, partway around the bend. The rock deflects the current with most of the water flowing to the right through the narrow passage between the rock and the shore. Unless there is trapped debris, paddlers can pass safely through this channel. To pass to the left of the rock, paddlers must draw the boat sharply toward midstream where there is less, but usually sufficient, water, except at low stream levels.

There are intermittent stretches of fast water in the mile between Roaring Branch and the takeout at Rochester Bridge.

🛶 Takeout:

Takeout is on river left, just upstream of the Rochester bridge on VT 313 in Arlington; public parking is available at the eastern end of the bridge. To reach the takeout by car, drive 0.3 mi west from Arlington on VT 313.

Batten Kill

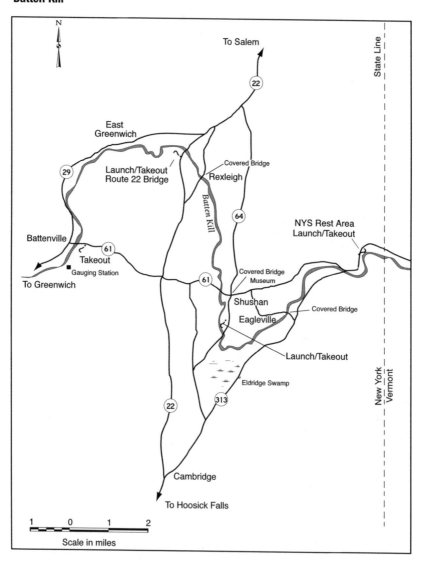

N

To Salem

22

State Line

East Greenwich

Covered Bridge

29

Launch/Takeout Route 22 Bridge

Rexleigh

Batten Kill

64

NYS Rest Area Launch/Takeout

Battenville

61

Takeout

Gauging Station

61

Covered Bridge Museum

To Greenwich

Covered Bridge

Shushan

Eagleville

Launch/Takeout

Eldridge Swamp

New York Vermont

22

313

Cambridge

To Hoosick Falls

1 0 1 2

Scale in miles

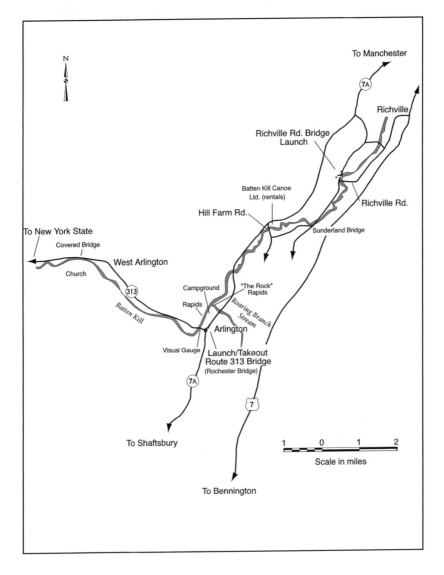

Upper Hudson Tributaries

Batten Kill

↕ **Segment:** Arlington, Vermont, to New York State Rest Area
☆ **County:** Bennington, Vermont; Washington, New York
↔ **Length:** 8.0 mi (12.9 km)
↘ **Drop:** 100 ft (30.5 m)
♦ **Difficulty:** Class I at medium water; Class II sections at high water; medium level, 2.5–3.5 on the visual gauge at Arlington (see discussion of gauges in Batten Kill introduction)
✳ **Problems:** Possibility of fallen trees or strainers
⚐ **Maps:** Pages 120–121, USGS Equinox (Vermont), Shushan (New York); DeLorme page 81
✍ **Contributor:** Al Fairbanks

! Caution:
If water levels are high, there is reduced clearance under the bridge.

⚓ Launch:
Access to the Batten Kill at Arlington is on VT 313, 0.2 mi west of the junction with VT 7A. There is a parking area at the east end of the VT 313 bridge. Boats can be easily launched upstream of the bridge.

✎ Description:
After passing under the bridge, it is a lively Class I paddle to a sharp right turn 0.5 mi from launch. After making the turn, there is a moderate drop through a rocky area. The river follows VT 313 fairly closely as it flows through a beautiful valley between Big Spruce Mountain on the left and Red Mountain on the right. Water tends to pile up at bends in the river, creating small wave trains which are best run near the center of the stream to avoid overhanging branches or downed trees. At 4.5 mi the river flows under a covered bridge where there is a beautiful white church and a picnic area just up from the left bank. This is a charming place to stop and rest a while.

After paddling about three miles beyond the covered bridge, between beautiful hills, the stream passes into New York State. Another 0.5 mi and the river makes a turn from west to south through a 90-degree arc. The takeout is reached shortly after leaving the turn.

🛶 Takeout:

The takeout is at a New York State rest area on river right. This area is close to both the river and NY 313; so carrying the boat to the car is an easy task. To reach the takeout by car, drive 7.0 mi west of Arlington on VT 313.

Upper Hudson Tributaries

Batten Kill

↕ **Segment:**	New York State Rest Area to Shushan
☆ **County:**	Washington
↔ **Length:**	6.1 mi (9.8 km)
↘ **Drop:**	80 ft (24.4 m)
♦ **Difficulty:**	Class I; medium water level, 2.5–3.5 ft on the visual gauge at the NY 313 bridge in Arlington (see discussion of gauges in Batten Kill introduction)
✳ **Problems:**	Possible strainers and logs
🏃 **Maps:**	Page 120; USGS Shushan; DeLorme page 81
✍ **Contributor:**	Al Fairbanks

🛶 Launch:

Launch at the New York State rest area on NY 313, 0.8 mi from the New York/Vermont line and 1.4 mi from the junction of NY 313 and County Route 61.

✎ Description:

Launch from the right bank opposite a steep wooded slope. The river flows along the base of the woods for about 0.8 mi before passing beneath NY 313. Downstream of the bridge, the river plain broadens and farmland becomes the dominating feature, particularly on river left. One and three-quarter miles from launch, the remnants of a broken dam extend across the river, forming the most serious obstacle of the route. The dam can be run straight at any point of its width except at very low water levels.

At about 2.0 miles, the river passes under the County Route 61 bridge. The Eagleville access is reached at 3.5 mi, and canoeists wishing to exit here should stay in the channel on the left side of the island. This is the main channel so there is little choice except at high water levels. Access is on the left side of a right-hand bend and, since the water is fairly swift, caution is advised for novices using this exit. There is a designated parking area at the access, which is 0.1 mi east of the Eagleville covered bridge. After passing under the covered bridge, the river flows past a campground and rural farmland. Two miles beyond the bridge, the river direction changes from its generally southwest course to a northerly course towards Shushan, 1.5 mi farther downstream.

🛖 Takeout:

The takeout is on County Road 64 on the right one mile upstream of Shushan and 6.0 mi from the launch site. To reach the takeout by car, drive west on NY 313 2.0 mi to County Route 61 entering on the right. Follow County Route 61 across the Batten Kill and left 2.5 mi into Shushan. The takeout is 1.0 mi south from Shushan on County Route 64 where it crosses the Batten Kill on the right. Parking for several cars is available.

Upper Hudson Tributaries

Batten Kill

↕ **Segment:**	Shushan to NY 22 Bridge
☆ **County:**	Washington
↔ **Length:**	5.4 mi (8.7 km)
↘ **Drop:**	40 ft (12.2 m)
◆ **Difficulty:**	Class I; medium water level, 2.5–3.5 ft on the visual gauge at the VT 313 bridge at Arlington (see discussion of gauges in Batten Kill introduction)
✳ **Problems:**	Possible strainers and logs
⌂ **Maps:**	Page 120; USGS Shushan, Salem; DeLorme page 81
✍ **Contributor:**	Al Fairbanks

⌇ Launch:

Drive east on NY 29 from Schuylerville to Battenville and turn right on County Route 61. Follow County Route 61 to Shushan. In the center of Shushan turn south on County Route 64 (the road immediately east of the railroad tracks). Proceed on County Route 64, paralleling the railroad tracks, for 1.0 mi to the point where the highway crosses the river. Parking and access are available at this point.

✎ Description:

About three-quarters of a mile downstream of the launch site, the Batten Kill makes an S-turn to the left. Another 0.5 mi and the river passes by Shushan under the County Route 61 bridge and the old covered bridge constructed in 1858. The bridge is now a museum and well worth a visit. Put ashore on river right after passing under the bridge and climb the steep bank. Spend an hour or so studying the old tools, farm machinery, and household artifacts from Washington County and environs. Next to the museum is an old country schoolhouse complete with desks, blackboards, maps, and old photos. Shushan is the terminal of the Batten Kill Railroad excursion train from Salem.

Below Shushan the river enters a well-forested area, crossing under the Batten Kill Railroad tracks at several points. Four and a half miles from the launch site the remnants of an old mill and a broken dam can be seen, and another 0.1 mi paddle carries the canoe beneath the Rexleigh covered bridge.

There is access just downstream of the Rexleigh bridge on river left with parking for a couple of cars and additional parking close by. This makes an interesting stop because there is a bronze plaque on the highway close to the bridge which tells some of the area's history. From here it is a 0.8 mile paddle to the takeout.

⌂ Takeout:

The takeout is just downstream of the NY 22 bridge on the left bank. By car from Schuylerville, drive about 14.0 mi to the intersection of NY 29 and NY 22. Follow NY 22 southwest 0.6 mi to the bridge over the Batten Kill. Cross and turn right onto a short access road leading to a parking area just downstream of the bridge on river left. The route back to the launch is a pleasant 2.5 mi drive south on NY 22 to Schoolhouse Lake and then 2.0 mi east on County Route 61 to Shushan. From Shushan take County Route 64 1.0 mi south to the launch site.

Batten Kill

↕ **Segment:**   NY 22 Bridge to Battenville
☆ **County:**   Washington
↔ **Length:**   5.8 mi (9.4 km)
↘ **Drop:**   40 ft (12.2 m)
◆ **Difficulty:**   Class I
✳ **Problems:**   Possible strainers and logs
🛖 **Maps:**   Page 120; USGS Salem, Cossayuna, Cambridge; DeLorme
          page 81
✍ **Contributor:**   Al Fairbanks

⛵ Launch:

Follow NY 29 east from Schuylerville about 14.0 mi to the junction of NY 29 and NY 22. Follow NY 22 southwest 0.6 mi to the NY 22 bridge over the Batten Kill. Cross the bridge and turn right onto a short access road leading to the launch site downstream of the bridge on river left. There is room to park several cars.

✏ Description:

From the NY 22 bridge, the Batten Kill flows west and gradually bends south. East Greenwich is reached after paddling 2.1 mi from the launch site. Below East Greenwich the river becomes somewhat wider with occasional islands. Downed trees may be a problem in this stretch of the river.

Some say that the Batten Kill gets its name from the many bats seen in the early evening around East Greenwich. Others believe it more likely that an early resident was nicknamed Bart or Batt, and the name of the stream evolved from Batts Creek to Batten Kill.

Battenville, the termination of the recommended canoeable sections of the Batten Kill, is reached after another 3.8 mi of paddling. Although the Batten Kill continues to the Hudson, canoeing below Battenville is not practical due to dams and development.

🏠 Takeout:

The takeout is by the bridge on County Route 61, just east of the intersection of NY 29 and County Route 61 in the center of Battenville. Just upstream of the bridge on river left is a tiny beach (at most water levels). From here, boats can be carried uphill a few yards to the railroad tracks and along the tracks to the road, where there are several good parking spots.

Upper Hudson Tributaries

Kayaderosseras Creek

↕ **Segment:**	Rock City Falls to Ballston Spa
☆ **County:**	Saratoga
↔ **Length:**	9.0 mi (14.5 km)
↘ **Drop:**	195 ft (59.5 m)
◆ **Difficulty:**	Class I, II, some Class III at high water; runnable in early spring during runoff Problems: Downed trees; tricky takeout near dam with potential hazards
🗻 **Maps:**	Page 129; DOT Middle Grove, Saratoga Springs; DeLorme page 80
✍ **Contributor:**	Ken Robbins

Note: The only way to assess the water level is to view the rapids from the NY 50 bridge in Ballston Spa and from the Galway Road bridge at Factory Village. If these rapids look runnable, the whole segment can be paddled.

🛶 Launch:

The put-in is reached from NY 29 about 7 mi west of Saratoga Springs in the village of Rock City Falls. Near the center of the village take Rock City Road 0.2 mi south to a bridge that crosses the creek. Just before the bridge turn left on Cottrell Lane, which runs close to the creek for a short distance. The launch site is on property owned by the Cottrell Paper Company; the company allows access with the understanding that canoeists will not block the road. Cottrell Lane is a residential street, so cars should be parked along Rock City Road after unloading.

🖉 Description:

The Kayaderosseras is canoeable in early spring (March–April) during runoff, and occasionally at other times of year after a heavy rain. The most significant danger is fallen trees forming strainers. In many places the stream is so narrow that a large tree can completely block the route. Since trees in or over the water will vary from year to year, the paddler needs to be prepared to pull out on short notice and carry around obstacles.

The Kayaderosseras is used today by local fishermen. In past years there were a number of dams along the creek to supply power to mills of various kinds. In 1870 an estimated thirty mills were operating along the Kayaderosseras in the vicinity of Ballston Spa and locations upstream. Perhaps one of the most famous was the Blood Scythe and Axe Works, which later became the American Axe and Tool Company. Around 1900 this mill produced 12,000 dozen scythes and sickles, 8,000 dozen axes and hatchets, and 10,000 dozen other tools each year. Today there are several places where remnants of dams are visible and round millstones can still be found along the creek bed.

From the put-in to the first bridge at 0.8 mi the rapids contain small rocks, which are easily avoided. In low water this stretch can be scratchy. The stream flows slowly meandering through an area frequented by wildlife such as ducks, muskrats, and beaver. At 1.4 mi the creek passes under a small, infrequently used bridge. About 0.5 mi farther the creek briefly touches property belonging to the US Department of Energy Kesselring Site. Just downstream the creek takes a sharp left where there is a short rapids. The route is flat for another 0.5 mi followed by an S-turn with a short stretch of Class II rapids. These rapids can be run starting on the right side and working left for the second turn. After the S-turn the current continues with no major obstacles. On river left are the remains of the foundation of one of the larger old mills.

Just downstream from the old mill foundation, the West Milton Road crosses the stream. Beyond this bridge are 3.0 mi of quiet water with easy rapids as the creek flows through relatively flat land. Downed trees are common in this stretch. Be prepared to carry around some of them. About 0.6 mi below the West Milton Road bridge on river right, the Glowegee Creek joins the Kayaderosseras. About 0.2 mi farther is a gauging station on the left. Continuing downstream one passes under the Lewis Road bridge, followed in 0.8 mi by the Middle Line Road bridge. About 1.2 mi beyond Middle Line Road is an access to the stream on river left, which is the right-of-way for a gas pipeline. This is a good takeout point for those

Kayaderosseras Creek: Rock City Falls to Ballston Spa

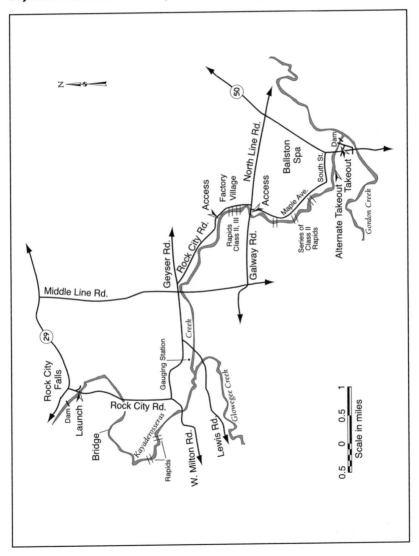

who do not wish to run the more challenging rapids downstream.

A few hundred yards downstream from the access point the stream narrows to form a chute leading into 0.5 mi of rapids. There was once a milldam here and some of the remaining stonework can be seen on river right. Run the chute near the middle, but be prepared to go right just downstream as there is a strong current pushing the boat left. The stream makes a series of turns where there are a number of large rocks with holes. These rapids are more difficult than any encountered previously. They are Class II, but can become Class II+ or III at high water levels. This stretch is likely to have downed trees, so scouting is advisable. The paddler must be prepared to avoid sweepers.

The creek now passes under the Galway Road bridge where there is an access point on river left. For the remainder of the trip to Ballston Spa, the stream runs through a deep valley with high ground on either side. The gradient increases in this stretch and there are a series of Class II rapids that require maneuvering. About 1.4 mi below the Galway Road bridge on river left are the remains of the Sythe and Axe factory. The Route 50 bridge is reached at 9.0 mi, just upstream from takeout.

🏠 Takeout:

It is important for paddlers to scout the takeouts in Ballston Spa before running the river. If there are hazards such as ice or very high water levels, it may be advisable to takeout at the Galway Road bridge access point.

In Ballston Spa, the best and safest takeout is up a bank on river right about 100 yd upstream from the NY 50 bridge on the private property of an old building which was formerly a chocolate factory. The building has been renovated and now houses a variety of businesses. There is a parking lot next to the river. When businesses are closed, parking on this private property may be acceptable. If businesses are open, paddlers should ask permission.

Just below the NY 50 bridge on river right is another possible takeout leading to the parking lot of the Napa Auto Parts Company. Paddlers should ask permission from the manager before leaving vehicles.

! Caution:

Do not takeout downstream of the Napa Auto Parts Company because of the low-head dam located just below a bridge that is downstream of the NY 50 bridge. The dam forms a hydraulic that turns into a "keeper" at high water levels. Rescue would be difficult because the dam has been enclosed with chain-link fence and is inaccessible. There is also a pipeline across the creek at the bridge that could block passage at high water. One can view the dam from the bridge by taking either Ford Street on the south side of the creek or Saratoga Avenue on the north side of the creek to the cross street over the bridge.

Upper Hudson Tributaries

Kayaderosseras Creek

↕ **Segment:**	Ballston Spa to Saratoga Lake	
☆ **County:**	Saratoga	
↔ **Length:**	12.0 mi (19.4 km)	
↘ **Drop:**	20 ft (6.1 m)	
◆ **Difficulty:**	Flatwater with occasional quickwater	
✳ **Problems:**	Downed trees and logjams	
♠ **Maps:**	Page 133; USGS Saratoga Springs, Quaker Springs; DeLorme page 80	
✒ **Contributor:**	Tom Gibbs	

⚟ Launch:

Launch at Kelly Park in Ballston Spa. From NY 50 in the center of town, turn east on Malta Avenue and drive 0.6 mi to the Kelly Park access road, entering on the left. There is parking and easy access to the creek. Kelly Park is open daily; the gates are locked at night.

As of spring 2005 there is a new canoe access off Grays Crossing Road 1.1 mi downstream of Kelly Park. This access is on New York state land purchased in 2004 as an extension of Saratoga Spa State Park. The Friends of the Kayaderosseras Creek joined forces with New York State to construct the access, a 6 car gravel parking lot and a loop trail along the creek.

✐ Description:

This section of the Kayaderosseras flows through lovely rural country; trees and fields line the banks, providing habitat for a variety of birds and wildflowers.

131

The first part of the trip passes farmland that gradually changes to heavily forested terrain as the creek nears Saratoga Lake. This latter area is particularly beautiful and offers many opportunities for viewing wildlife.

The first 2.0 mi are characterized by quickwater and frequent turns with the possibility of downed trees. In summer, when the water is low, it may be difficult to find an open channel. The Mourning Kill joins on the right at 1.4 mi followed by the bridge where Grays Crossing Road crosses the stream. There is parking here and easy access for those who prefer a shorter trip.

Continuing downstream there are occasional tight corners, shallow spots, and trees that partially block the stream. In very low water you may have to walk the boat. At 3.6 mi Saratoga Spa State Park bounds the creek on the left. Numerous birds, including great blue herons and kingfishers, frequent this area.

At 4.5 mi Geyser Brook enters on the left. This paddler found a beaver dam in the entrance and a tree across the brook a few yards upstream; once around those obstacles it was an easy paddle about a mile farther through an area that was formerly a swamp. Geyser Brook starts above Saratoga Spa State Park and flows under the pedestrian bridge at the Performing Arts Center, where it passes the well-known mineral geyser, "Island Spouter." If you have a small boat and water levels are high, it is possible to paddle down Geyser Brook from the East-West Road in the State Park and into the Kayaderosseras, where you can choose to takeout at any of the available access sites.

At 6.0 mi US 9 crosses the creek. Access is possible here, although parking is marginal. At 7.2 mi you pass under I-87 and, shortly thereafter, the Nelson Avenue Extension bridge.

The Lake Lonely outlet enters on the left at 9.2 mi. A lovely 0.8-mile paddle upstream in the outlet brings you to the Lake Lonely boat livery, an excellent access point. There may be a small fee for boat launching. The drive from Grays Crossing to Lake Lonely is 8.0 mi. Taking out at the livery shortens your trip by 2.0 mi. However, the most beautiful part of the river is still to come.

About 0.2 mi downstream from the outlet is a major logjam that can usually be negotiated. Occasionally a short portage on the left bank is necessary.

Below the Lake Lonely outlet the banks of the Kayaderosseras are thickly forested with branches overhanging the water. Their reflections provide a sense of great tranquillity. Here you may see muskrat and hear the splash of a beaver's tail. There are many species of birds and you are likely to hear the raucous call of the kingfisher signaling his knowledge of your presence.

Kayaderosseras Creek: Ballston Spa to Saratoga Lake

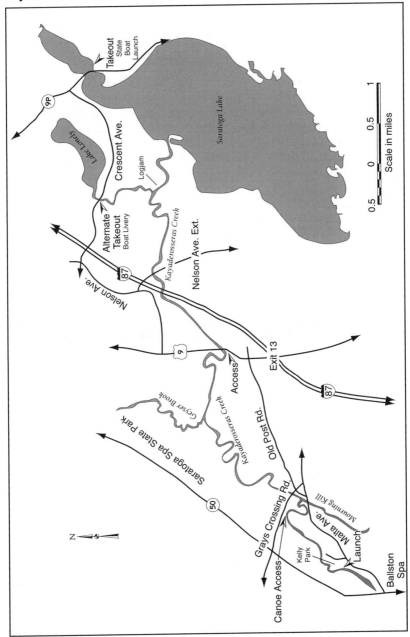

The next mile or so brings you to Saratoga Lake. There is a point on the left shore as you enter the lake where you can take a break before heading out into the "big waters." It is about 1.6 mi north on Saratoga Lake to the takeout at the state boat launch. Be prepared to deal with the possibilities of wind, waves, and the inevitable powerboats as you cross the lake. If you're paddling into a north wind, it is a long mile and a half. The safest route is to follow the west shore past Waters Edge Townhouses toward the bridge and cross the channel to the boat launch.

🛖 Takeout:

Takeout at the state boat launch on the right, just after passing under the NY 9P bridge at the northern end of Saratoga Lake. You can shuttle to the launch by following NY 9P to I-87, south to Exit 13N, north a short distance on US 9, and then west on Old Post Road to either Grays Crossing Road or Malta Avenue in Ballston Spa.

Upper Hudson Tributaries

Fish Creek

↕ **Segment:**	Saratoga Lake to Grangerville	
☆ **County:**	Saratoga	
↔ **Length:**	4.5 mi (7.3 km); additional 3.0 mi (4.8 km) round-trip from takeout to Grangerville Dam	
↘ **Drop:**	Negligible	
◆ **Difficulty:**	Flatwater	
✳ **Problems:**	None	
🛖 **Maps:**	Page 136; DOT Quaker Springs; DeLorme pages 80, 81	
✍ **Contributors:**	Don Butler and Gwenne Rippon	

🛖 Launch:

Take NY 9P from the center of Saratoga Springs approximately 3.7 mi east to a New York State boat launch site on Fish Creek near Saratoga Lake. Immediately after crossing Fish Creek, turn left into the parking lot. Stores and a private campground are located nearby.

✐ Description:

There are any number of Fish Creeks in New York. This one flows from Saratoga Lake to the Hudson River. The section described here is entirely flatwater and can be paddled in two to three hours. Motorboats use the entire area above Staffords Bridge, especially on summer weekends. Skidmore College and high school rowing shells, a pleasanter kind of traffic, use this route during the crew season. Both sections of Fish Creek described in this guide provide excellent nature-oriented excursions. Many birds, animals, and plants common to wetlands live here. Fishing for warm water species is said to be good. Because the current is negligible it is almost always possible to make a trip downstream and return to the launch point.

At the boat launch, the creek is much like a pond or small lake. It is up to half a mile wide with swampy wooded shores and some camps on sections of higher ground. Two miles from the launch at Staffords Bridge a privately owned campground with a marina and restaurant (river right) provides an intermediate access for a shorter trip.

Below Staffords Bridge the creek remains wide and relatively unspoiled. After passing through the pilings of an old railroad bridge, a number of camps come into view. At about 4.0 mi the stream comes close to NY 29 and the sounds of traffic may intrude on the paddler for a short distance. Several looping bends lead to Bryants Bridge, 4.5 mi from launch.

⌂ Takeout:

The takeout is at Bryants Bridge just downstream from the bridge on river right. To reach the takeout by car follow NY 29 east from Saratoga Springs. Four miles east of I-87 underpass turn right onto Bryants Bridge Road; continue 0.3 mi to a bridge over Fish Creek. There is parking for one or two cars; canoeists should be careful not to block the private drive. A very steep bank leads to the stream. A private citizen has placed a small trash can here. Use it.

Note: For those who wish to extend the trip, it is possible to continue 1.5 mi beyond the takeout to Grangerville Dam. Since there is no public access at the dam the paddler must return to Bryants Bridge for a round-trip total of 3.0 mi. This section of the creek is narrower with wooded shores interspersed with camps.

Fish Creek: Saratoga Lake to Grangerville

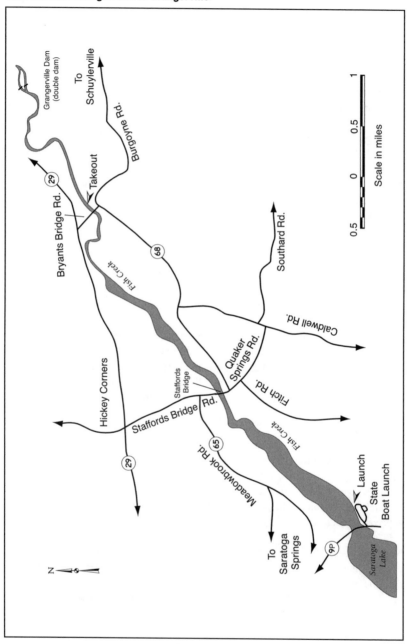

!Caution:

A series of buoys alerts the paddler to the proximity of two small dams joined
by an island. It is usually not difficult to turn around here and paddle back to
the takeout, except in spring when high water may create a strong current.
Below the dam is very heavy whitewater; in places logs may completely block
the creek.

Upper Hudson Tributaries

Fish Creek

↕ **Segment:**	Grangerville to Victory Mills
☆ **County:**	Saratoga
↔ **Length:**	4.0 mi (6.5 km)
↘ **Drop:**	10 ft (3.0 m)
◆ **Difficulty:**	Flatwater; quickwater at start
✳ **Problems:**	Old mill dam; logjams
⚑ **Maps:**	Page 139; DOT Quaker Springs, Schuylerville; DeLorme page 81

✍ **Contributors:** Don Butler and Gwenne Rippon

Launch:

Drive east on NY 29 from Saratoga Springs. Seven miles past the I-87 overpass
take a right on Hayes Road, just east of the westernmost NY 29 bridge in
Grangerville. Hayes Road leads to a gravel loop that accesses the creek. There is
ample room to park.

Before launching, paddlers should scout the riffles under the bridge and
over the broken dam some 50 ft below the bridge to select the best route. Scout
from the bridge and from a side road which runs downstream along the left side
of the creek.

Description:

After passing under the bridge and over the dam remnants, the creek loops
behind the hamlet of Grangerville and under the second NY 29 bridge. The paddler will enjoy this attractive wooded countryside. Although the current is
noticeable, it will not prevent paddling upstream at any point. About 1.5 mi

from the launch the creek passes under Burgoyne Road and, a mile farther, under NY 32. Either point provides access. Just before the NY 32 bridge, the paddler passes the private clubhouse and campgrounds of the Fish Creek Rod and Gun Club on river left. These grounds are open to members only. Shortly after NY 32 the pilings of an old railroad bridge come into view.

For the next mile the creek flows through a wild, swampy forest reminiscent of a bayou. The naturalist will enjoy identifying the varieties of plants and birds that live in this area. Brushy logjams are possible. After looping back on itself, Fish Creek enters the village of Victory Mills.

Takeout:

Paddlers must not go beyond the first bridge (Mennen Road) in Victory Mills because of hazardous ledges, heavy whitewater, and a hydroelectric dam farther downstream. These areas are not canoeable. Mennen Road is the next highway bridge beyond the NY 32 bridge. Takeout on river right just upstream of the bridge.

To reach the takeout by car from the launch, follow Hayes Road south, turning sharply left at a fork after 0.5 mi; continue 2.3 mi and turn left on NY 32. About 2.0 mi east of this intersection, Mennen Road enters on the right and immediately crosses Fish Creek. Parking is available on the right.

At most water levels one can reverse the trip by launching at the takeout and paddling upstream to Grangerville and back.

Note: Paddlers can take a trip back in time by visiting the nearby home of Revolutionary General Phillip Schuyler. Drive west on Mennen Road a short distance and turn right on NY 32. Follow NY 32 1.3 mi to US 4 and turn south. Almost immediately the Schuyler House comes into view on the left, between US 4 and the Hudson River.

General Schuyler built the present house in 1777 just after the Revolution. The previous house was burned by order of British general John Burgoyne. Following the British surrender at Saratoga, Burgoyne came to regret his order, having become personally acquainted with General Schuyler, who treated his prisoner well. Schuyler used the house as his summer residence until his death in 1804. The Schuyler House is open to the public throughout the summer.

Fish Creek: Grangerville to Victory Mills

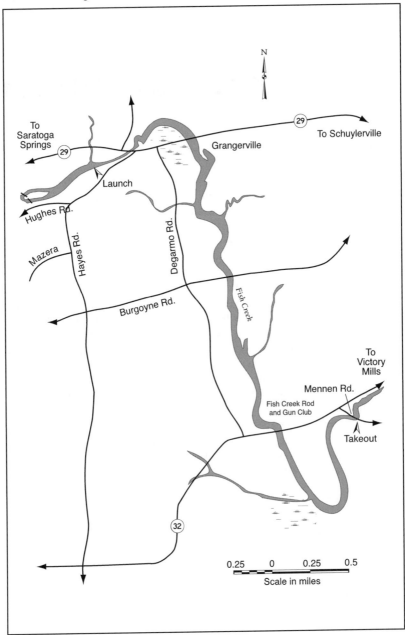

Upper Hudson Tributaries

Hoosic River

Introduction

The name Hoosic, Indian for "stony place," is also spelled Hoosick or Hoosac; the usual spelling, Hoosic, is used here. The river rises in the Berkshires near Pittsfield, Massachusetts, and flows through North Adams, Williamstown, and the southwest corner of Vermont before entering New York. It joins the Hudson River at Stillwater.

There are some attractive runs on the lower stretches of the river, but there are also stretches of flatwater impounded by dams, impassable cataracts in ravines, and places where access is restricted. The upper segments described in this guide are delightful at medium to high water, with only a few places where the paddler need be alert to small rapids and other obstacles. Except where the stream passes through villages, the terrain is rural with fields and trees lining the banks. Warblers, goldfinch, red-winged blackbirds, kingfishers, ducks, and other species of birds will reward the birdwatcher paddler. Beaver and river otter also frequent isolated stretches of the river.

The Hoosic above Buskirk is not canoeable at low water. At medium levels, paddlers will have to avoid rocks and gravel shoals, most of which are covered at high water. There is a gauge at Eagle Bridge that reads the water level several times a day in the sections above Buskirk. Access the gauge through the Internet or call Waterline (see Appendix D). A gauge reading of 4.5 ft provides a good moderate water level with fast-moving current. At 3.3 ft conditions are too scratchy for reasonable running. An acceptable minimum level is probably no lower than 4.0 ft. Paddlers can also judge the water level by scouting from bridges and banks. A good vantage point is Eagle Bridge where NY 67 crosses the river.

Below Buskirk, water impounded by the Johnsonville Dam permits paddling through the summer and fall as far as Johnsonville. Water levels in the stretch from Johnsonville Dam to Valley Falls are dependent on rain and water released from the dam impoundment. The dam at Valley Falls creates a pool, which creates adequate water for paddling the last two miles to the village.

Upper Hudson Tributaries

Hoosic River

↕ Segment: North Pownal, Vermont, to Hoosick Falls, New York
☆ County: Bennington, (Vermont); Rensselaer, Washington, (New York)
↔ Length: 13.5 mi (21.8 km)
↘ Drop: 100 ft (30.5 m)
♦ Difficulty: Class I, II; runnable at 4.5 ft or above on the Eagle Bridge gauge (see Appendix D, entries 1–3 to access water level data)
✳ Problems: Rock ledge; scratchy rocks at low water level
🎋 Maps: Page 143; USGS Albany (New York) (30x60); DeLorme (New York) page 67
✍ Contributor: Warren Broderick

🛶 Launch:

Launch at North Pownal, Vermont. Drive south 6.0 mi on NY 22 from Hoosick Falls to North Petersburg, then east on state Route 346 3.3 mi to North Pownal. A small bridge crosses the stream just downstream from an older bridge and a boarded-up tannery. Launch the boat from the south bank just downstream of the older bridge. Ask permission to park behind the country store.

An alternate easier launch is 2.4 mi below North Pownal at the Route 346 bridge crossing the river at the New York state line. Launch on river left below the bridge; park cars on the road shoulder.

✐ Description:

Immediately after launching the paddler passes between the remnants of an old dam on the left and rocks on the right. At 0.7 mi Washtub Brook enters on the right followed by a large S-shaped bend. Just beyond the bend a gravel bar in the stream requires a choice. At medium to low water, maneuver left, avoiding the bank; at high water, the right channel is recommended, as the rocks will be covered.

About 2.0 mi from the launch the stream passes under the state line bridge (NY 346) followed by the Boston and Maine Railroad Bridge. The navigable channel is right of the bridge pier. The course runs more or less parallel to the state line for about a mile. After several turns the river comes close to the railroad on the left. At this point the stream narrows and waves signal a short Class II rapid caused by a ledge and a two-foot drop. At medium to low water, boats may scrape the ledge; at high water, boats will slide over and meet some turbulence at the bottom.

The river meanders away from the tracks, sometimes offering multiple channels. About 5.5 mi from the launch are two small gravel islands; at high water, these are completely covered. At lower levels, the only passable channel is between the two. Just before reaching the County Route 95 bridge at Petersburg Junction there is a possible access along County Route 96 on river right opposite the Green family farm. There is room to park along the road.

Beyond Petersburg Junction the river widens and becomes shallower; at low water it may be necessary to get out occasionally and walk a few yards. Just beyond the County Route 95 bridge the Little Hoosic River enters on the left, causing some turbulence at high water. Shortly thereafter, the route passes old railroad abutments at a small island. The better channel is river right. For the next mile, the river runs beside the B&M Railroad on the right.

Undercut sand and gravel banks on the left provide homes to colonies of bank swallows. About 9.0 mi from North Pownal the Hoosic passes under NY 7 where there is a popular swimming hole and some midstream rocks, which are easily avoided. Paddlers may encounter sweepers in the one-mile stretch upstream of the bridge. There is an excellent access 0.3 mi north of the NY 7 bridge. The Hoosick Falls Central School is on the left and there are attractive farms in the area.

About 12.0 mi from North Pownal at a right bend, the remains of a dam may necessitate a short carry or drag. Now the river bends left, constricts, and leads to quickwater, which can become Class I or even II at high water. About 0.5 mi farther the paddler passes under the NY 22 bridge in the village of Hoosick Falls. The takeout is another 0.5 mi on river left before the railroad bridge.

! Caution:

Under no circumstances should one go beyond the railroad bridge. Beyond the bridge are rapids leading to impassable falls that are contained within steep concrete walls.

Hoosic River: North Pownal to Hoosick Falls

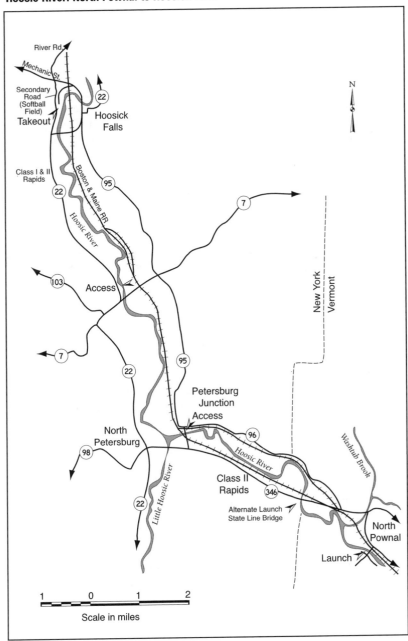

ADK Canoe and Kayak Guide • • • •

Takeout:

To reach the takeout by car, take NY 7 to NY 22. Drive north 3.0 mi on NY 22 to a traffic light before 22 goes right across a bridge. Go straight at the light on River Road, 0.75 mi. Turn right on Mechanic Street, 0.25 mi, then right on a short gravel road, 0.1 mi. Park near the gate. Find a path through the thick vegetation leading to the river.

Identify landmarks so that you can spot the takeout from the water.

From the river the takeout is left of a low grassy island. Carry the boats about 50 yd to the parking area.

Upper Hudson Tributaries

Hoosic River

↕ **Segment:**	Hoosick Junction to Johnsonville Dam
☆ **County:**	Rensselaer, Washington
↔ **Length:**	11.0 mi (17.7 km)
↘ **Drop:**	20 ft (6.1 m)
◆ **Difficulty:**	Class I; flatwater below Buskirk; runnable above Buskirk at 4.0 ft or above on the Eagle Bridge gauge (see Appendix D, entries 1–3 to access water level data)
✳ **Problems:**	Upper part cannot be run at low summertime levels
⚑ **Maps:**	Page 145; USGS Albany (30x60); DeLorme page 67
✍ **Contributors:**	Will Holt and Warren Broderick

Note: The upper part of the run, from Hoosick Junction to somewhat below Eagle Bridge, is usually too shallow to paddle at low summertime levels. A trip in May, 1999, with a reading of 4.4 ft on the Eagle Bridge gauge, found a good level with fast moving water. On another occasion, a visual inspection at 3.3 ft on the gauge showed conditions to be too scratchy for reasonable paddling, suggesting that the minimum level for this section of river is not much lower than 4.0 ft. If gauge readings are not available, inspection of the river where the NY 67 bridge crosses will show what to expect in the upper part.

Hoosic River: Hoosick Junction to Johnsonville Dam

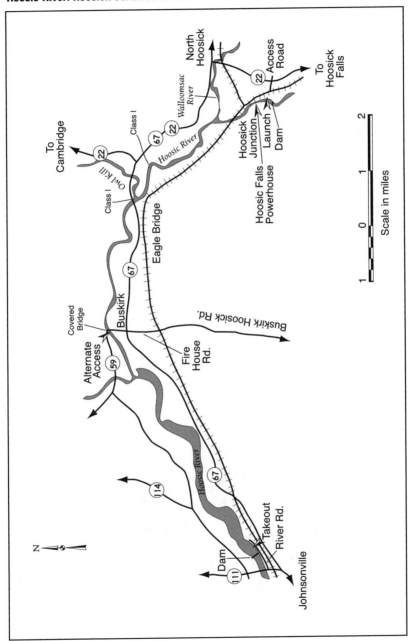

Scale in miles

At a point between Eagle Bridge and Buskirk, the river becomes deeper as water backs up from the Johnsonville Dam. From this point down, the Hoosic can be paddled through the summer and fall. If the upper river is too low, start the trip at Buskirk and go 5.0 mi downstream to Johnsonville.

ᗧ Launch:

Launch in Hoosick Junction near a small hydroelectric generating plant. Follow NY 22 about 0.3 mi north of the Hoosick Falls village line to a gravel road which leads west and is identified by the sign Hydro Project 2487; there are wooden transmission towers nearby. If traveling south, the gravel road is about 1.2 mi from the point where NY 22 and NY 67 join. Take the road across the railroad tracks and turn right to reach a parking lot near a small hydroelectric generating plant. Carry canoes down a short hill and launch immediately below the plant.

If starting at Buskirk, launch on the south side of the river downstream from the bridge. The covered bridge is reached by turning north off NY 67 onto Fire House Road.

Covered Bridge at Buskirk on the Hoosic   Warren F. Broderick

✏ Description:

This attractive and interesting stretch of the Hoosic River flows through farm country and forest, and passes the settlement of Eagle Bridge and the towns of Buskirk and Johnsonville. Eagle Bridge was the home of Grandma Moses, a self-taught artist whose primitive-style paintings captured the essence of life in rural New England.

Starting from the launch site at Hoosick Junction, the river passes through attractive forested country and alternates between fast-moving smooth water and short Class I drops. Several islands split the river flow, requiring the paddler to choose the best channel. The Walloomsac River enters from the right at 1.0 mi from the launch, adding significantly to the flow. The Eagle Bridge gauge and cable are passed at about 2.0 mi. A Class I drop occurs at 3.0 mi under a stone railroad bridge. A bridge pier splits the river and there are short steep drops in both channels. A half-mile farther, the Owl Kill enters from the right, upstream from the highway bridge at Eagle Bridge; there are Class I drops above and below the bridge.

Downstream from Eagle Bridge the river is generally wider and shallower as it passes through farming country. Low river levels can be a problem until just above Buskirk where the paddler reaches the area of backup water from the Johnsonville Dam. At 6.0 mi, Buskirk is recognized by a covered bridge; an access site is located below the bridge on river left. This is the alternate launch if the water levels are low.

Below Buskirk the river continues as flatwater with only minor current. The country is mostly forested and there are several side channels into marshy terrain, offering good opportunities for observing wildlife. Wind from the west can sometimes be a hindrance. Houses appear as the paddler reaches Johnsonville at 11.0 mi.

⌂ Takeout:

The takeout is in a small bay on the left side of the river within sight of the dam and power station. Extensive weed growth late in the summer makes it somewhat difficult for the paddler to find passages to the shore.

To reach the takeout by car, turn north from NY 67 onto County Route 111. After a short distance, turn right on River Road and follow the river upstream past the dam to a parking area next to the small bay. Ownership of the land is not clear.

Hoosic River: Johnsonville Dam to Valley Falls

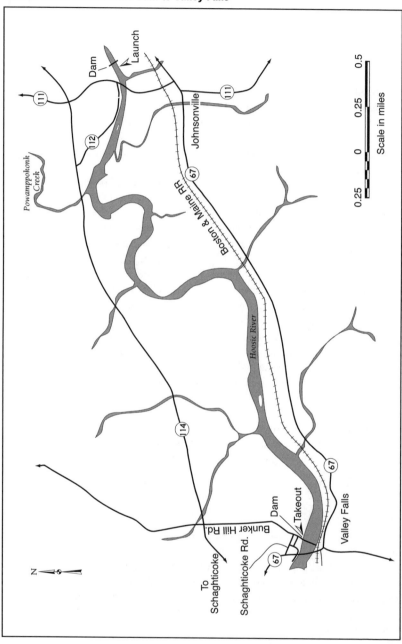

Upper Hudson Tributaries

Hoosic River

↕ **Segment:**	Johnsonville Dam to Valley Falls
☆ **County:**	Rensselaer
↔ **Length:**	4 mi (6.5 km)
↘ **Drop:**	20 ft (6.1 m)
◆ **Difficulty:**	Class I; water levels dependent on rain and dam releases; segment located between two dams so Eagle Bridge gives only a general idea of water level; gauge above 3.5 ft suggests adequate water. (See Appendix D to access gauge readings.)
✳ **Problems:**	Occasional rocks at low water level
⌖ **Maps:**	Page 148; USGS Schaghticoke; DeLorme page 67
✍ **Contributor:**	Warren Broderick

⚓ Launch:

Access is on the south side of the river just below the dam in Johnsonville. From NY 67 drive a short distance north on NY 111 (Bridge Street) and, just before the bridge, turn right on Axe Factory Road. From here it is 0.2 mi to the put-in below the dam. There is room for a few cars to park along the roadside. The power company has plans to improve the parking facilities.

✎ Description:

This short pleasant run passes through forested lands with no visible buildings except at the beginning and near the takeout. The gradient is not steep, but there are numerous boulders in the stream to keep the paddler alert. Rocks covered at high water can provide an interesting slalom course at lower levels. In spring, the water level is generally adequate, but in summer or fall, paddlers must take into account any recent rainfall and whether water is being released from the Johnsonville Dam.

The first half of this trip involves some rock dodging, especially at low water levels. Almost immediately after launching, the route passes the ruined pillars of the old Greenwich and Johnsonville railroad trestle, dismantled in 1932. At 0.6 mi Powamppokonk Creek enters from the north, almost unnoticed.

At about 2.5 mi, the river flattens out as it enters the pool created by the

Round Lake and Anthony Kill

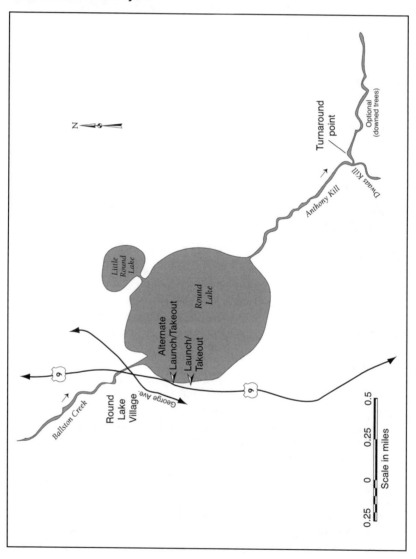

Upper Hudson Watershed

dam at Valley Falls. About 3.0 mi from launch, there is a large island in mid-stream. Take the right channel because the last couple of miles may involve a stiff paddle against a strong headwind. At about 3.5 mi from launch, the dam at Valley Falls and the James Thompson textile factory are seen ahead. Keep to river right from here to the takeout.

🛶 Takeout:

The takeout is on river right at a boat launch with a small parking area. To reach the takeout by car from the intersection of NY 67 and NY 40 north of Schaghticoke, drive 1.2 mi east on NY 67 to the bridge over the Hoosic at Valley Falls. Immediately before crossing the bridge, turn left (east) on Schaghticoke Road. About two blocks from NY 67, Schaghticoke Road joins Bunker Hill Road. Turn right on Bunker Hill Road. It is less than 0.1 mi to a dead end at the river. Here, a sign reads, "J. T. Hydro" and a short, grassy lane leads left to the access point.

! Caution:

It is possible to portage the dam on the right, but it is not recommended. After a short stretch of relatively easy water below the dam, the river enters Power Mill rapids, Class III–IV or higher. There is no good takeout before the rapids.

Upper Hudson Tributaries

Round Lake and Anthony Kill

↕ **Segment:**	All
☆ **County:**	Saratoga
↔ **Length:**	5.2 mi (8.4 km) round-trip
↘ **Drop:**	None
♦ **Difficulty:**	Flatwater
✳ **Problems:**	None
▲ **Maps:**	Page 150; DOT Round Lake; DeLorme page 66
✍ **Contributor:**	Norm Dibelius

In ancient times, water from Lake Erie ran eastward through the Mohawk Valley until it reached Schenectady, where it turned north through the valley now occupied by Ballston Lake, then east through Shanantaha Park, and Round Lake, south along the route of Interstate 87, and emptied into the Hudson River south of Albany. The last continental glacier changed the course of the waterway. When the glacier retreated, it deposited a moraine of sand and gravel near Schenectady that blocked the northward flow of the river. The river, now the Mohawk River, was thus diverted to its present course where it continues to run east from Schenectady and empties into the Hudson River at Cohoes after it cascades over the spectacular Cohoes Falls. The best view of the falls is from the cliffs on the north side of the river. The ancient riverbed is easily identified when flying over the area in a small aircraft.

To step back in time, walk through the village of Round Lake. It was founded in 1867 as a Methodist summer retreat. Affluent Methodists built ornate Victorian homes on minuscule lots adjacent to buggy-width streets. The village, now a tight-knit community of 750 people, is an island of quaintness. The 3,000-seat auditorium in the center of the village houses an antique Ferris wooden tracker organ with more than 1,000 pipes, the small pipes metal and the large ones wood. The unheated auditorium is still used for summer concerts. A walk through the village is a must for people interested in American history.

⛏ Launch:

There are two parking areas on the east side of US 9 and on the west shore of Round Lake. These parking areas are just south of the traffic light at the intersection of US 9 and George Avenue, which leads to the village of Round Lake.

✐ Description:

The shore of Round Lake is three miles around, most of which is surrounded by swampy wetlands, excellent for birdwatching, identifying water plants, and looking for signs of beaver. From the southernmost parking lot it is 1.1 mi, counterclockwise, of interesting paddling along the south shore of the lake to the entrance of Anthony Kill.

Anthony Kill meanders through wetland for another 1.1 mi. There are many opportunities for curious canoeists to explore the swamps on both sides of the stream. In spring, spawning carp can be seen and heard breaking the surface of the water in the shallows of the swamp. At 1.1 mi from the inlet the paddler often encounters one or two beaver dams, sometimes several feet high. The Dwaas Kill enters from the right; at some water levels this tributary can be paddled a mile or so upstream. Where the Dwaas Kill enters, the Anthony Kill makes a sharp left turn. This is the usual turnaround point. A grassy pasture beside the bank provides a convenient lunch spot. Adventurous paddlers can continue downstream on the Anthony Kill, but there are many trees that have fallen completely across the creek. It is difficult to drag the canoe up and over these trees. The creek eventually empties into the Hudson River at Mechanicville. The lower half of the Anthony Kill is the site of the Tenendaho White Water Race in early spring.

Upon returning to Round Lake, turn right (counterclockwise) along the swampy edge of the lake. Three-quarters of a mile farther is the channel that connects Round Lake with Little Round Lake. In the summer, when the channel is overgrown with vegetation, it is easily missed. Another 0.6 mi along Round Lake leads to the outlet of Ballston Creek. At high water, the creek is canoeable for a few thousand feet, under two bridges and through a culvert. The creek is not canoeable at low water. From here it is another 0.6 mi back to the starting point.

🛖 Takeout:
Same as launch.

Upper Hudson Tributaries

Grafton Lakes

↕ **Segment:**	Long Pond, Second Pond, Mill Pond, Shaver Pond, and Martin-Dunham Reservoir
☆ **County:**	Rensselaer
↔ **Length:**	Long Pond, 2.5 mi (4.0 km); Martin-Dunham Reservoir, 3.0 mi (4.8 km)
↘ **Drop:**	None
◆ **Difficulty:**	Flatwater
✳ **Problems:**	Shaver Pond requires a carry for access; wind can sometimes be a problem on open lakes
🏕 **Maps:**	Page 154; DOT Grafton; DeLorme page 67
✏ **Contributor:**	Will Holt

Grafton Lakes

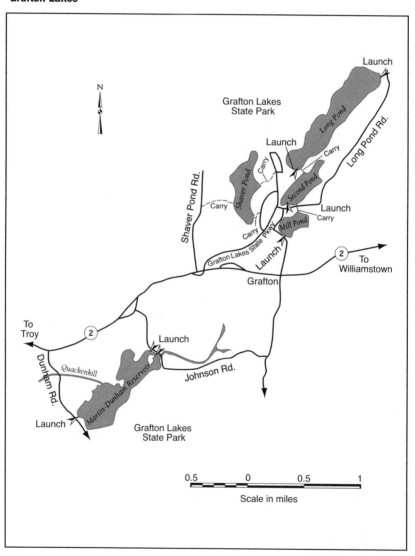

🎓 Launch:

From the Hudson River at Troy, follow NY 2 14.5 mi east to Grafton Lakes State Park. The park entrance is 0.8 mi west of the center of Grafton. Launches for these lakes are shown on the accompanying map.

📝 Description:

The Grafton Lakes are small as lakes go, but they are attractive and offer a few hours of paddling within a short distance of New York's Capital District. Area clubs hold races here during the summer and fall. The longest trip in the main portion of the park is on Long Pond, which has a good launch site at its northeast corner. A paddle along the shoreline of the lake covers about 2.5 mi. The shore is forested and unoccupied, except at the south end where there is a beach and other park facilities.

Second and Mill Ponds are similar to Long Pond but smaller. Each has its own launch site, but it is also possible to carry from Long Pond to Second Pond into Mill Pond. Shaver Pond, also in the main portion of the park, offers more isolated paddling but launching requires a carry of 0.1–0.3 mi from a park road or about 0.5 mi from a town road. Boats can be wheeled along the trails to these points.

Isolated paddling is also found on Martin-Dunham Reservoir, located to the southwest of the main portion of the park. A dam forms the western end of this irregularly-shaped body of water, no longer used as a reservoir. A paddle along the forested shoreline will cover about 3.0 mi including about 0.3 mi of the inlet stream, which enters through an attractive marshy area at the eastern end.

🛖 Takeout:

The same sites can be used to launch or takeout.

Lower Hudson Watershed

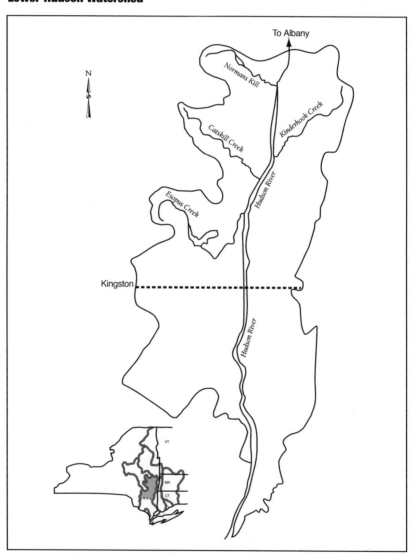

Lower Hudson Tributaries

Kinderhook Creek

Introduction

The Kinderhook Creek is a wonderful trip to start the paddling season. Although convenient to the Capital District, few paddlers come here. It is a spring runoff creek, often runnable when other streams are still too high. Having no upstream lake or reservoir, the creek loses its water soon after the snow melts. However, two or three days of steady rain in summer or fall will bring up the water level so that paddlers can enjoy the river for a day or two before it recedes again. Several small hamlets are passed as the creek flows through scenery varying from mixed hardwood and conifers to farmland.

There are no gauges for reading water levels. Those familiar with the Kinderhook say that paddlers can judge runnability by assessing the river level from the three bridges where US 20 crosses the creek between Nassau and Brainard.

!Caution:

First time paddlers on the Kinderhook should consider joining a scheduled ADK Schenectady Chapter trip or asking a person who knows the river to come along because of the downed trees and dangerous strainers that are often encountered.

✍ **Contributor:** Jim Pirman

Kinderhook Creek

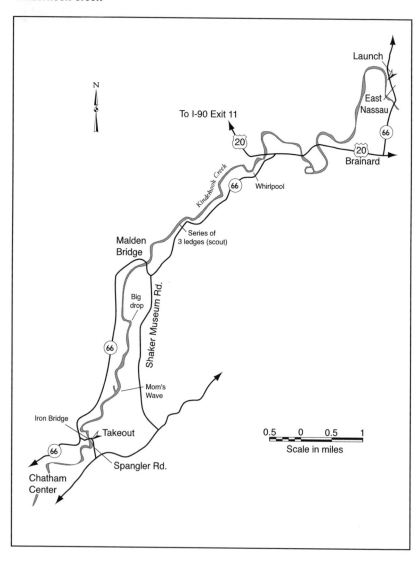

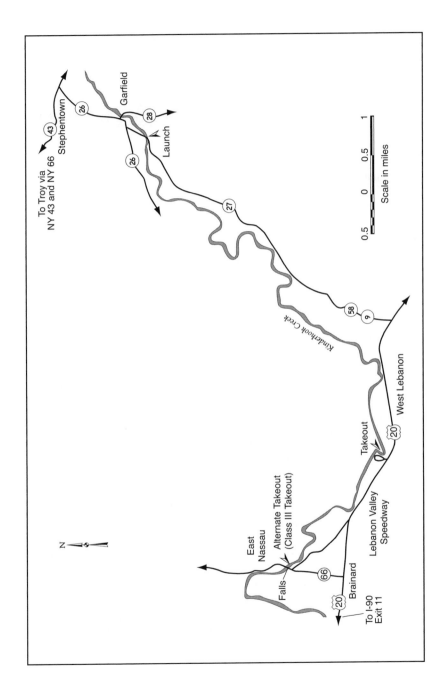

Lower Hudson Tributaries

Kinderhook Creek

⬍ **Segment:**	Stephentown to West Lebanon
☆ **Counties:**	Rensselaer, Columbia
↔ **Length:**	7.7 mi (12.4 km)
↘ **Drop:**	225 ft (68.6 m)
◆ **Difficulty:**	Class I with occasional minor Class II riffles (see Note on extending the trip 2.3 mi through a gorge with a Class III takeout)
✱ **Problems:**	Numerous strainers; possible stream-wide downed trees
⚲ **Maps:**	Page 159; DOT Stephentown Center, Canaan; DeLorme pages 53, 67
✍ **Contributor:**	Jim Pirman

🕮 Launch:

From I-90 take Exit 11 and drive 12.0 mi east on US 20 to Brainard. Continue east 3.5 mi on US 20 past the Lebanon Valley Speedway to the junction where US 9 enters on the left. (You will pass the loop road for the takeout where you may leave a shuttle car; see Takeout.) Drive north on US 9 (which becomes NY 27) 5.0 mi to the bridge over the Kinderhook.

The launch site can also be reached by taking NY 66 southeast out of Troy 12.0 mi to NY 43 entering on the left. Follow NY 43 9.0 mi to junction of County Route 26 just west of Stephentown. Take County Route 26 south 1.2 mi, then go left on County Route 27 0.2 mi to the bridge.

The put-in is just downstream of the County Route 27 bridge. Park along the shoulder of County Route 27 or just downstream of the bridge via a short gravel path which angles to the right from County Route 27. This site is at the edge of a farmer's field, so paddlers should ask permission.

There is an alternate put-in 0.2 mi upstream (northeast) where the bridge on County Route 28 crosses the creek at the intersection of County Route 26 and County Route 28. A few cars can be parked in a grassy area between County Route 26 and the bridge. There is an easy put-in above the bridge, but a row of small boulders directly under the bridge must be negotiated.

Description:

This segment of the Kinderhook is a leisurely, scenic day trip easily accessible from the Capital District. At the launch the Kinderhook is a small winding stream about 25-feet wide with riffles. In its nearly 8-mile course to the takeout, the stream flows between forested banks interspersed with areas of attractive farmland.

There are a few easy Class II sections, mostly where the stream passes under bridges. Watch for sweepers at bends in the creek.

Note: Experienced paddlers may wish to extend the trip another 2.3 mi. Adding this extension increases the total drop by 34 feet.

!Caution:

Do not attempt to run the trip extension without first scouting the Class III Takeout. There is a falls that ends in a nasty 15-foot drop just downstream of the takeout.

Paddlers running the extension will pass the Lebanon Valley Speedway at 8.0 mi; at 9.0 mi the creek makes a left turn and descends into a boulder-strewn gorge. At the end of the gorge there is a sharp drop with a house-sized rock in the middle of the creek. Most of the water passes left of the rock, but since the takeout is on the right, just beyond the rock, it is safer to stay right of the rock if there is enough water. If one paddles river left it is essential to eddy out behind the rock and ferry hard right to the shore to avoid being swept over the falls just below. **Do not miss this takeout. The second half of the falls is a nasty 15-foot drop.**

Takeout:

The takeout for the Class I trip is at an informal fisherman's access on river left with a convenient gravel beach and short trail where cars can be parked. The trail is located on the east side of a loop road located about 1.7 mi east of Brainard off US 20. The loop road encloses an unattractive area that seems to be a repository for defunct machinery. This is 0.3 mi east of the Lebanon Valley Speedway—possibly the source of the machinery carcasses!

To reach the launch from the Class I takeout, follow US 20 2.0 mi east to the junction with County Route 9. Turn left (north) on County Route 9 (which becomes County Route 27) for 4.5 mi to the put-in site.

The Class III takeout for the extended trip is on river right at a fisherman's access area. From I-90, Exit 11 take US 20 to the town of Brainard. Turn north on NY 66 at about 0.9 mi, crossing the bridge over the Kinderhook. Immediately after the bridge turn right on Tayer Road and follow the river 0.1 mi to the small fishing access area on the right.

Lower Hudson Tributaries

Kinderhook Creek

↕ **Segment:**	East Nassau to Chatham Center
☆ **Counties:**	Rensselaer, Columbia
↔ **Length:**	11.0 mi (17.7 km)
↘ **Drop:**	260 ft (79.3 m)
♦ **Difficulty:**	Class II; runnable in early spring or after two to three days of rain
✳ **Problems:**	Numerous strainers; downed trees
▲ **Maps:**	Page 158; DOT Stephentown Center, Nassau, East Chatham; DeLorme pages 53 and 67
✍ **Contributor:**	Jim Pirman

☵ Launch:

From I-90 take Exit 11 and drive east on US 20 about 12.0 mi to the junction with NY 66 in Brainard. Take NY 66 north 1.0 mi to East Nassau. Continue north on NY 66 through East Nassau an additional 0.2 mi to the launch site at a parking area on the left, next to the river.

✐ Description:

This segment of the Kinderhook is an active Class II play river featuring a boulder gorge, holes, surfing ledges, exciting drops, and a whirlpool. The river runs north from the launch site about 1.5 mi before bending west and then southwest through a small boulder-strewn gorge. The first of three US 20 bridges is reached 2.5 mi from the launch.

!Caution:

In the 1.0-mile section between the first and second US 20 bridges the paddler is sure to encounter strainers, logjams, and cutoffs. Extreme caution is a must in this section.

After passing under the second bridge, one encounters high waves where the river bends south. The third US 20 bridge crosses at 4.6 mi. At 5. 2 mi look for the whirlpool where (if you are still right side up) you can hone your play skills crossing the strong eddy line.

At 7.0 mi there is a series of three ledges. It is wise to scout these and fun to watch as others try their luck playing in the waves. Half a mile farther Malden bridge crosses the creek. There is a series of ledges at the bridge which are run most easily on river right.

Continuing south, the river passes under the New York State Thruway and comes to the Big Drop at 8.8 mi. Scout this drop by climbing a gravely hill on river right. After negotiating the upstream waves, most paddlers run the final ledge either far right or far left.

A mile before the takeout the river brings you to the most popular play spot of all, Mom's Wave. Enthusiasts can surf to exhaustion before heading down the last stretch to the takeout at Iron Bridge.

Takeout:

The takeout is on river left, upstream of the blocked-off Spangler Road iron bridge, at the foot of a steep bank.

!Caution:

Be careful to stay upstream of the bridge to avoid the broken dam just below. This can be big trouble in high water.

There is room for a few cars on Spangler Road on the east side of the bridge. Do not block the road, as it appears to be a gravel access road to property upstream of the bridge on the east side of the river.

To reach the takeout by car, take I-90 to Exit 11. Drive southeast 9.0 mi on US 20 to the junction with NY 66. Turn right (south) on NY 66 and drive 7.5 mi to the intersection with County Route 28. Turn left (east) on County Route 28 and drive 0.8 mi to County Route 13 entering left. Drive north on

County Route 13 0.6 mi to Spangler Road entering on left. Follow Spangler Road 0.5 mi to the takeout at Iron Bridge.

An alternate takeout is on river right, immediately past the bridge pier. The advantage is a more gradual grade up the bank to the road; if you stay close to the bridge you can avoid posted property. The disadvantages of this takeout are the narrow landing spots that will accommodate only one boat at a time and the close proximity to the broken dam downstream. There is room for several cars on the old unused road leading to the blocked-off Spangler Road bridge.

To reach this alternate takeout drive west on US 20 1.0 mi from Brainard to NY 66 branching to the left. Follow NY 66 7.0 mi to Spangler Road, a gravel road entering on the left. Follow Spangler Road 0.1 mi to the blocked west end of the Spangler Road iron bridge.

Note: There is an additional 7.0-mile Class I stretch of the Kinderhook starting just below the old broken dam and ending upstream of a dam south of Valatie. The creek passes through woods and farmland. At present there is no public access to takeout. All the property adjacent to the creek is private and posted. At a later time this attractive part of the Kinderhook may become available to the public.

Normans Kill

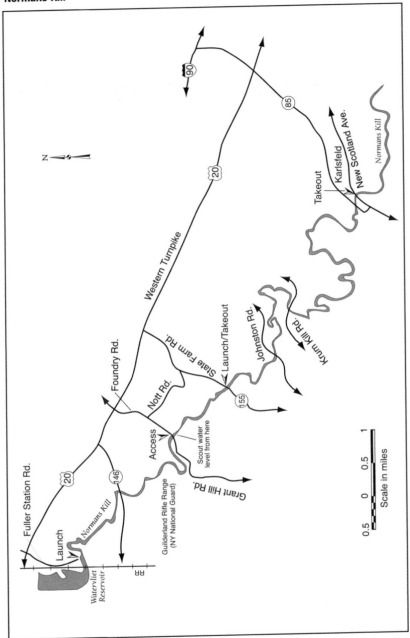

Lower Hudson Tributaries

Normans Kill

↕ **Segment:**	Watervliet Reservoir to New Scotland Avenue
☆ **County:**	Albany
↔ **Length:**	14.0 mi (22.5 km) (or shorter segments as described in text)
↘ **Drop:**	55 ft (16.8 m)
◆ **Difficulty:**	Swift water up to Class II; runnable in early spring or after significant rain
✳ **Problems:**	Downed trees, strainers
♠ **Maps:**	Page 165; DOT Voorheesville, Albany; DeLorme page 66
✍ **Contributor:**	Sally Dewes

⚓ Launch:

Although the 14-mile trip on the Normans Kill can be completed in one day, the paddler can also choose shorter segments, depending on available time. The segment from Fuller Station Road just below the Watervliet Reservoir to the NY 155 bridge at State Farm Road is 5.0 mi.

From this point to the takeout at New Scotland Avenue is an additional 9.0 mi. Another good access with parking is about 4.0 mi downstream of the reservoir, at the bridge where Grant Hill Road crosses. Accessing the stream at the bridges where Johnston Road or Krum Kill Road cross is difficult and not recommended.

To reach the launch below the Watervliet Reservoir, turn south from Western Turnpike (US 20) on Fuller Station Road. Drive about 1.0 mi to where the road ends on the north bank of the Normans Kill. Although some maps may show the road crossing the stream, this bridge is closed.

There is a large pull-off where you can easily park cars downstream on river left. It is advisable to inform the Guilderland police that you plan to park near the reservoir (518-351-1501). Unidentified cars left in this location may precipitate an investigation. Launch from the north bank below the railroad bridge.

To reach the launch at NY 155, turn south from Western Avenue on State Farm Road and drive about 1.5 mi to the bridge over the stream. There is room for one or two cars in a parking turnout on river left, just upstream of the bridge.

To reach the access at Grant Hill Road, turn south from Western Turnpike on Foundry Road and drive 0.6 mi to a fork where Foundry Road ends and Grant Hill Road branches right; continue another 0.5 mi on Grant Hill Road to the bridge over the river.

✐ Description:

Normans Kill is an interesting run through Albany County that can easily go unnoticed. It can be paddled only during spring runoff and after big rain events. Since there are no gauges, the only way to know if there is enough water for a run is to view the stream. A good scouting spot is the bridge at Grant Hill Road. What you see is what you get! If it looks like a bump and grind, it will be a bump and grind all the way from the reservoir.

From the reservoir to New Scotland Avenue, the stream is swift water to Class II with the gradient lessening as you travel downstream. There are strainers of all sizes and great care must be taken to avoid entrapment. You should expect to get out of your boat at least once and be prepared to move quickly if necessary.

! Caution:

About 4.0 mi from the reservoir, the Normans Kill flows through a National Guard rifle range. The guardsmen are not always there, but you should call the superintendent before making the trip to make sure you will not be part of the target practice. First call the scheduling office at 518-786-4810; explain that you want to run the river, how many boats will be going, and what time you expect to pass through. The scheduling office should refer you to the Range Keeper(s) at the site. Call this individual and again provide the details of your trip. This procedure will assure your safety.

From the launch site the stream flows northeast; very shortly you will see a small green sign on the right bank that identifies a pipe State Pollutant Discharge Elimination System (SPDES) discharge location.

About 0.3 mi into the trip the stream takes a turn to the right (southeast); at 0.8 mi a steep cliff rises on the left. The stream continues to meander and wind as it varies between fast moving water and Class II. At about 2.0 mi the NY 146 bridge passes overhead.

Approximately 1.0 mi after the bridge the river doglegs to the right and then arcs to the left through a 180-degree turn. The stream gets steeper and drops through a long Class II rapid. As the river bends left a very high cliff of black sedimentary rock appears on the right. During periods of heavy runoff there are beautiful, high waterfalls cascading down the cliff face.

As you pass this cliff you are entering the National Guard Rifle Range. As stated above, **call before launching to alert the range superintendent that you will be traveling through.** Now the river turns right and you will see a high cliff on your left which has been severely eroded by target practice. Immediately after passing the rifle range you will pass under the bridge at Grant Hill Road. The access is on river left and can be used as a takeout or launch site. Continue another mile to the takeout at State Farm Road (NY 155).

If you choose to launch at State Farm Road, the put-in is on river left upstream of the bridge. You are now below the Class II rapids. This section of the Normans Kill is an easy coast down a scenic meandering stream which drops only 40 ft in 9.0 mi. The terrain varies from flat to steep embankments of over 100 ft at sharp bends in the river. At 1.3 mi the stream flows under the Johnston Road bridge and at 4.0 mi the Krum Kill Road bridge passes overhead. Another 5.0 mi brings you to the takeout on river left, just upstream of the bridge at New Scotland Avenue.

Takeout:

To reach the State Farm Road, takeout by car, drive 1.5 mi south on State Farm Road (NY 155) from Western Turnpike (US 20) and leave the shuttle car in the parking turnout on river left just upstream of the bridge over the Normans Kill.

To reach the New Scotland Avenue bridge from I-90 Exit 4, drive south on NY 85 about 4.5 mi to New Scotland Avenue. Turn left and drive less than 0.5 mi to the bridge over the Normans Kill. There is room to park several cars just upstream of the bridge on river left.

! Caution:

Although the 4.0 mi between New Scotland Avenue and Delaware Avenue is easy, there is no good takeout at the Delaware Avenue bridge. Directly below the bridge is a series of dangerous Class V ledges where the river drops 10 ft in 0.1 mi!

Lower Hudson Tributaries

Catskill Creek

↕ **Segment:**	Cooksburg to East Durham
☆ **Counties:**	Albany and Greene
↔ **Length:**	9.5 mi (15.3 km)
↘ **Drop:**	310 ft (94.5 m)
◆ **Difficulty:**	Class III (may be Class IV in high water); runnable in early spring or after a significant rain; check the Schoharie Creek gauge at Prattsville for a level of at least 5.0 ft (see Appendix D, entries 1–3 to access water level data)
✳ **Problems:**	Frequent sweepers; rocky areas; several significant ledges; high crumbly banks in some places, which could fall without warning
▲ **Maps:**	Page 171; USGS Durham, Greenville, and Freehold; DeLorme pages 51, 52
✍ **Contributor:**	Charles Beach

🛶 Launch:

Take Exit 21 from I-87. Drive west on NY 23 to Cairo and take NY145 from Cairo to the junction with NY 81 in Cooksburg. There is no formally designated launch site for the Catskill. Paddlers must pick an appropriate place to park that does not interfere with traffic or private property. At this writing it possible to park along the side of NY 81 or in a vacant field adjacent to the creek between the junction of NY 81 and NY 145. A sizable stream joins the Catskill from the west at this site. The launch is just upstream of the NY 81 bridge.

Note: NY 145 passes within 1.0 mi of the takeout in East Durham, making it convenient to leave a shuttle car on the way from I-87 to the launch site at Cooksburg.

✒ Description:

The Catskill Creek flows through a charming rural landscape of farms, fields, and small towns. Meeting other paddlers is unlikely, as the creek is not known by many whitewater enthusiasts.

Water levels are high enough for paddling only during spring runoff or after a prolonged wet period. Although the map shows a gauging station at Oak Hill, it is no longer in operation. When the Prattsville gauge on the Schoharie Creek reads 5 ft, water in the Catskill is probably adequate.

From Cooksburg to Durham Road bridge in Oak Hill, the stream flows 4.0 mi through a wooded valley with scattered houses and camps along the banks. This section has stretches of lively Class II. Approximately 1.0 mi below the launch, the stream runs into an undercut wall as it turns sharply to the right. Approach this turn with caution.

Paddlers who wish to access the creek in Oak Hill can do so from the area around the Durham Road bridge, providing they can find an appropriate place to park. In the 1.3-mile section between this bridge and the one at Deans Mill Road, there is a series of ledges that may require scouting. The first ledge is easily run. Upstream of the second ledge there is a series of diagonal ledges before the stream drops abruptly into a pool on river left. The third ledge is short, dropping into a pool which has a large rock right of center. In some years, trees are caught by the rock and held across part of the stream. It is advisable to scout, as the ledge is scratchy on the left with rocks in the middle and on river right.

From the bridge at Deans Mill Road to the takeout at East Durham the stream flows through a wooded valley with several views of scenic cliffs. Approximately 1.7 mi downstream of the bridge there is a large ledge extending into the stream from a rock wall on the left. This ledge is about 3.0 ft high at the wall, becoming lower as it slopes to the right into the stream. Paddlers usually run the drop on the right; scouting is advisable.

⛵ Takeout:

The takeout is on river right about 200 ft above the County Route 67A bridge in East Durham. To reach the bridge take NY 145 to the junction with County Route 67A about 0.8 mi east of East Durham. Follow County Route 67A north about 1.0 mi to the bridge. Park wherever you can find an appropriate place. Ask permission if you think it may be private property.

Note: If water levels are adequate, paddlers who are interested in a longer trip can continue 6.7 mi to Woodstock. The river drops an additional 135 ft. Below the bridge at East Durham the flow is relatively gentle until one reaches a right turn with houses on the right shore. The next three rapids have small ledges; the third may require scouting.

Catskill Creek

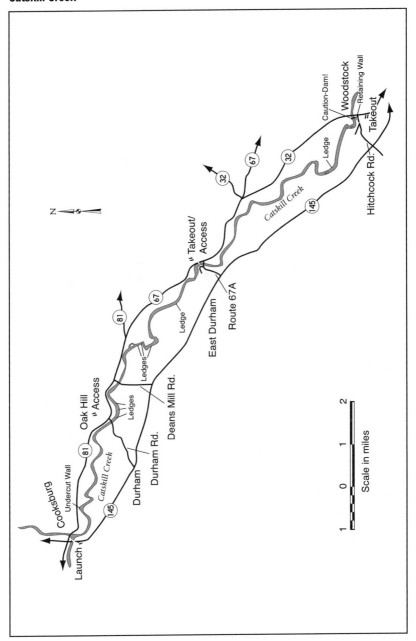

! Caution:

There is a partially broken dam above the NY 32 bridge in Woodstock; if approached too closely the dam can be dangerous because of the strong current flowing through holes in the structure.

There is a retaining wall on the top of the right bank extending upstream from the dam about 200 ft. Paddlers should plan to takeout before reaching the upstream end of the retaining wall. Scout this area before attempting to use it! There is no known public access above the dam, so permission must be obtained to takeout between the houses along the shore.

Lower Hudson Tributaries

Esopus Creek

↕ **Segment:**	Allaben to Boiceville
☆ **County:**	Ulster
↔ **Length:**	11.0 mi (17.7 km)
↘ **Drop:**	354 ft (107.9 m)
♦ **Difficulty:**	Class II–III; runnable in early spring and all summer during scheduled water releases; gauge reading of 5.3 ft at Cold Brook is a good medium level (see Appendix D, entries 1, 2, or 3 for water level information).
✳ **Problems:**	Congestion from other paddlers, rafts, and inner tubers in summer; canoe/kayak slalom racers at Railroad Rapids
⚲ **Maps:**	Page 175; DOT Phoenicia; DeLorme page 51
✍ **Contributor:**	Kathleen Magee

⚓ Launch:

Leave I-87 at Exit 19. Follow NY 28 west 28.0 mi to Allaben. There is a small, gravel parking area alongside the Shandaken Tunnel Aqueduct. Cars can be parked there or along the northeast side of the highway. To reach the creek, carry the canoe across the highway (generally not too busy), over a guardrail, and down a short embankment. There is a generous amount of poison ivy growing along the banks of Esopus Creek—beware.

✐ Description:

Esopus Creek is a beautiful, challenging whitewater creek that reinvents itself from year to year. It is a pleasure to paddle it for the first time in the spring and discover how the course has changed over the winter. This is a steep, intimate mountain stream, easily influenced by the forces of nature. It is also a very popular creek for summer paddlers, inner tubers, and fly fishermen. While one part of its personality is isolated beauty, the Esopus can also be a social butterfly.

The Esopus can be paddled in early spring on its natural flow or after a substantial rainfall, but most paddlers take advantage of occasional water releases from Schoharie Reservoir, 18.0 mi away. The water travels to the Esopus through an aqueduct that goes under the Catskill Mountains. Water then flows down the Esopus to the Ashokan Reservoir, providing water to New York City residents. In recent years, the releases have generally been scheduled monthly: the first weekend in June, second weekend in July, occasionally a weekend in August, one in September, and then the first weekend in October. Certain designated paddling groups request releases from New York State DEC Bureau of Water Resources for the purpose of races or safety instruction. Releases may be cancelled for water conservation or other reasons. The Bureau of Water Resources can be reached at 518-457-1626. Ernie Gardner of Cold Brook Canoes in Boiceville (914-657-2189) is an additional source of information about releases.

When the gauge at Cold Brook reads between 4.8 and 5.8 ft the level is good for paddlers. At 4.7 ft the creek is scratchy; 6.0 ft is too high for the average paddler. According to New York USGS data, 11.0 ft is flood level.

The drive from the takeout in Boiceville to the put-in can be used to scout the two biggest rapids on the creek, Elmers Corner and Railroad Rapids. Elmers Corner is located on a sharp bend immediately below Phoenicia. There is no good place to park to scout; just pull over to the side of the road.

Scout Railroad Rapids from High Street in Phoenicia; crossing the creek on the Woodland Valley bridge places you immediately above the rapid. There is parking along High Street and an easy bank to walk to see the full rapid.

Because of its changing nature, it is not possible to offer a detailed guide to the creek without risking obsolescence by the next paddling season. There are several consistencies, however. There are small islands, often built-up gravel bars, throughout the run, with the preferred channels changing from time to time. A truism about the Esopus is that if you go with the flow, you will probably find a large boulder or hole in the midst of it! In other words, paddlers should pay attention to what is ahead, approach each bend with caution, and maintain control of their boats at all times.

The 3.5-mile section from Allaben to Railroad Rapids consists of fastwater, occasional strainers, and lots of turns. There are several good play holes along the way; they will probably be identified by a cluster of kayaks waiting their turn. The creek is approximately 40 ft wide at this point and generously supplied with large rocks, creating small ledges, holes, standing waves, and eddy spots.

The Woodland Valley bridge marks the approach of Railroad Rapids. During the first weekend of June and October this is also the scene of canoe and kayak slaloms. If a race is going on, an official will ask through-paddlers to wait for a break in the race before going through the rapids. Slalom gates across the creek make scouting easier; many paddlers simply determine which gates they will go through rather than which rocks to avoid.

Railroad Rapids is a work in progress. Previously consisting of a steep drop followed by standing waves, a storm in 1996 shifted boulders and made it less technical. After the excitement of running the drop, many paddlers like to stop and sit on the large erosion-control boulders lining the right bank, eat lunch, and watch other paddlers and tubers negotiate the rapid.

Below Railroad Rapids is a small rock garden followed by a shute, before turning the corner and approaching Phoenicia. The Phoenicia rock garden is more substantial, bounded by the NY 28 and NY 155 bridges. Water tends to be deeper on the right side of the creek. On the left is an exit point for most tubers; below Phoenicia, the creek becomes much less populated.

The first turn below the NY 155 bridge marks the beginning of the second big rapid on the creek, Elmers Corner. It has the effect of a spiral staircase, making a nearly 90-degree turn with a steep gradient. There is room to eddy out just below the rapid on either side; below are several small ledges and then a quiet, wider stretch.

In the next 6.5 mi, Esopus Creek becomes an interesting and scenic Class II stream, still with dancing water and challenging maneuvers, but on a less technical level. There is a put-in (or takeout) on the left bank, just past a small water station. The creek flows by campgrounds, a scenic railroad, and a final exit point for tubers before it goes by Mount Tremper. Note the rock cairns and sculptures, a variety of miniature and temporary Stonehenges, placed along the rocky shore by idle sun worshippers, just before the Mount Tremper bridge.

Esopus Creek

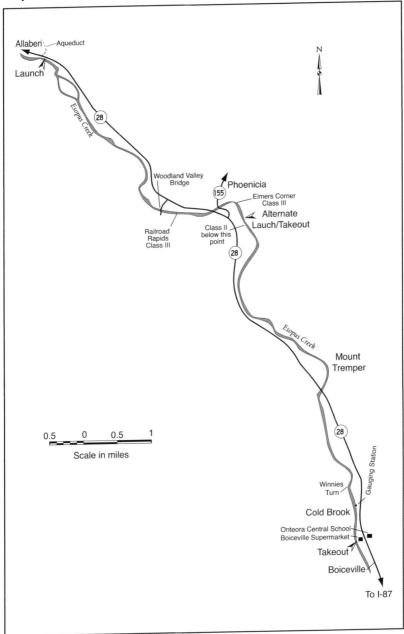

Soon after Mount Tremper, the creek passes under NY 28 once again, then speeds directly toward a steep mountain, creating an interesting whirlpool eddy on the right just before the creek makes an abrupt left turn.

The next mile is a mix of flatwater and rapids, with smooth, flat rocks decorating the edges of the creek. This is a good area to see mergansers, sometimes with up to twelve ducklings in tow.

At approximately 10.0 mi, one approaches the final sets of rapids. The first is an S-turn, Winnies Turn, with boulders above, below, and in the middle. At the end of the turn is a short stretch of ledges and boulders; at the bottom right is an excellent play hole. The creek continues by the old Cold Brook bridge and gauge station and then the NY 28A bridge is seen in the distance.

Takeout:

The takeout is 0.5 mi from the Cold Brook bridge, on the left. To reach the takeout by car from NY 28, drive through the parking lot of the Boiceville Supermarket, all the way to the Stucki Embroidery parking lot near the creek's edge. While parking is not permitted, the lot can be used to load boats and gear after the trip. The best parking option is the Onteora Central School parking lot across NY 28.

Railroad Rapids on Esopus Creek   Dana Garber

Lake Champlain Drainage

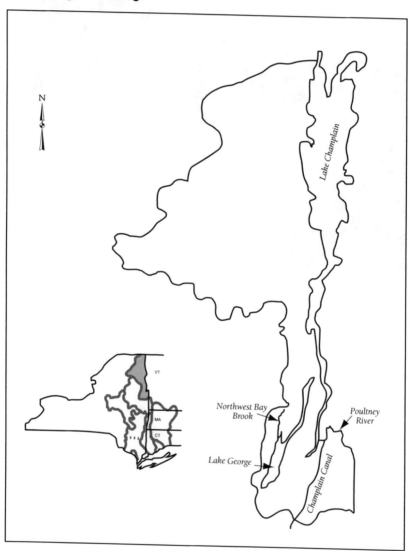

Lake Champlain Drainage

Lake George

↕ **Segment:**	Northwest Bay Brook	
☆ **County:**	Warren	
↔ **Length:**	2.5 mi (4.0 km) round-trip to the lake plus any desired distance on Northwest Bay	
↘ **Drop:**	Negligible	
♦ **Difficulty:**	Flatwater	
✳ **Problems:**	Rough water on lake in windy weather; rattlesnakes on land	
⛰ **Maps:**	Page 180; USGS Bolton; DeLorme page 89	
✍ **Contributor:**	Will Holt	

🛶 Launch:

Launch at a state fishing access site on the east side of NY 9N about 5.0 mi north of Bolton Landing. Bolton Landing is on the west shore of Lake George and can be reached from I-87, Exit 24, as well as by NY 9N from north or south.

📖 Description:

This trip combines a winding Adirondack stream in marshy terrain and the very attractive shoreline of Lake George's Northwest Bay. The brook can be paddled a short distance upstream before heading downstream to the right at the launch site. Paddling downstream, the brook is flatwater with little current. It turns sharply to the right after about 0.3 mi and continues toward the lake. A left turn at the bend leads the paddler to at least two interesting backwater branches. The stream and backwaters are surrounded by a marshy area, which is several hundred yards wide and bordered by forested shores. The backwaters can be explored at the beginning of the trip or on the way back.

Continuing downstream, the marsh narrows and the brook enters Northwest Bay about 1.3 mi from the launch. The Nature Conservancy maintains the area as a preserve for the plants, birds, and other animals that flourish in this habitat. Rattlesnakes are occasionally sighted on shore.

Northwest Bay is a large body of water which can be very rough, even life-threatening for canoeists, when a strong south wind is blowing. A northwest

Lake George: Northwest Bay Brook

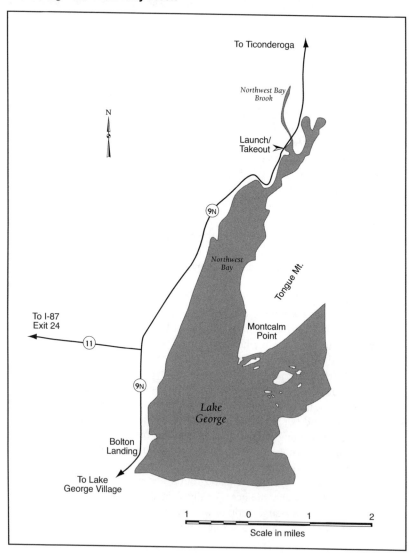

wind can also be pushy but does not produce such large waves. If conditions are favorable, the best canoeing is along the beautiful east (left) side of the bay which is the west side of Tongue Mountain. This is an attractive shoreline with clear water, steep rocky banks, tall overhanging trees, and a succession of points and bays. It is state land with no sign of human presence except a sometimes-visible footpath. There are places where canoes can be landed for hiking. The trail is noted for the variety of wildflowers that bloom in succession during the seasons. Canoeists can turn around at any point and return to the launch site.

About 4.0 mi from the launch is Montcalm Point at the extreme southern end of Tongue Mountain. Here Northwest Bay opens into the main lake where there are many islands and fine views in all directions. Boat traffic is sometimes heavy, producing significant waves even when the wind is calm. There are good places for swimming off the rocks at Montcalm Point, but be alert for rattlesnakes!

🛶 Takeout:

Takeout at the launch site. A short walk north on NY 9N leads to informal paths to waterfalls on the west side of the highway.

Lake Champlain Drainage

Poultney River

↕ **Segment:**	West Haven, Vermont, to Whitehall, New York
☆ **Counties:**	Washington, New York; Rutland, Vermont
↔ **Length:**	6.0 mi (9.7 km)
↘ **Drop:**	Negligible
♦ **Difficulty:**	Flatwater
✳ **Problems:**	Downed trees; low water
♠ **Maps:**	Page 183; DOT Thornhill, Whitehall (New York); DeLorme (New York) page 89

✐ **Contributor:** Ed Miller

At one time Lake Champlain was an arm of the sea and more recently (10,000 years ago), the region was slowly uncovered by the retreating continental glacier. This segment of the Poultney River is part of the border between New York State and Vermont. Only along this stretch of the river do Vermont state lands lie west of New York state lands.

⛵ Launch:

From I-87 Exit 20, drive east on NY 149 to the intersection with US 4 in Fort Ann. Follow US 4 north to Whitehall. After crossing the canal, turn north (left) on County Route 9 (Williams Street) and continue for about 1.0 mi to County Route 10 (Doig Street), which enters on the left. Follow County Route 10 north 5.5 miles to the Poultney River. Immediately after crossing the bridge, turn left on a dirt road. A good put-in is about a mile downstream of the bridge, where parking is available for a few cars. Do not block the road.

✏ Description:

The Poultney River flows north through Fair Haven, Vermont, then turns west. When it turns south, the current slackens and remains quiet all the way to the East Bay of Lake Champlain, north of Whitehall. In the spring, the water level of Lake Champlain is high enough to back water all the way to the put-in. In summer and fall, the lake drops and the water may be too shallow in the upper sec-

Poultney River

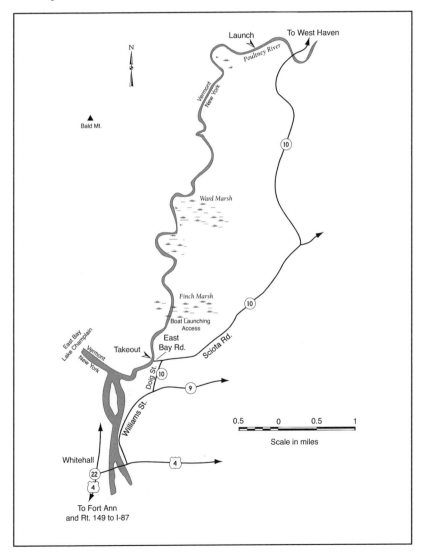

tion. However, one can paddle upstream from the takeout at any time and it is still a good trip. The bluffs along the river are limestone, and their erosion has contributed to the rich soil and the biological diversity of the area. Both New York and Vermont Nature Conservancy chapters have acquired land along the river to protect rare and endangered species of plants and animals. Of particular interest are the rare fresh water mussels that live in the river. Please do not disturb them. Golden corydalis blooms early on the few rock ledges visible from your canoe. In the summer you should find flowering rush, a pretty but alien species that so far seems to be limited to the Lake Champlain watershed.

There are very few homes along the river. Most of the land is flooded in the spring and you will likely see flood debris in trees at surprising heights above your canoe. Three miles from the put-in, a clearing on the New York State side marks the Ward Marsh wetland complex protected by The Nature Conservancy. It may be your best bet for a lunch stop. Across the river is Bald Mountain, which is protected by the Nature Conservancy and the state of Vermont as a nesting site for peregrine falcons. At 6.0 mi the Finch Marsh wetland appears on the New York side of the river. You can probably get over the beaver dam that blocks this wetland. Even without access, you should see ducks, geese, herons, and lots of sunning turtles. In spring yellow iris, dame's rocket, and other flowers adorn the riverbanks. Finch Marsh can be accessed by boat from a launching area on County Route 10.

You will probably not be tempted to swim in the river, but the muddy, shallow water is a perfect habitat for many animals. There are signs of beaver along the entire distance and at least one otter slide, and you can expect to see mink and muskrat. Bird calls make a continuous chorus. Bring along someone who can identify birds by their calls since it is difficult to use binoculars from a drifting canoe. The takeout at the County Route 10 bridge appears all too soon after the wetland area. The half-mile below the bridge is very pleasant and the current is usually slight enough so that paddling down and back to the takeout is no problem.

🏠 Takeout:
Takeout at the bridge at East Bay Road. County Route 10 is about 0.1 mi east of the bridge. If you travel north on County Route 10 to the launch site, a shuttle car can be left conveniently at the East Bay Road takeout before you begin the trip.

Lake Champlain Drainage

Champlain Canal

Introduction

Technically, the state refers to all locks and short, canalized stretches of the Hudson north of Troy as the Champlain Canal. However, this guide describes the Champlain Canal as the section that connects the Hudson River at Fort Edward to Lake Champlain at Whitehall. There are five locks in this section: Lock 12 at Whitehall to Lock 7 at Fort Edward. Lock 10 was never built. The canal system was constructed in the mid-1820s.

The highest elevation of this waterway is between Locks 8 and 9. From here, water flows north to Lake Champlain and south to New York City. To provide water for the flow in both directions, the Glens Falls Feeder Canal was built to bring water from the Hudson above Glens Falls to the high point of the Champlain Canal, the pool between Locks 8 and 9. Although there is little current here, it flows in opposite directions on either side of the junction with the Feeder Canal. Travel can be in either direction, but for convenience, this guide describes the canal as it would be encountered in a canoe paddling south from Whitehall to Fort Edward.

Paddlers will have no problem passing through any of the locks on the Champlain Canal, or any other part of the New York State Barge Canal System. Lock operators are happy to "lock through" one or more small boats any time that the locks are open, during daylight hours from about May 1 to late November. There are tolls on the canal system for powerboats, but not for any boat without an engine.

It is advisable to notify in advance the lock operator at the first lock the paddler plans to "lock through" and ask the lock operator to phone ahead to the next lock, with a request that he or she do the same when (s)he sees the boat(s) approaching. It is sometimes difficult to get out of the boat and walk to the lock house, and usually impossible to shout loud enough to be heard. A convenient way to notify the lock operator is by cell phone.

Paddlers can call the Barge Canal Division in Albany for information on all the locks: 518-471-5055. Phone numbers for individual locks are given in the trip descriptions as needed.

Commercial traffic on the canal is not heavy; pleasure boats traveling in excess of the speed limit present a greater problem to canoes and kayaks than barges.

Whitehall is an historic town whose past commerce was heavily dependent on the canal system. The town claims, and is considered by many, to be the "Birthplace of the U.S. Navy." Colonial troops under the direction of Benedict Arnold built a fleet of small ships here to fight the British on Lake Champlain. Although the fleet was defeated, the tactic served to delay the British advance on Saratoga, where they were defeated by the American Revolutionary Army. At that time Whitehall was known as Skenesborough.

✍ **Contributors:** Mark Freeman and Chet Harvey

Lake Champlain Drainage

Champlain Canal

↕ **Segment:**   Whitehall to Fort Ann
☆ **County:**   Washington
↔ **Length:**   10.5 mi (16.9 km)
↘ **Drop:**   Elevations increase and decrease, but only at locks
♦ **Difficulty:**   Flatwater
✳ **Problems:**   None
▲ **Maps:**   Page 187; DOT Whitehall, Fort Ann; DeLorme page 81, 89
✍ **Contributor:** Mark Freeman

🌊 Launch:

The village of Whitehall maintains good access in Skenesborough Park, near the ruins of the *USS Ticonderoga*, which dates back to 1812. Launch down a grassy ramp from Main Street in Whitehall, just north of US 4, and south of Lock 12. There are toilet facilities and parking for several cars.

✎ Description:

This section of the canal is a quiet paddle through farmland and low-lying marsh country. Great numbers of birds, including great blue herons, kingfishers,

Champlain Canal: Whitehall to Fort Ann

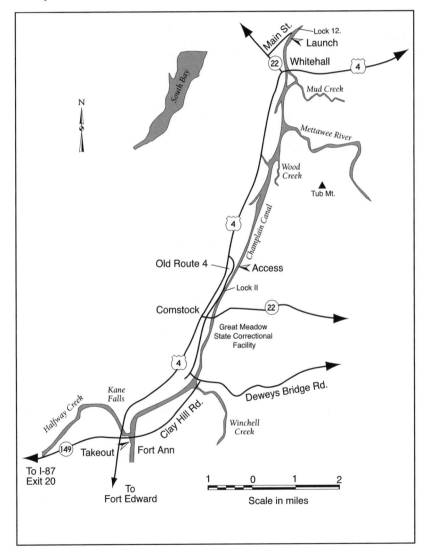

ducks, and red-winged blackbirds, inhabit the area. The paddler is also likely to glimpse muskrat, beaver, and other animals.

Before construction of the canal 180 years ago, Wood Creek and the Mettawee River joined about 1.0 mi south of Whitehall and the combined flow followed a meandering course north and northwest to Lake Champlain's East Bay. The mouth of the old riverbed enters the canal almost directly across from the launch site.

For the first 1.5 mi the canal is a straightened and deepened modification of the combined riverbeds of the Mettawee River and Wood Creek. Beyond the junction with the Mettawee, the canal continues another 2.5 mi as a modification of the bed of Wood Creek. Remnant arcs of the old riverbeds offer fascinating bayou-like backwaters that invite exploration. Paddlers can travel up any stream that enters the canal for some distance before encountering obstacles.

The canal passes under US 4 and a bridge of the Delaware & Hudson Railroad less than 0.5 mi from launch. The unusual round shape of Tub Mountain rises 400 ft above the surrounding flat, marshy land on the left. The Delaware & Hudson and US 4 parallel the canal on the right for almost the entire length of this section. There are no roads on the left and the terrain is low-lying and swampy.

The first lock encountered is Lock 11 at Comstock, about 6.5 mi from launch. (Lock Operator phone: 518-639-8964.) There is a fairly good access point on the right 1.0 mi before the lock. It can be reached by car via Old US 4, which passes the lock and ends at the access point. There are no difficulties in locking through. Below Lock 11 the vast installation of Great Meadows Correctional Facility stretches for about a mile on the left.

At 7.0 mi NY 22 crosses the canal. About 1.5 mi farther Winchell Creek enters from the left at the Deweys Bridge Road crossing. About 10.5 mi from launch, in the center of Fort Ann, Clay Hill Road crosses the canal and Halfway Creek enters on the right. Usually one can paddle up Halfway Creek to the foot of beautiful Kane Falls.

🛶 Takeout:

The takeout is on the right, just after passing under the Clay Hill Road bridge. To reach this takeout by car from I-87 take Exit 20 and drive east on NY 149 to the traffic light at US 4 in the center of Fort Ann. Clay Hill Road joins into this intersection from the east. Parking for the takeout is on Clay Hill Road about 0.1 mi east of the traffic light on the right, just before crossing the bridge.

Champlain Canal

↕ **Segment:**	Fort Ann to Fort Edward	
☆ **County:**	Washington	
↔ **Length:**	12.3 mi (19.8 km)	
↘ **Drop:**	Elevations increase and decrease, but only at locks	
♦ **Difficulty:**	Flatwater	
✳ **Problems:**	None	
🛉 **Maps:**	Page 190; DOT Fort Ann, Hartford, Hudson Falls; DeLorme page 81	
✍ **Contributor:**	Mark Freeman	

🌊 Launch:

Launch at the Clay Hill Road bridge in the center of Fort Ann. This is the take-out point described in the Whitehall to Fort Ann segment of the canal.

✐ Description:

Paddling this segment of the canal provides the opportunity to pass through Locks 8 and 9. As mentioned in the introduction to the Champlain Canal, it is a good idea to notify the lock operator at the first lock in advance and ask him/her to phone ahead to the next lock. (Phone for Lock 9: 518-747-6021; Lock 8: 518-747-5520)

From Fort Ann to Fort Edward, the Delaware & Hudson Railroad runs parallel to the canal on the west. US 4 follows as far as Baldwin Corners Road where it turns west and NY 149 continues south to Smiths Basin. The canal passes through farmland similar to that found between Whitehall and Fort Ann; however, there is more high ground and less marsh.

Baldwin Corners Road crosses the canal about 1.5 mi from the launch. Another 2.5 mi brings the paddler to the hamlet of Smiths Basin where NY 149 crosses the canal and Big Creek enters from the left. Lock 9 is just south of these landmarks. There is no Lock 10. By some accounts, every section of the New York State Barge Canal has at least one phantom lock.

The highest point on the Champlain Canal system is between Locks 8 and 9, where water flows north from Lock 9 and south from Lock 8. In order to pro-

Champlain Canal: Fort Ann to Fort Edward

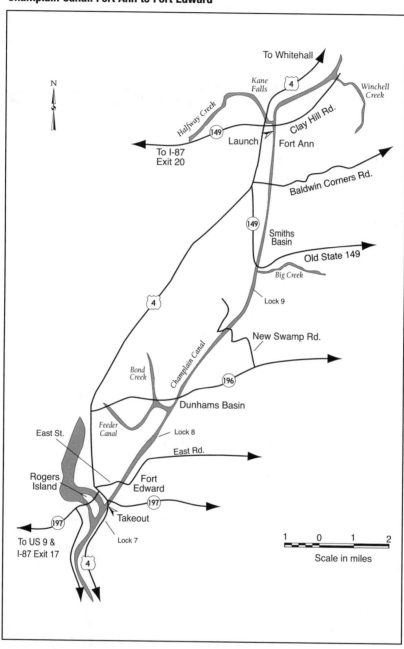

vide adequate levels to maintain flow in both directions, the Glens Falls Feeder Canal brings water 7.5 mi from the Hudson River just south of Glens Falls and empties into the canal between the two locks.

Six miles from Fort Ann, the aptly named New Swamp Road crosses, and 2.5 mi farther, the paddler reaches Dunhams Basin and the NY 196 bridge. Bond Creek enters on the right, just below the bridge. Bond Creek connects the modern canal with the original canal built in the early nineteenth century. The remains of the old canal are visible along almost the entire route, and are particularly impressive in Fort Edward near Lock 7. Building the modern canal required dredging about a quarter of a mile of Bond Creek to form a connection from the old canal to the Glens Falls Feeder Canal, through which water is introduced to today's waterway.

About 10.0 mi from Fort Ann, the paddler reaches Lock 8. About 1.0 mi beyond the Lock, East Street bridge crosses and at 11.8 mi the paddler passes under NY 197. The takeout is another 0.5 mi, just before Lock 7.

🛶 Takeout:

The best access is on the left bank just north of Lock 7, where a steep dirt road angles down from the Lock 7 access road. The Lock 7 access road connects to US 4 near the east end of the US 4 bridge over the canal. There is plenty of parking in the general area.

Lake Champlain Drainage

Glens Falls Feeder Canal

↕ **Segment:**	Feeder Dam to Martindale Avenue
☆ **Counties:**	Warren, Washington
↔ **Length:**	5.5 mi (8.9 km)
↘ **Drop:**	Slight
◆ **Difficulty:**	Flatwater
✳ **Problems:**	None
⚲ **Maps:**	Page 193; DOT Glens Falls, Hudson Falls; DeLorme page 81
✍ **Contributor:**	Kathleen Kathe

⚓ Launch:

A boat dock is conveniently located at the Moore Memorial Bridge at the Feeder Dam Park in Glens Falls. To reach the park take Exit 18 from I-87; drive east on Main Street 0.6 mi and turn right on Richardson Street for another 0.6 mi to the end of the street. There is room to park a few cars. Carry the boats around a gate to the dock.

There are no public restrooms along the Feeder Canal and the only access points are the launch and the takeout at Martindale Park. Almost all of the land along the canal is private property.

✒ Description:

The Feeder Canal is steeped in history. It was built in 1824 to bring water from the Hudson River at Glens Falls and carry it eastward about 7.5 mi to the highest point on the Champlain Canal. This water assured adequate levels in the Champlain Canal, both north to Lake Champlain and south to its junction with the Hudson at Fort Edward. The first feeder canal and dam constructed in 1822 at Fort Edward were abandoned after a flood destroyed the dam. In 1824 a new dam was built across the Hudson River upstream from Wings Falls (now Glens Falls) and construction of a new Feeder Canal began; it ran seven miles eastward to join the Champlain Canal, guaranteeing adequate water at its summit between Locks 8 and 9.

In 1832 the canal was widened and deepened to accommodate barge traffic. Mills and factories soon lined the banks and the canal became a major

Glens Falls Feeder Canal

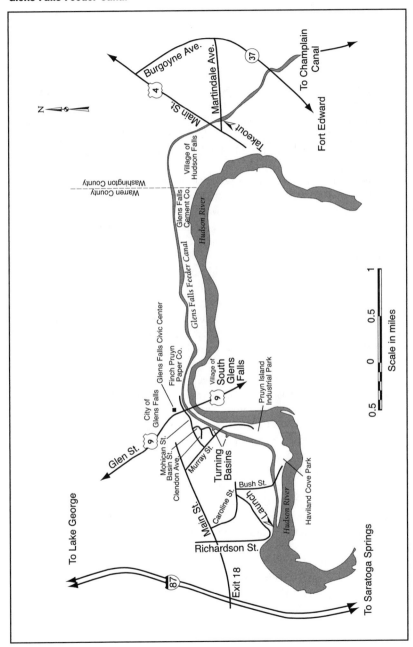

shipping route for the next 100 years. In its heyday, the canal carried the products of a booming Glens Falls economy to the outside world. Lumber, lime, paper, apples, potatoes, and other items moved via this route. The trip required thirteen locks to negotiate the steep 130-foot drop east of Hudson Falls. Although no longer able to lift boats, the locks remain and may be seen at the end of the trip.

The Feeder Canal Alliance, a group of dedicated volunteers, has cleaned and refurbished the canal over the past decade so that paddlers can fully enjoy this nostalgic return to the route as it was in days long gone. The Alliance has also built attractive picnic facilities at each end and a jogging and bike route the length of the canal. The Glens Falls Feeder Canal is listed on the National Register of Historic Places.

About 0.5 mi from launch, paddlers pass under the Bush Street bridge and through the Glens Falls City Park at Havilands Cove. There is a slight but definite current in the canal, flowing from west to east. The remains of an old turning basin come into view on the left about 1.3 mi from launch; 0.2 mi farther on is a second basin adjacent to Clendon Basin Avenue. The boats that navigated the canal were very long, and narrow, capable of changing direction only at these basins!

Between the two basins Murray Street passes over the canal, providing vehicle access to Pruyn's Island, an industrial park between the canal and the river. A short distance beyond Murray Street the canal passes under Glen Street (US 9), past the Glens Falls Civic Center, and through the busy complex of the Finch Pruyn Paper Company. Until the canal was closed to navigation in the 1920s, Finch Pruyn shipped many loads of newsprint to New York City via this route. At high water the paddler may have to duck under an open structure supporting a pipe across the canal.

Soon the canal passes the ghostly chalk-white buildings of the Jointa Lime Company. At one time more than eighty limekilns lined the banks; industrial products produced from the lime were shipped from Glens Falls via the Champlain Canal.

About 4.5 mi from launch, the canal rounds a bend and passes the Glens Falls Cement Company before crossing into Washington County. This rural wooded area is particularly popular with birdwatchers, and indicates the approach of the takeout about a mile downstream.

⌂ Takeout:

The takeout is at Boat Basin Park on Martindale Avenue in Hudson Falls. Martindale Avenue runs west to east between Main Street (US 4) and Burgoyne Avenue (County Route 37) crossing the canal about 0.1 mi east of Main Street. Here, on the site of a filled-in basin, there are docks, benches, and a small park, as well as room to park a number of cars. Paddlers will find it worthwhile to walk a short distance along the canal beyond the takeout to view the old locks, especially the steep group called the Five Combines.

Mohawk River Watershed

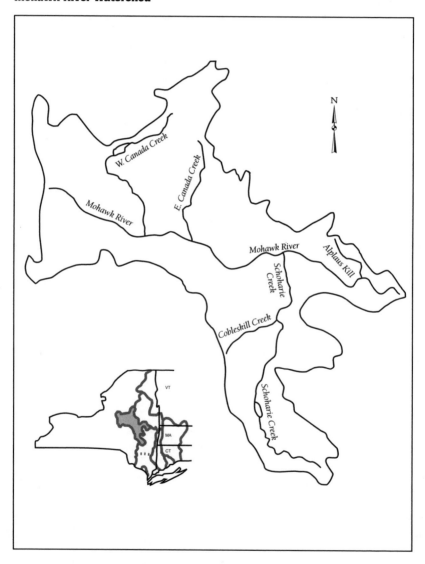

Mohawk River Tributaries

West Canada Creek

Introduction

Early in the century, West Canada Creek carried logs from the west central Adirondacks mills downstream. Today, the creek provides enjoyable boating, including flat- and whitewater paddling, tubing, fishing, camping, and other outdoor recreational activities. The creek is drawn from the many small, little-known lakes and vleis of the central Adirondacks. Notable sources are T Lake, located on a plateau above Piseco from which the spectacular Piseco flume descends, and the West Canada Lakes, which lie in one of the largest wilderness areas of the Adirondack Park. Branches from different sources converge, emptying into Hinckley Reservoir about 4.0 mi upstream of the village of Trenton Falls. The dam drops water from the reservoir through the power station into an impressive gorge from which the creek, now more the size of a river, flows southward 32 mi to the Mohawk River. En route the river passes five towns, the largest of which is Herkimer, located at the confluence with the Mohawk.

Paddlers should not leave the valley without viewing it from above. NY 29, heading east from Middleville, climbs high above the surroundings for a stunning view. Here on Barto Hill you are 1000 ft above the river and can see the West Canada Valley sweep down into the Mohawk Valley.

The upper creek cascades 17 mi over a rugged plateau through forested wilderness. Some upper sections can be paddled by advanced paddlers, depending on the water level, but this guide focuses on the three more reliable stretches beginning near the mouth of the Trenton Gorge and ending close to the confluence with the Mohawk River. The challenges and rewards increase as one paddles farther down the river. You choose how much you want to do!

There are no less than six state access sites along the river. If you need shuttle help between your chosen put-in and takeout, the West Canada Creek Campground offers rides for a modest fee, determined by the trip length. Give them a call to confirm: 315-826-7390. The river is best paddled when the flow rate is 800–2000 cfs. Water release information is available by calling Waterline (see Appendix D, entry 2); the code for West Canada Creek is 365124. Waterline will give you the time and duration of the release. Plan your trip carefully, keeping in mind that it takes about one hour for the water released from

Hinckley Dam to reach Trenton Falls, and eight or nine hours for it to reach Middleville.

✍ **Contributors:** Larry and Esther Denham

Mohawk River Tributaries

West Canada Creek

↕ **Segment:**   Trenton Falls to Poland
☆ **Counties:**   Oneida, Herkimer
↔ **Length:**   6.2 mi (10.0 km)
↘ **Drop:**   40 ft (12.2 m)
◆ **Difficulty:** Class I; runnable at 400 cfs or higher; use Waterline (see Appendix D, entry 2) for release schedule at Hinckley Dam
✳ **Problems:**   Downed trees, especially around islands
⚑ **Maps:**   Page 199; DOT Remsen, South Trenton, Newport; DeLorme page 77

✍ **Contributors:** Larry and Esther Denham

⛵ Launch:

From the west, take Exit 31 from I-90 in Utica. Follow NY 12 to the intersection with NY 28 at Barneveld Station. Follow NY 28 east and southeast 3.0 mi to the bridge over West Canada Creek. The launch site is at a New York State fisherman's access on the east side of the river upstream of the bridge. There is a good-sized parking lot.

From the east, take Exit 30 from I-90 at Herkimer and drive north on NY 28 about 23 mi to the launch site. An alternate, unofficial access is 0.5 mi west of the bridge on NY 28 at a bend in the river. This launch offers a 5-mile trip to Poland.

Note: This segment can be extended to 9.0 mi by launching at the Downers Hill Road bridge in Trenton Falls. However, access is difficult due to guardrails along the road beside the creek and "no parking" signs on streets adjacent to the bridge. To reach Trenton Falls, take NY 28 to Trenton Falls Road and continue

West Canada Creek: Trenton Falls to Poland

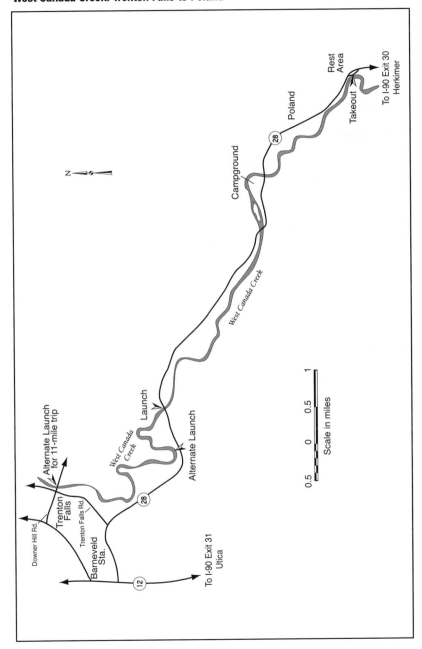

north to Downer Hill Road. If you choose this option, you can start paddling about one hour after the water release from Hinckley Dam.

✐ Description:

Unless the water release from the power station at the Hinckley Reservoir is continuous, it is important to know the time the release is scheduled to begin. This information should be available on the Waterline phone (Code 365124). If the river is below 400 cfs there will not be enough water to paddle. It will take only a short time for the water to travel from the dam to the launch site at the NY 28 bridge. Plan to paddle about an hour and a half after the scheduled release time.

This section of the river offers about two to three hours of casual flatwater paddling. High water levels will move you along quickly and some sections may have riffles.

For most of the way, the creek is distant from the highway, providing a quiet peaceful ambience for paddlers and fishermen. Graceful cedars line the banks along some sections. Ducks, geese, and other wildlife frequent the river, and old bridge remains speak of travel patterns from the past. At about 3.0 mi the river passes under a bridge and shortly thereafter around a large island. A campground appears on the right bank about 4.0 mi from the launch site. One hardly notices the village of Poland as the stream continues to the takeout at about 6.2 miles.

⌂ Takeout:

The takeout is on the left bank at a rest area on NY 28, about 1.2 mi south of Poland. The rest area provides ample parking.

Mohawk River Tributaries

West Canada Creek

↕ **Segment:**	Poland to Middleville
☆ **County:**	Herkimer
↔ **Length:**	8 mi (12.9 km)
↘ **Drop:**	105 ft (32.0 m)
◆ **Difficulty:**	Class II; runnable at 800 (low) to 2000 (high) cfs; may also be run when the dam is spilling, but expect bigger waves; use Waterline (Code 365124) (see Appendix D, entry 2) for release schedule at Hinckley Dam
✳ **Problems:**	Downed trees; variable water levels due to dam releases
♟ **Maps:**	Page 202; DOT Newport, Middleville; DeLorme pages 77, 78
✍ **Contributors:**	Larry and Esther Denham

⛵ Launch:

Take I-90, Exit 30 at Herkimer and drive north on NY 28 about 17.0 mi. The put-in is at a rest area on the left side of NY 28 about 1.2 mi south of Poland. Nearby is a stream flowing in from Oklahoma Gulf, reported to be an interesting ravine for persons interested in exploring the area.

✐ Description:

If the power station at the Hinckley Reservoir is not releasing water on a continuous basis, it is important to know the time of the release. It takes six hours for the release to reach Poland and the trip must be planned accordingly. This information should be available on the Waterline phone.

The river quickly leaves the highway and enters a large sweeping turn to the right. There are several miles of Class I and II rapids. After about 1.4 mi the creek divides around a large island; choose either channel.

Another 1.6 mi brings you to the Newport dam. Paddle down the flat backwater to start the portage on the left shore; a log barrage and warning signs direct you to the landing. The carry is 200 yds across the road and around the dam. Choose the farthest put-in to avoid a steep scramble down the bank.

Back in the water the river widens and you are surrounded by islands with

West Canada Creek: Poland to Middleville

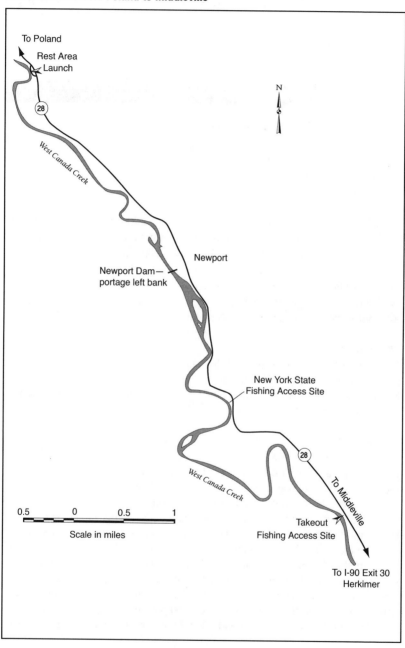

To Poland

Rest Area
Launch

28

West Canada Creek

Newport

Newport Dam—
portage left bank

New York State
Fishing Access Site

28

To Middleville

West Canada Creek

Takeout
Fishing Access Site

To I-90 Exit 30
Herkimer

N

0.5   0   0.5   1
Scale in miles

Class I and II chutes. Always choose a main channel. The river unites, passes close to the highway, and swings away for 1.0 mi of pleasant, quiet paddling. You pass a fishing access site 1.8 mi downstream from the Newport dam as the river bends back to the road. Across the meadows and between the trees on the right shore are glimpses of high hills around the valley, some forested and rising 1000 ft above the river.

A short distance downstream the river flows to the right around a bend, passes under an old railroad bridge, and flows about half a mile west away from the highway and straight toward 150-foot high sand cliffs. After rounding a left bend at the foot of the cliffs, the creek follows along the base of the cliffs rising steeply from the right bank. After 1.0 mi, a sharp left bend leads away from the cliffs and back toward the highway. Another 1.7 mi of paddling leads to the takeout.

🛶 Takeout:

The takeout is at a state fishing access site on the left bank, 1.2 mi north of Middleville and adjacent to NY 28. Middleville is at the intersection of NY 28, NY 29, and NY 169.

Mohawk River Tributaries

West Canada Creek

↕ **Segment:**	Middleville to Kast Bridge
☆ **County:**	Herkimer
↔ **Length:**	7.2 mi (11.6 km)
↘ **Drop:**	135 ft (41.2 m)
♦ **Difficulty:**	Class II, II+ or possibly III if water is spilling over the dam; runnable at 800 (low) to 2000 (high) cfs; use Waterline (Code 365124) (see Appendix D, entry 2) for release schedule at Hinckley Dam
✳ **Problems:**	Strainers, especially around islands; variable water levels due to dam releases
🏃 **Maps:**	Page 204; DOT Middleville, Herkimer; DeLorme page 78
✍ **Contributors:**	Larry and Esther Denham

West Canada Creek: Middleville to Kast Bridge

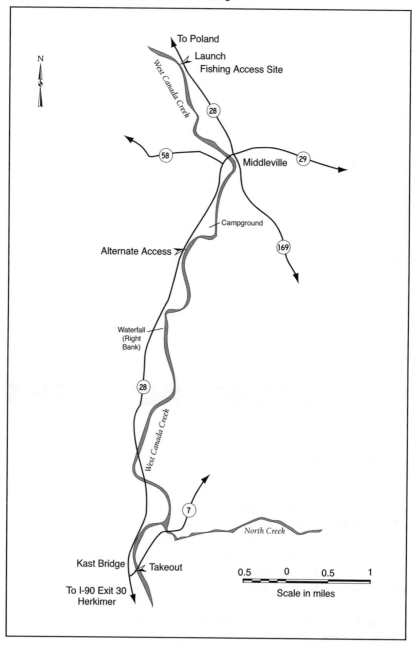

⚓ Launch:

Take Exit 30 from I-90 at Herkimer and drive north on NY 28 about 11 mi. The put-in is at a fishing access on the left side of NY 28 about 1.2 mi north of Middleville.

✐ Description:

If the power station at the Hinckley Reservoir is not releasing water on a continuous basis, it will take eight or nine hours from the time of the release for the water to reach Middleville. Plan your trip accordingly. This information should be available on the Waterline phone.

As you enter the river, a series of boulders provide excellent opportunities to practice eddy turns. Shortly thereafter is a tricky bend to the right with impressive hydraulics at high water levels. This bend leads to a whirlpool on river left; with the surrounding rocks, this makes an interesting play area.

Stay in the main channel as you pass old bridge abutments and a succession of islands. It takes about a half hour to reach Middleville, where the river narrows and runs swiftly under the bridge. For the next few miles the riverbanks are high; the river moves swiftly, accompanying the highway southward. Stay away from the concrete retaining walls on the right bank.

High sand cliffs in the distance signal the approach of a Class II rapid. There are many opportunities in this area for practicing eddy turns and surfing in and out of rapids. At 2.5 mi from the launch there is a wide bend in the river where a KOA campground is located on the right bank near the Herkimer Diamond Mine. Just below, on a left bend, is another rapid where boulders create a slalom course just right of center. Watch for strainers on the right bank. About half a mile below the campground an informal access is possible where the highway is close to the river.

Now the river leaves the highway. Steep banks signal the approach of a fun rapid with numerous boulders. Watch for the waterfall on the right bank at the foot of the rapid. The creek spreads out and could be shallow at low water.

As you pass a high bank of evergreens, riffles and gravel beds keep your attention. Pastures border on the right bank. The water is clear with washed stones near the surface. Soon a Class II rapid with a significant drop gives you a choice of two channels. Both offer practice in boulder avoidance and exciting standing waves, especially at high water. A large gravel bar keeps you to the right and a blue farmhouse comes into view. Minutes later the river channels right and forms a rapid with large standing waves. Run them straight or along the right shore to avoid the biggest waves.

Soon you pass North Creek tumbling down from the east and creating additional waves. The scenery is now cornfields. A large gravel bar provides numerous channels to cut across. Soon Kast Bridge is in sight. Pull in to the right bank before the bridge for a well-graded climb up the bank.

⛰ Takeout:

From Exit 30 on I-90 take NY 28 4.0 mi to the town of Kast Bridge. Turn right on NY 7 for about 250 yds to the bridge. Park off the road in a dirt parking area on the west side of the river.

Mohawk River Tributaries

East Canada Creek

↕ **Segment:**	Stratford to Dolgeville
☆ **County:**	Herkimer and Fulton
↔ **Length:**	10.0 mi (16.1 km)
↘ **Drop:**	280 ft (85.4)
♦ **Difficulty:**	Class II–III; runnable only during spring runoff or after a prolonged rain; no gauge; may be runnable when the gauge at Hope on the Sacandaga River indicates more than 5.5 ft (see Appendix D, entries 1–3 to access water level data)
✳ **Problems:**	Downed trees, especially in upper sections; takeout difficult
♠ **Maps:**	Page 207; USGS Stratford, Oppenheim, Little Falls; DeLorme page 78
✍ **Contributor:**	Charles Beach

⛴ Launch:

Take Exit 29A from I-90 at Little Falls and follow NY 169 northwest about 2.0 mi to the junction with NY 5. Turn right on NY 5 and drive about 0.7 mi to NY 167 branching to the left. Follow NY 167 approximately 7.0 mi to Dolgeville. You may wish to leave some cars here at the takeout. This is the time to scout

East Canada Creek: Stratford to Dolgeville

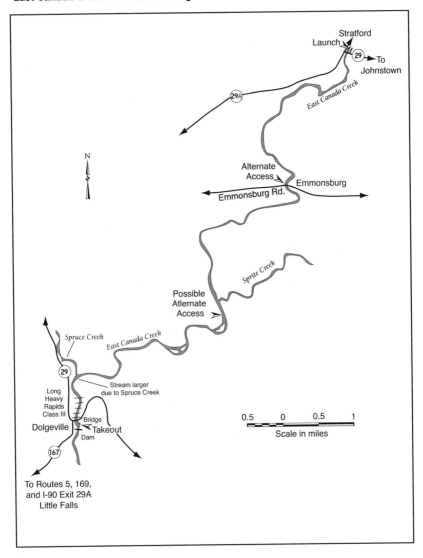

the rapids leading to the pool above the dam. The rapids can be seen from the bridge over the creek. If you want a broader perspective, cross the bridge, turn left, and drive a short distance up a hill; park and walk down through the woods until you have a view of the river.

!Caution:

The takeout in Dolgeville is from a pool above a high dam. A long Class III rapid just above the dam is dangerous in high water or in the event of a capsize; paddlers and/or equipment could be swept over the dam. Scout before running the creek.

From Dolgeville turn left on NY 29 and follow it 3.0 mi north to Salisbury Center. Turn right on NY 29A and follow it for 5.5 mi to Stratford. Cross the bridge and immediately turn left and park off the dirt road beside the creek. Launch from a convenient spot along the bank.

From the east, the launch site can be reached via NY 29A out of Johnstown or Gloversville.

✍ Description:

Drainage for the creek is from small headwater ponds that provide enough water for paddling only in the very early spring when there is still apt to be significant snow along the banks and occasional ice floating in the water. It may be possible to paddle after very heavy rains later in the season, but the water level drops quickly from one day to the next.

Before committing to the trip, look carefully at the many small rocks in the stream above and around the bridge. Most should be covered with water or the stream is too low to paddle. If you can see a reasonable route from the bank to the far side of the bridge, the creek is runnable. Launch the boats from the side where you have parked. Don't be surprised to see local people watching your departure; few paddlers come here, so you are likely to be alone on the water.

Paddling the East Canada in early spring is a true delight. You must go when the water is up, for if you wait a day, the opportunity may be gone. Leaving Stratford, the stream flows almost entirely through a scenic, wooded valley. The first few miles are Class I and II. The stream turns frequently and there are apt to be sweepers partially obstructing the course. It is 3.0 mi to the bridge at Emmonsburg; this is the only road crossing and can serve as an alternate put-in or takeout point.

As the trip continues, the rapids gradually increase in frequency and size. After another 3.1 mi Sprite Creek enters on the left. Just below this confluence the map shows a road on the right; it may also provide an access or exit. There are scattered houses in the vicinity. Below Sprite Creek is a stretch with islands where the stream flattens out.

It is another 3.2 miles to Spruce Creek, which tumbles in on river right. Spruce signals the beginning of heavier water and a buildup of rapids leading to the half mile of Class III before the pool above the dam in Dolgeville. This stretch of rapids has some big waves and pourovers on river left. However, one should be careful to avoid the right side, particularly as the bridge comes into view.

! Caution:

It is important to pull strongly left as you pass under the bridge. The right shore is built up with a vertical stonewall along which a strong current leads to the lip of the dam. **This is especially dangerous in high water.**

Once in the pool, paddle left to the broad grassy (or snowy, as the case may be) area where it is easy to land and carry the boats to the cars.

🏠 Takeout:

To reach the takeout, follow the launch directions to Dolgeville. From the center of town cross the NY 29 bridge over East Canada Creek and immediately turn right. It's a short distance to an open area beside the millpond above the dam. Park at the edge of the road.

Mohawk River Tributaries

Schoharie Creek

Introduction

Schoharie Creek drains one of the largest watersheds in New York State. From its source southeast of Hunter Mountain in the Catskills, the river courses north ninety miles to Fort Hunter on the Mohawk River. Two dams between Prattsville and North Blenheim form the Schoharie and Blenheim-Gilboa Reservoirs, which supply water and power to New York City and much of the rest of southeastern New York.

From the covered bridge in North Blenheim to remnants of the old Erie Canal at Fort Hunter, the river flows through beautiful historic terrain. There are near-vertical cliffs, farmland, forests, and pre-Revolutionary War villages. The valley was settled in the early eighteenth century and became the scene of skirmishes and pillaging in the French and Indian War. The village of Schoharie is the third oldest in upstate New York, and Central Bridge was the birthplace of inventor George Westinghouse.

This guide describes the segments of the river most often paddled, the fifty miles from North Blenheim to the Mohawk River. Paddlers of all abilities can find a segment to their liking, from Class I and II above Esperance to lively Class III between Esperance and the Mohawk. However, ratings can change quickly when sudden rainstorms fill the streams in this large watershed. In 1987 a group from the Schenectady Chapter of ADK cancelled a trip on the Class III segment from Esperance to Power House Road after learning from the evening weather report that the river level was expected to exceed twelve feet by morning. This was the flash flood that destroyed the New York State Thruway bridge over Schoharie Creek, causing the deaths of several motorists in the waters below.

The river is normally run at levels between 1.8 and 3.0 ft as measured on the gauge at Burtonsville. Readings above 4.0 ft can indicate difficult, even dangerous conditions in most segments. A level of 6.0 ft indicates flooding. See Appendix D for more water level information.

✍ **Contributors:** Chet Harvey and Kathie Armstrong

Mohawk River Tributaries

Schoharie Creek

↕ **Segment:**	North Blenheim to Middleburgh
☆ **County:**	Schoharie
↔ **Length:**	13.5 mi (21.8 km)
↘ **Drop:**	160 ft (48.8 m)
◆ **Difficulty:**	Class I to I+; medium level, 1.8 to 3.0 ft on Burtonsville gauge (see Appendix D, entries 1–3 to access water level data); normally runnable in April and early May or after a storm which causes Schoharie Dam to spill
✳ **Problems:**	Possible strong headwind from North; possible downed trees; floating debris in high water
⚘ **Maps:**	Page 212; DOT Gilboa, Breakabeen, Middleburgh, DeLorme pages 51, 65
✍ **Contributor:**	Jack Daniels

⚓ Launch:

Drive south on NY 30 from Middleburgh to North Blenheim. Cross the NY 30 bridge over Schoharie Creek to North Blenheim on the west bank. A sharp right just after the bridge gives access to the river under the bridge.

✎ Description:

This segment of the Schoharie Creek is usually paddled at water levels in the range of 1.5 to 3 feet. Below 1.5 ft the creek is too shallow. Above 4 ft the current is swift with high waves and possible floating debris. Flood stage is 6 ft.

Just upstream from the present NY 30 bridge is the old Blenheim Bridge, said to be the world's longest single-span, wooden covered bridge at 232 ft. From 1855 to 1930 it was operated by the town as a toll bridge. In 1964 the bridge was named a National Historic Landmark. It is open to pedestrians only. The sign above the entrance reads: "$500 Fine To Ride Or Drive This Bridge Faster Than A Walk."

Further south on NY 30 is the Blenheim-Gilboa Pumped Storage Power Project. There is a visitor center and nearby is Lansing Manor Museum with his-

Schoharie Creek: North Blenheim to Middleburgh

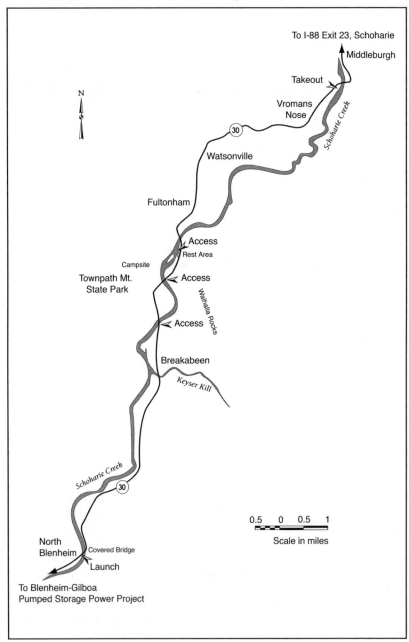

To I-88 Exit 23, Schoharie

Middleburgh

Takeout

Vromans
Nose

Schoharie Creek

30

Watsonville

Fultonham

Access

Rest Area

Campsite

Townpath Mt.
State Park

Access

Walhalla Rocks

Access

Breakabeen

Keyser Kill

Schoharie Creek

30

North
Blenheim

Covered Bridge

Launch

To Blenheim-Gilboa
Pumped Storage Power Project

N

0.5   0   0.5   1

Scale in miles

toric exhibits. Camping in season is available at Max V. Shaul State Park on NY 30 between Breakabeen and Fultonham.

This trip is perfectly suited for proficient Class 1 paddlers in open boats. Although the river runs close to NY 30 for most of the way, there is a feeling of rural isolation. The scenery is beautiful and the rapids are fun. From North Blenheim to the rest area at NY 30 there are a number of drops, interspersed with sections of flatwater. As the river bends, water piles up on the outside of the turns, forming wave trains that vary in size depending on the water level. Paddlers must be able to maintain control and avoid being swept into possible strainers in the fast water.

About 2.5 mi from the launch, the stream makes a sharp left turn at the base of near-vertical cliffs rising to 800 ft. In another 2.2 mi the Keyser Kill enters on the right at Breakabeen. One and three quarters miles beyond the confluence of the Keyser Kill, the imposing 600-foot cliffs of Walhalla Rocks rise up from the river. The rest area south of the village of Fultonham is about 1.5 mi beyond the cliffs, and affords a view of Townpath Mountain rising abruptly from the opposite shore.

Three bridges cross the creek between Breakabeen and Fultonham, offering intermediate access points. Of these, the NY 30 rest area just south of the northernmost bridge is the most convenient. Picnic tables make this an enjoyable lunch spot.

From the rest area to Middleburgh, the frequency of swift water decreases and the sections of flatwater are longer. Four and a half miles beyond the picnic spot the paddler passes within a half-mile of the prominent hill known as Vromans Nose. This landmark rises 600 ft above the creek on the left side. It is another 1.5 mi to the takeout in Middleburgh. Paddling time for the trip is three or four hours, excluding breaks.

During a recent run at the low level of 1.7 ft we encountered a potentially dangerous situation just before the takeout. Here the river curves right and then left. Coming around the bend we found rocky shoals on the left and a large downed tree across the deep water on river right. The trick was to stay left of the strainer to avoid being swept into it, and still find enough deep water to stay off the rocks. Over the years, of course, obstructions come and go; the point is that paddlers must stay alert and be prepared to take quick action. There can always be a surprise around the next bend.

⛰ Takeout:

The takeout is on river left at a public recreation field just before the NY 30 bridge in Middleburgh. To reach the field by car from NY 30, take the first left after crossing the bridge from the north.

Mohawk River Tributaries

Schoharie Creek

↕ **Segment:**	Middleburgh to Esperance
☆ **County:**	Schoharie
↔ **Length:**	18.0 mi (29.0 km); 13.0 mi (21.0 km) for shorter trip to the Esperance Fishing Access Site
↘ **Drop:**	60 ft (18.3 m)
♦ **Difficulty:**	Class I to I+; runnable from 1.8 to 3.0 ft on the Burtonsville gauge; minimum level is probably about 1.5 ft (see Appendix D, entries 1–3 to access water level data)
✳ **Problems:**	Wind; fallen trees and other debris during and after spring high water
♠ **Maps:**	Page 215; DOT or USGS: Middleburg, Schoharie, Esperance; DeLorme page 65

✍ **Contributors:** Al Andrejcak and Betty Lou Bailey

⛰ Launch:

From east or west, take I-88 to Exit 23 and drive south on NY 30 to Middleburgh. At the traffic light, turn right and cross the bridge over the Schoharie. After crossing the bridge, continue south on NY 30 a few hundred feet and turn left on a small dirt road to the pumping station and the access site.

From the launch it is approximately 18.0 mi to the takeout at the US 20 bridge in the village of Esperance, and approximately 13.0 mi to an alternate takeout at the Esperance Fishing Access Site on NY 30A.

✎ Description:

Schoharie Creek changes dramatically with water level. Uprooted trees and

Schoharie Creek: Middleburgh to Esperance

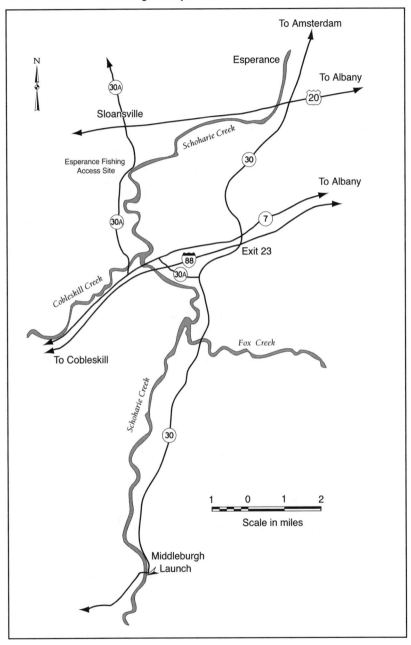

debris in tree limbs above the banks indicate the damage caused by high water during storms and spring runoff.

The first few miles meander through rural farmland with large trees on both sides, creating an atmosphere of quiet isolation. A variety of birds are seen and heard in this area, especially swallows that nest in holes in the high sand banks. About 7.5 mi from the launch, and just before Fox Creek enters on the right, cliffs appear on the left, rising to 400 ft above the valley floor.

Another 4.0 mi brings the paddler to Cobleskill Creek, entering on the left. The currents can be quite strong and pushy in this area, depending on the river level. For the next 0.5 mi, grass, leaves, and other debris high in the tree limbs and stacks of large downed trees attest to the power of the river at high water.

Paddlers who wish to takeout after 13.0 mi will find a convenient access to NY 30A at the Esperance Fishing Access Site on the left bank.

The next 5.0 mi to the takeout at US 20 in Esperance is quiet water with very little current, especially at low water. Wind can be a problem because the creek is wider and the surrounding land is more open. Upstream of the takeout, camps on the left bank signal the approach to the village. As one rounds the final bend the US 20 bridge comes into view. At low water, a shoal extends almost across the river upstream of the bridge. The takeout is on river right, just below the bridge.

🏠 Takeout:

The takeout for the 13-mile trip is at the Esperance Fishing Access Site on NY 30A. From Middleburg, drive north about 7.0 mi on NY 30 to the point where NY 30A branches to the left. Follow NY 30A to the intersection with NY 7, just north of I-88. Turn left (west) on combined NY 7/30A, cross the Schoharie, and turn right on NY 30A where it exits to the north. Drive approximately 2.5 mi north to the access site on the right.

From Esperance, drive west on US 20 to Sloansville, turn left (south) on NY 30A and continue south about 1.0 mi to the access site on the left.

The takeout for the 18-mile trip is at the US 20 bridge in Esperance. Follow NY 30 from either north or south and turn west on US 20 at the traffic light. The takeout is 0.5 mi from the traffic light, on the right (downstream) side of the US 20 bridge over the Schoharie. Access is on a narrow strip of state land between the highway and an auto repair garage. There is parking space at the garage, but it is private property, so be sure to ask permission from the owner.

Schoharie Creek: Esperance to Power House Road

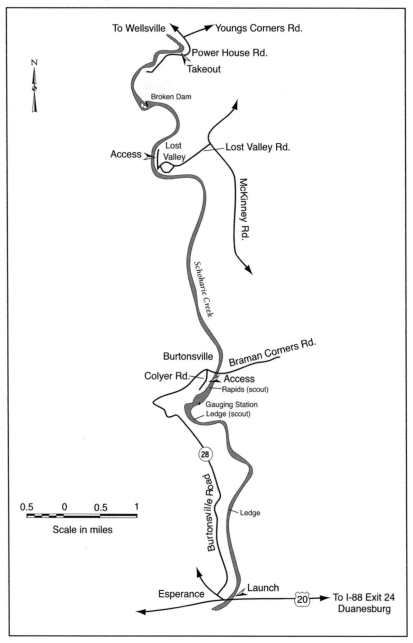

Mohawk River Tributaries

Schoharie Creek

↕ **Segment:**	Esperance to Power House Road
☆ **Counties:**	Schoharie and Montgomery
↔ **Length:**	10.4 mi (16.8 km)
↘ **Drop:**	175 ft (53.4 m)
◆ **Difficulty:**	Class II and III; medium level is 1.8 to 3.0 ft at Burtonsville Gauge; runnable in April and early May or later after a heavy rain (see Appendix D, entries 1–3 to access water level data)
✳ **Problems:**	Undercut ledges above Burtonsville create dangerous hydraulics at high water; possible downed trees; possible strong winds
♠ **Maps:**	Page 217; USGS Esperance Quadrangle; DeLorme page 65
✍ **Contributor:**	Charles Beach

🛶 Launch:

From I-88 Exit 24 drive west approximately 6.0 mi to the east end of the US 20 bridge at Esperance. Access is downstream of the bridge via a narrow strip of state land between the highway and an auto repair garage. There is parking space at the garage, but since it is private property, be sure to ask permission from the owner.

Other access points are at Burtonsville from Braman Corners Road, and Lost Valley via Lost Valley Road leading to the river from McKinney Road.

✐ Description:

This wide scenic stream flows past farms, a few cottages, through a wooded valley, and below shale cliffs towering to 200 ft. In some places waterfalls drop directly from the cliffs into the river.

The best water levels are between 1.8 ft and 3.0 ft on the Burtonsville gauge. Higher levels can raise the difficulty to Class IV.

From the put-in, approximately 1.0 mi of relatively calm water leads to a low ledge which diagonals downstream from the right, increasing in height toward the left bank. The easiest passage is on the right, where the main channel drops over the ledge and then flows left toward the center.

About 2.0 mi below the ledge the river enters a gorge. Part way through the gorge, the river makes a slight right turn and drops over a significant ledge that should be scouted. Stop in the eddy on the right shore to plan your route. Many paddlers run this ledge on the far left; if you choose this route be ready to brace, as there is often a mean pour-off from the left wall that can capsize the unwary. At medium water levels and above, there is a passage near the right bank where you may scrape the bottom of the boat. Some paddlers choose to run the ledge in the middle where there is a 2- to 3-ft drop.

After a short, moderate rapid and a flatwater stretch, the rapids above Burtonsville begin. These rapids contain several undercut ledges and should be scouted from the left shore. Scouting can be done from Colyer Road in Burtonsville during the drive to the launch site. Burtonsville is 4.1 river miles below the launch at Esperance. There is an island just upstream of the rapids that directs most of the flow to the left and over the ledges. At higher river levels, some paddlers take the difficult right passage, but most stay close to the left bank in the left channel to avoid the large waves caused by the ledges.

The next 3.8 mi from Burtonsville to Lost Valley are Class I. From Lost Valley to the takeout at Power House Road there are 2.5 mi of rapids, some of which are Class III. There is an interesting drop at a broken dam, all that remains of a power source built many years ago. Occasionally otter or beaver provide entertainment in the quiet water created by the dam on river right. From the broken dam to the takeout the river flows over smooth bedrock where several small ledges provide enjoyable surfing.

🛖 Takeout:

The takeout is on river right at a fisherman's access on Power House Road. To reach the takeout by car, drive north or south on NY 30 to the intersection with NY 161. This is Mill Point Road. Drive west on Mill Point Road about 5.0 mi to Schoharie Creek. Before crossing the bridge turn left on County Route 143 through the settlement of Wellsville to the junction of Youngs Corners Road and Power House Road. Turn right on Power House Road and drive less than a half-mile to the takeout. Since the access is on private land, it is best to park on the road.

The trip can be extended 2.0 mi by paddling the Class I and II rapids to Mill Point where boats are taken out at the NY 161 bridge.

Mohawk River Tributaries

Schoharie Creek

⇡ **Segment:**	Power House Road to the Mohawk River
☆ **County:**	Montgomery
↔ **Length:**	8.2 mi (13.2 km)
↘ **Drop:**	100 ft (30.5 m)
◆ **Difficulty:**	Class II; medium level: 1.8–3.0 ft on Burtonsville Gauge; runnable April and early May or after a significant rain causing the Schoharie Dam to spill (see Appendix D, entries 1–3 to access water level data)
✳ **Problems:**	Possible strong headwind from north; floating debris in high water
♠ **Maps:**	Page 222; DOT Tribes Hill, Esperance; DeLorme page 65
✍ **Contributor:**	Jack Daniels

🛶 Launch:

From NY 5S near Amsterdam, take NY 30 south for about 2.5 mi. Turn right on NY 161 (Mill Point Road). In about 4.0 mi NY 161 crosses Schoharie Creek at Mill Point. Before crossing the bridge turn left on County Route 143; drive through the settlement of Wellsville to the junction of Youngs Corners Road and Power House Road. Go right on Power House Road for less than 0.5 mi. The launch is at an informal fishermen's access on the right where the road is beginning to turn left. This access is private property; it is no longer posted, but cars should be parked on the road after unloading. Paddlers should help keep the area free of trash.

✐ Description:

Although it is possible to run this section of the river as low as 1.5 ft as measured on the gauge at Burtonsville, it is quite scratchy at that level. A level of 2.0 to 3.0 ft provides a lively ride. At 4.0 ft the river becomes dangerous due to swift current, high waves, and possible floating debris. Flood level is 6.0 ft.

The most challenging part of the trip is the first 2.0 mi from the launch to Mill Point bridge. From the put-in the river bends right and then left under the cliffs of Power House Road. This section is Class II with standing waves and some rocks that are fairly easy to negotiate. The river splits around two islands; paddlers usually take the right channel where there is more water. About 0.3 mi upstream of the Mill Point bridge there is a tricky spot with a high standing wave, which requires some maneuvering.

The bridge at Mill Point was recently rebuilt and a major bank stabilization program completed. These construction projects, coupled with the effects of flooding, have dramatically changed the channel. Paddlers may wish to scout their route from the deck of the bridge. There is usually a significant wave across the river under the bridge; it will not cause a problem if run head-on.

For paddlers who wish to avoid the Class II section, there is access to the river just below the Mill Point bridge on river right. Downstream the river broadens and the gradient is less steep. The scenery is beautiful, with high bluffs and ravines; there are many attractive rock beaches for a snack or lunch break. Birds are abundant in spring. There are few signs of human habitation, except for an occasional farm field, until one reaches the Thruway bridge, about 6.0 mi below Mill Point.

In April of 1987 a disastrous flood eroded the old bridge piers, causing the collapse of some sections of the bridge and the deaths of a number of motorists. The flood and subsequent rebuilding of the bridge changed many of the channels in the Schoharie.

From the Thruway bridge to the takeout is about 0.8 mi. Total paddling time, not counting breaks, is about two hours, but could be longer in a strong head wind.

Some of the most interesting historic sites are found in Fort Hunter, where the creek enters the Mohawk River. On Railroad Street, just down from the "low water" takeout (see description below), are exhibits and a visitors center depicting the era when the old Erie Canal crossed the creek on the Schoharie Aqueduct. Near the Schoharie Crossing boat launch are the remnants of the old aqueduct arches. Near the end of the Schoharie Crossing parking lot is a memorial to the victims of the 1987 Thruway bridge collapse.

Takeout:
There are two recommended takeouts in Fort Hunter, depending on the level of the river. If the trip is run in April, the dam in the Mohawk River at Fort Hunter will probably not be adjusted for seasonal boat traffic through the locks on the Erie Barge Canal. Water in the Schoharie will be too low to conveniently use the

Schoharie Creek: Power House Road to Mohawk River

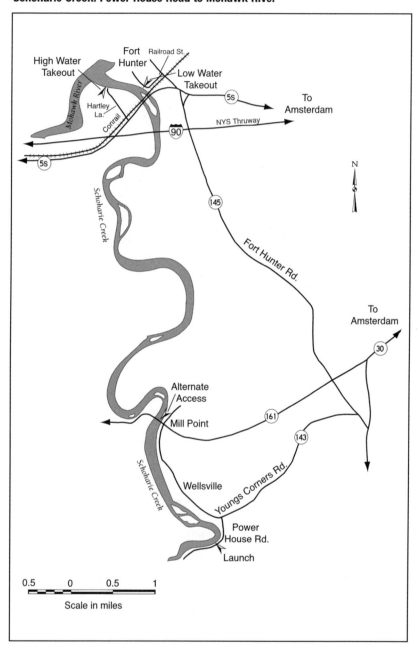

Schoharie Crossing boat launch on the left bank. There will likely be large mud-flats in the river in front of the ramp and possibly unplowed snow on Hartley Lane, the road leading to the launch parking area. In May, after the dam is adjusted for boat traffic, water backs up into the Schoharie, providing easy access to the boat launch.

When water at the mouth of the Schoharie is low (early spring), the pre-ferred takeout is on the east bank (river right), just downstream of an island and bridge abutments from the NY 5S bridge and the old railroad bridge. A steep, rocky path leads from the river to Railroad Street. To reach the path by car from the east, take the right fork off NY 5S on County Route 27, cross the railroad tracks and turn left on Railroad Street. The path to the river is just beyond the bend, where Railroad Street turns right. When spotting a car for the shuttle, be sure to scout a course for maneuvering the boat around the abutments to reach the path from the river.

When the water at the mouth of the Schoharie is high (May and later), the preferred takeout is at the Schoharie Crossing boat launch on the west bank. To reach the launch by car, turn north from NY 5S onto Hartley Lane and continue to the launch, where there is a parking area.

To drive from the takeout to the launch at Power House Road, head east on NY 5S a short distance to County Route 145 (Fort Hunter Road) and contin-ue 4.2 mi to NY 161. Follow NY 161 to County Route 143 and Power House Road, as described previously under launch.

Mohawk River Tributaries

Cobleskill Creek (Tributary of Schoharie Creek)

↕ **Segment:**	Cobleskill to Sagendorf Road
☆ **County:**	Schoharie
↔ **Length:**	7.0 mi (11.3 km)
↘ **Drop:**	200 ft (61.0 m)
◆ **Difficulty:**	Class II with a Class III drop; runnable in early spring or after significant rain; check the Schoharie Creek gauge at Burtonsville for a level over 4 ft (see Appendix D, entries 1–3 to access water level data)
✳ **Problems:**	Possible downed trees and sweepers; steep ledge in Barnerville
♠ **Maps:**	Page 225; USGS Cobleskill and Schoharie Quadrangles; DeLorme page 65
✍ **Contributor:**	Charles Beach

⚓ Launch:

Take Exit 22 from I-88 and drive north on NY 145 to NY 7. Follow NY 7 west about 4.0 mi and turn left (south) on Grand Street in Cobleskill. Drive about 0.5 mi to the bridge over the creek; park in a gravel lot on river left. This is not a parking area designated for paddlers, but it seems to be public land.

✐ Description:

A tributary of Schoharie Creek, the Cobleskill is a narrow creek situated at the base of a beautiful terraced valley. The stream winds through woods, farmland, and rural towns. In many sections the stream flows between walls so steep that roads and railroad tracks must be located on terraces high above the sides of the creek. The Cobleskill can only be paddled during spring runoff or after a heavy rain. There is no gauge, but water levels may be high enough when the Burtonsville gauge on the Schoharie Creek is over 4 ft.

For the first 2.0 mi the stream flows at a leisurely rate with a few mild riffs. The current picks up as buildings start to appear along the shore. As one approaches Barnerville, there is a series of runnable small to medium ledges. In Barnerville choppy water leads to a 3-foot diagonal ledge that must be scouted.

Cobleskill Creek

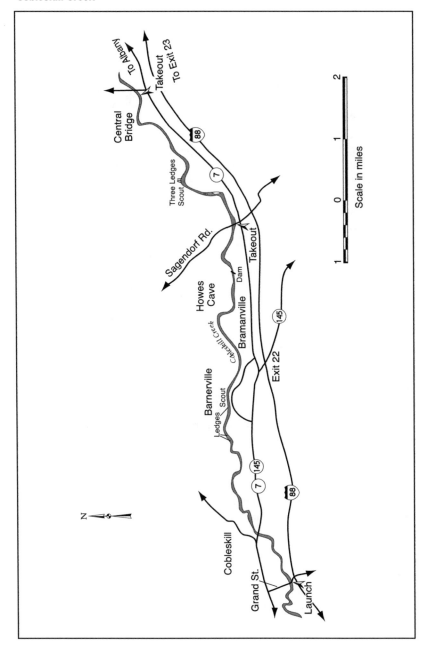

As the stream makes a slight left turn in the community, pull off on river right. This ledge can also be viewed from the road before launching by taking Barnerville Road off NY 7 and driving about 0.5 mi to the creek. There is a bridge across the stream about 0.3 mi downstream of the ledge. At the ledge the flow splits three ways with most of the water divided between the left and right sides. On the left the precipitous drop has boulders that make the run quite hazardous. The right side has a short, straight chute that is not difficult, providing one chooses a good line.

The 4.0 mi below Barnerville are Class I and II with some big waves, which at high water levels might be Class III. The creek passes under two bridges about a half-mile apart in the village of Bramanville. About 0.8 mi farther there is a 1 ft low-head diversionary dam just above the old Howes Cave cement plant. This dam is no problem for paddlers. The dam diverts some of the creek into a pool. Looking back upstream after passing the dam one can see a short falls on river left where the water from the pool returns to the creek. One mile below the dam, Sagendorf Road passes over the creek. This is the recommended takeout to avoid the dangerous 5-foot ledge between Howes Cave and Central Bridge. See the note below for a description of the 3-mile run to Central Bridge.

🏠 Takeout:

Take NY 145 to NY 7 as described in the launch. Follow NY 7 east 2.5 mi to the bridge over the creek at Sagendorf Road. Park well off the road in a place convenient to the creek. There is no designated parking area. Be sure to get permission if you park on private land.

Note: The 3-mile trip from Sagendorf Road to Central Bridge drops 100 ft. At 1.3 mi the stream turns sharply right. A high stone wall which supports the railroad track appears on the left. Immediately after the turn the paddler encounters a series of three ledges. The first two are low; the third is a 5-foot high streamwide drop which is undercut.

! Caution:

A spill over this ledge could be very dangerous. Due to the wall on the left, the only portage is on the right, which is very ledgy. Portaging requires lifting the boat up over the ledges and lowering it down about 5 ft to the pool below. It is essential to stop on river right before this hazardous drop. The ledge is adjacent to the railroad but not close to any road.

Those who chose to paddle to Central Bridge will not encounter any difficult rapids after the ledge. The takeout is adjacent to the NY 30A bridge in Central Bridge. To reach this takeout one may continue east past Sagendorf Road on NY 7 about 2.5 mi to NY 30A. Turn left about 0.8 mi to the bridge. Look for a place to park near the bridge that will not interfere with traffic or private land.

Paddlers who plan to end their trip in Central Bridge may wish to take Exit 23 from I-88, drive north on NY 30A, and left on NY 7 in order to leave a car near the bridge in Central Bridge en route to the launch. Those who choose to paddle to Central Bridge will not encounter any difficult rapids after the ledge. The takeout is adjacent to the NY 30A bridge in Central Bridge. To reach this takeout, continue east past Sagendorf Road on NY 7 about 2.5 mi to NY 30A. Turn left and continue about 0.8 mi to the bridge. Look for a place to park near the bridge that will not interfere with traffic or private land.

Paddlers who plan to end their trip in Central Bridge may wish to take Exit 23 from I-88 and drive north on NY 30A to NY 7, turning left on NY 7, in order to leave a car near the bridge in Central Bridge en route to the launch.

Mohawk River Tributaries

Alplaus Kill

Introduction

The Alplaus Kill deserves to be better known. It offers canoeing that ranges from easy to fairly difficult, often in a near-wilderness setting, and only a short drive from the city of Schenectady. The Kill rises at Consalus Vly in the town of Galway and empties into the Mohawk just south of the hamlet of Alplaus, a few miles from downtown Schenectady.

The influence of the early Dutch settlers is evident in many words and place names still in use. Vly is a Dutch term for marsh or swamp. Alplaus is derived from the Dutch word *aalplaats* meaning eel place; Alplaus Kill means eel creek. Dawson Mill, one of numerous eighteenth and nineteenth century mills along the Alplaus Kill had a Leffell turbine that would become clogged with eels during the eel run. After the construction of the dam on the Hudson River at Troy, it became impossible for the immature eels to make their way up the Mohawk River to the Alplaus Kill. Eels are born in the sea and return to spend most of their adult lives in the same fresh rivers where their parents lived before returning to the sea to spawn.

This guide describes two paddling segments of Alplaus Kill: Charlton Road (County Route 51) to VanVorst Road and below the falls at Kristels Inn (NY 50) to the Mohawk River. Although it is possible to paddle above Charlton Road with sufficient water, most access points require permission from landowners, and barbed wire, downed trees, and ledges present more difficulties than most paddlers would want. Between Van Vorst Road and Kristel Falls is a 4-foot ledge just upstream of the NY 50 bridge; this section is negotiable only by experts.

The Alplaus Kill can be paddled only at high water level when it is fed by melting snows, or later in the season after several days of steady rain. Although there is no official gauge, an informal gauge is painted on the upstream side of the bridge pier on river right at Van Vorst Road. A gauge reading between four and seven feet indicates good levels for paddling. In the early spring, the creek can rise to ten or even twelve feet as measured on this gauge. These are flood conditions and paddlers should not attempt a trip.

✍ **Contributor:** Mark S. Meyers

Mohawk River Tributaries

Alplaus Kill

↕ **Segment:**	Charlton Road to Van Vorst Road
☆ **Counties:**	Saratoga, Schenectady
↔ **Length:**	6.4 mi (10.3 km)
↘ **Drop:**	200 ft (61.0 m)
♦ **Difficulty:**	Class I, II; runnable only in early spring or after a heavy rain when the informal gauge on the Van Vorst Road bridge pier reads between 4 and 7 ft
✳ **Problems:**	Downed trees and sweepers
▲ **Maps:**	Page 233; USGS Pattersonville, Burnt Hills; DeLorme page 66
✐ **Contributor:**	Mark S. Meyers

☗ Launch:

The launch site at Charlton Road bridge is located on Charlton Road (County Route 51) about 6.0 mi west of the junction with NY 50 in the town of Ballston Center. The Charlton Road bridge can also be reached by driving 0.5 mi east from Sacandaga Road (NY 147). A few cars may be parked with care, on the shoulder of the road, away from the bridge. Access is on river right, either downstream of the bridge or upstream where a tiny tributary enters.

✐ Description:

About 0.3 mi south of the launch, the Alplaus Kill makes a sharp 180-degree bend to the left and heads back to the north. It then turns south again and at the 1.2 mi point is joined from the right by Crab Kill, flowing out of Taylor Pond. About 2.0 mi from launch the stream passes under Crane Street and after an additional mile under Swaggertown Road just south of the center of Charlton. Here, in a residential area, the stream narrows and flows between shale cliffs up to 25 ft high. Several ledges at this point create Class II rapids where the paddler is likely to encounter strainers.

At 4.8 mi, the stream turns gradually north, then sharply south, and passes Little Troy Park, a private recreation area on the left. It flows under Stage Road and, 1.6 mi farther, under Van Vorst Road. There are brief Class II rapids just upstream of each of these bridges. The section between the bridges may have numerous strainers and downed trees. LaRue Creek enters left at the Van Vorst Rd bridge. With the added volume from this creek, the Alplaus Kill is now about 25 ft wide.

Note: Some experts paddle from here to Kristel Falls. This has always been hazardous and difficult because of the 4-foot ledge extending across the creek just upstream of the NY 50 bridge. The land above and below the ledge is private. The current below the ledge is swift and dangerous because it leads directly to the falls. For these reasons, this guide recommends taking out at Van Vorst Road.

🏠 Takeout:

The takeout at Van Vorst Road is on river right, either upstream or downstream of the bridge. Although the owner of the private land adjoining the highway right-of-way has given permission for paddlers to cross his property at the take-out site, paddlers should confirm this status.

To reach the takeout by car, take NY 50 to the traffic light in Burnt Hills, turn west and follow Lake Hill Road 1.0 mi to the junction with Van Vorst Road. Lake Hill Road turns right and Van Vorst Road goes straight ahead. Continue straight on Van Vorst Road another 0.2 mi to the bridge over the Alplaus Kill. Cross the bridge and immediately take a short dirt road left to a flat area beside the creek, where a few cars can be parked downstream of the bridge.

Mohawk River Tributaries

Alplaus Kill

↕ **Segment:**	Kristel Falls to the Mohawk River
☆ **County:**	Saratoga, Schenectady
↔ **Length:**	5.5 mi (8.9 km)
↘ **Drop:**	60 ft (18.3 m)
♦ **Difficulty:**	Class I, II; runnable in early spring or after heavy rains when the informal gauge at Van Vorst Road reads between 4 and 7 ft
✳ **Problems:**	Strainers and downed trees
▲ **Maps:**	Page 233; USGS Burnt Hills, Schenectady; DeLorme page 66
✍ **Contributor:**	Mark S. Meyers

Launch:

Take NY 50 north 5.5 mi out of Scotia or south 1.0 mi out of Burnt Hills to the NY 50 bridge that crosses Alplaus Kill. Immediately north of the bridge is a long driveway to the Kristel's Inn parking lot (the Inn is not visible from the highway). Be sure to ask permission from the owners of the Inn before leaving your car in the parking lot.

A path from the far end of the parking lot leads 100 yds to the top of a 15-foot ledge above the pool below Kristel Falls. The 15-foot falls was once the site of the High Mills Grist Mill, a name still used for the area in the vicinity of the former mill. Boats must be lowered down the ledge to launch in the pool. The first rapid begins as you exit the pool and now is the time to scout it!

Description:

In addition to the gauge at the Van Vorst Road bridge, there are two places where the paddler can view the creek to determine if it is runnable. From the corner of NY 146 and Glenridge Road in Rexford take Glenridge Road west down a hill to the first bridge that crosses the Alplaus Kill. Look downstream; if the shallows are well covered, the creek is runnable. For the second view, from the intersection of NY 146 and Glenridge Road, take Blue Barnes Road (County Route 110) 2.0 mi north to a field on the left where the road comes within 100 ft of the creek and you can see the water. Walk across the field along a jeep/ATV trail to an overlook; if the water covers most of the rocks, the creek is runnable.

The first few miles after launch include some interesting Class II rapids. Below the falls, the stream flows through a wilderness gorge with walls rising 20 to 50 ft above the creek. It is hard to believe that a city is only a few miles away.

From the put-in, paddle across the pool and enter a chute on river right that leads to a Class II rock garden. A tributary drops over the cliff on river left as a lovely waterfall. The creek flows through the beautiful steep-walled gorge for about 1.0 mi, paralleling Blue Barns Road on the left. At this point, the Alplaus crosses from Ballston into the town of Clifton Park.

As one leaves the gorge there is an access on river left for those who wish to repeat the 1.1-mile Class II run from Kristel Falls. Here the Alplaus Kill is about 100 ft from Blue Barns Road, as described above. Paddlers can carry their boats along the jeep/ATV trail to cars parked along the road and drive back to the put-in. Of course this requires someone to shuttle cars and boats.

At 3.6 mi the Indian Kill enters on the right, and at 3.8 mi one paddles under the Glenridge Road bridge. Below the bridge a short swift water leads into the quiet backwaters of the Mohawk River. About 0.3 mi downstream from the Glenridge Road bridge, the stream passes under a railroad bridge with interesting marble stonework and erosional patterns. The paddler is now passing the campsite used by the French and Indians the night before the Schenectady Massacre in 1690. A marker on the fire department grounds in Alplaus commemorates this event.

The Alplaus Avenue bridge crosses at 5.0 mi; from here it is a quiet paddle past attractive residential back yards to the Mohawk River. The takeout is reached by paddling across the Mohawk and continuing a short distance downstream to a dock and boathouse just upstream of the Rexford Bridge. As with any wide water, motorboats, wind, and waves can be a hazard on the Mohawk.

🛖 Takeout:

Takeout at the public park and launch area on the right side of the Mohawk by the Aqueduct Rowing Club. There is a dock and beach; parking is available near the landing. The Boathouse, a paddlers' specialty store, is located just up the bank at 2855 Aqueduct Road in Niskayuna.

To reach the takeout by car take NY 146 7.0 mi west from Exit 9 on I-87. NY 146 turns south (at the corner of Glenridge Road) and crosses the Mohawk over the Rexford Bridge. Aqueduct Road, the Boathouse paddling store, and the launch site are immediately to the right after you cross the bridge.

Alplaus Kill

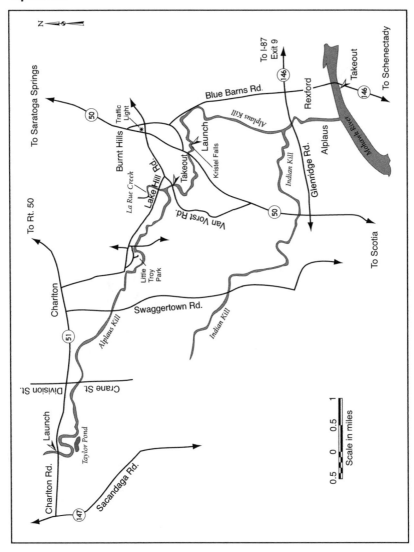

Lower Connecticut and Housatonic Watersheds

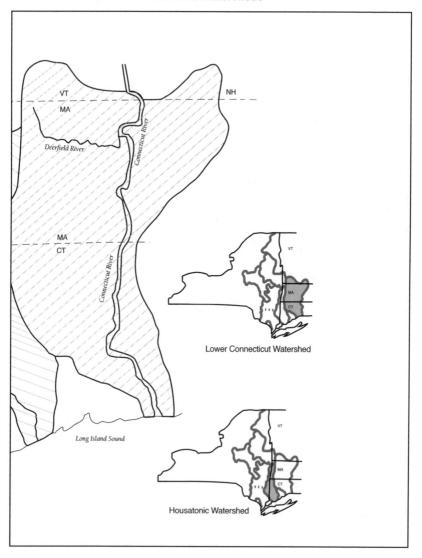

Lower Connecticut Watershed

Housatonic Watershed

Lower Connecticut and Housatonic Watersheds

Deerfield River, Massachusetts

↕ **Segment:**	Fife Brook to Charlemont
☆ **County:**	Berkshire and Franklin, Massachusetts
↔ **Length:**	8.5 mi (13.7 km)
↘ **Drop:**	118 ft (36.0 m)
✦ **Difficulty:**	Class II, with one Class III+ drop at Zoar Gap (at around 1000 cfs); runnable all summer during water releases from Fife Brook dam; use Waterline (Code 251144) for daily water volume release (Appendix D, entry 2); call Zoar Outdoor (Appendix F, whitewater) or New England Power Company (413-625-8414) for season schedule
✳ **Problems:**	Drop at Zoar Gap not visible from upstream; caution advised!
♠ **Maps:**	Page 237; USGS Rowe (Massachusetts) 7.5' x 15' quadrangle, DeLorme (Massachusetts) page 21
✍ **Contributor:**	Mark Graber

Note: For expert paddlers who are looking for a real challenge there is an upstream segment of the Deerfield River between Monroe bridge and the Dunbar Brook picnic area that is rated Class IV+. The Monroe bridge segment is not included in this guide.

⚓ Launch:

Drive east or west on MA 2 to the bridge where MA 2 crosses the Deerfield River, just west of the town of Charlemont, Massachusetts. Near the east end of the bridge, Zoar Road enters from the north. Drive 8.5 mi north along the river on Zoar Road to the launch site, about 0.1 mi below the mouth of Fife Brook. There is a 30-car parking lot with portable toilets. Along the way, Zoar Road crosses the river just below Zoar Gap rapids; paddlers not familiar with this part of the river are advised to stop and scout the rapids; they cannot be seen when approaching from upstream.

🖋 Description:

The Deerfield River provides great whitewater recreation through the summer months and is a training ground for many whitewater competitors. Water releases are usually scheduled every week from Thursday or Friday through Sunday from May through September. The annual Deerfield River Festival is usually held the first weekend in August. Call Zoar Outdoor (Appendix F) for information, to rent equipment, or to arrange for a guided trip.

The scenery is outstanding as the river follows wide, sweeping curves through a deep valley with walls rising steeply to more than 1000 ft in places. The mountain setting gives a feeling of remoteness, which, on weekends, the paddler may expect to share with many other whitewater enthusiasts.

The run starts with a few easy Class II rapids that provide opportunities for eddy hopping and surfing. From the launch site, the river flows southwest for 1.3 mi where it passes under a railroad bridge and then turns southeast. The bridge carries the Boston to Albany railroad tracks to the Hoosac tunnel, 1.0 mi west of the river. The tunnel is 5.0 mi long and took many years to build (1851–1873). At the time, it was among the world's longest tunnels and was considered an outstanding engineering feat. Midway in the tunnel, a 1028-foot ventilation shaft rises to the surface.

After the railroad bridge, the paddler can enjoy 3.8 mi of intermittent Class I riffles until the river enters a Class III+ drop called the Zoar Gap. One mile above Zoar Gap the river turns due south and follows a straight course to the entrance of the rapid. The Zoar Road highway crosses the river on Florida Bridge just below the rapid. The bridge can be seen from upstream, but the rapid itself is not visible. The river narrows to less than 25 ft as it sluices through the boulder strewn gap, dropping approximately 10 ft in the 75-foot passage. Zoar Gap rapid can be scouted from either side of the river.

The easiest route is to start along the right shore and then cut toward the center below the last of the heavy hydraulics to avoid a rock covered by turbulent water near the right bank. Some paddlers enter left and immediately eddy out behind a large rock outcropping before aligning the boat for the rest of the descent. A few take the more hazardous route down the center where open boats often swamp in the large hydraulics. However you run it, expect a crowd of spectators along both banks.

Paddlers who decide to portage can do so along the railroad tracks on the left or over the rocks on the right. Don't fall off a rock into the poison ivy that

Deerfield River

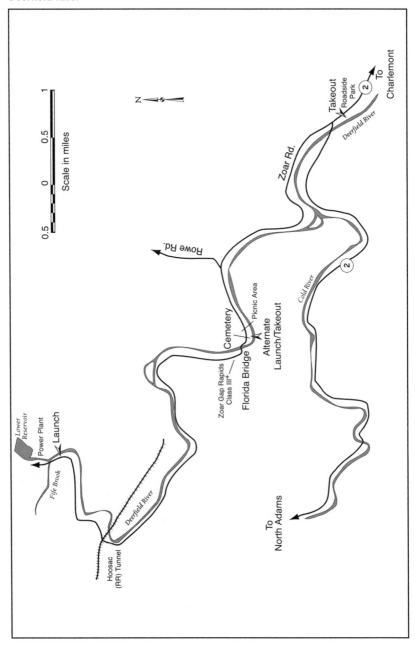

seems to carpet the banks, particularly the left bank and along the railroad tracks above it.

After the bridge below the rapids, the river turns sharply left and passes the New England Power Authority day-use picnic area on the left bank. This spot is 5.0 mi into the trip, a good place for lunch, and serves as an alternate put-in or takeout site for those who are not paddling the entire river segment. It is a pleasant, wooded area with picnic tables, portable toilets, and parking for about fifty cars. The old Nelson family cemetery is located nearby.

Below the picnic area, the river continues through 2.0 mi of boulder gardens with enough space between rocks to make this an easy but exhilarating Class II run.

Below the rock garden there is an island; the left side is a straight run with few obstacles. Just below the island the Cold River enters from the west, significantly increasing the volume of the river. After passing a railroad bridge, the rapids become less busy, and soon the MA 2 highway bridge comes into view. The takeout is 0.3 mi beyond the bridge on river left. Paddlers who want to continue can enjoy an additional 2.0 mi of Class I canoeing and takeout at the town of Charlemont.

🛶 Takeout:

Put ashore at the Massachusetts state roadside park, on river left 0.3 mi below the MA 2 bridge. Parking for about fifty cars is available. The area is conveniently located only 0.3 mi east of the Zoar Road/MA 2 intersection.

Zoar Gap on the Deerfield   Barbara Brabetz

Lower Connecticut and Housatonic Watersheds

Housatonic River

Introduction

The Housatonic River originates near Pittsfield, Massachusetts, and flows south for 142 mi through Connecticut to the sea in Long Island Sound near Bridgeport. The segments described here are particularly scenic with wooded hills rising from both banks much of the way. *Housatonic* is the Indian name that means river beyond the mountains, appropriately named as it flows though the valley between the Berkshire and Taconic ranges.

This guide describes the Housatonic River between Falls Village and Kent. Experienced, skillful paddlers seeking greater challenge may wish to search other references for information on the Class III–IV rapids above Falls Village and the Class IV–V rapids between Kent and Gaylordsville.

The new power plant relicensing agreement has discontinued scheduled water releases, which was of benefit to boaters. Flow is now run-of-the-river. Boaters are hoping to re-open the license in order to negotiate future releases.

Lower Connecticut and Housatonic Watersheds

Housatonic River, Connecticut

↕ **Segment:**	Falls Village to West Cornwall	
☆ **Counties:**	Canaan and Kent, Connecticut	
↔ **Length:**	7.5 mi (12.1 km)	
↘ **Drop:**	70 ft (21.3 m)	
◆ **Difficulty:**	Class I–II; flow is run-of-the-river; runnable above 500 cfs; medium level, 800–1800 cfs; experienced boaters, 2400 cfs and higher. For information call 888-417-4837 and press 1 twice for Falls River flow.	
✳ **Problems:**	Possible strong headwinds	
☖ **Maps:**	Page 240; USGS South Canaan, Cornwall (Connecticut); DeLorme (Connecticut) page 49	
✍ **Contributor:**	Jack Daniels	

Housatonic River: Falls Village to West Cornwall

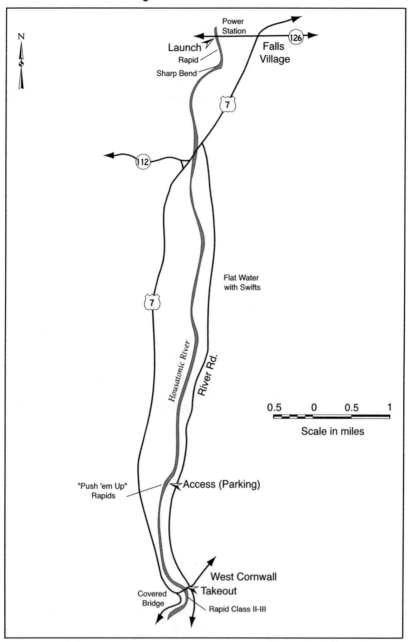

◤ Launch:

The put-in is just below the dam that feeds the Falls Village power station. From US 7 take CT 126 into Falls Village and follow Main Street through the business district. Turn right on Water Street, left through an underpass, right past the power station, cross the river, and turn left into the parking area.

✐ Description:

The run to West Cornwall is a short Class II trip, requiring about half a day for most paddlers. For a longer trip, it can be combined with all or part of the West Cornwall to Kent segment, which has several access points along the way.

Water level is controlled by generation at the Falls Village power station.

The only significant whitewater is a Class II rapid located at the start; scout from the launch area. The easiest route appears to be along the far left side, although this may change, subject to water level. The river goes around a sharp bend just below the rapid which novices should scout, especially at high water. The run to West Cornwall is mostly flatwater with a few swifts.

◤ Takeout:

Exit the river at either of the launch sites described in the next Housatonic segment, West Cornwall to Kent, or for a longer trip, at any of the access points below West Cornwall described in the text. Paddlers need to be aware that the takeout/launch at West Cornwall is on river left, just upstream of a Class II–III rapid under the bridge. Stay on river left as you approach the bridge. You can pullout about 100 ft upstream and end the trip here or scout the rapid before continuing downstream.

Lower Connecticut and Housatonic Watersheds

Housatonic River, Connecticut

⬍ **Segment:**   West Cornwall to Kent, Connecticut
☆ **County:**   Litchfield, Connecticut
↔ **Length:**   13.0 mi (21.0 km)
⬎ **Drop:**   120 ft (36.6 m)
◆ **Difficulty:**   Class II with one Class II–III rapid at the covered bridge at West Cornwall. Flow is run-of-the-river; runnable above 500 cfs; medium level, 800–1800 cfs; experienced boaters, 2400 cfs and higher. Call 888-417-4837 and press 1 twice for Falls River flow.
✳ **Problems:**   Possible strong headwind from south
⚑ **Maps:**   Page 243; USGS Cornwall, Ellsworth, Kent (Connecticut); DeLorme (Connecticut) pages 40, 49
✍ **Contributor:** Jack Daniels

⛵ Launch:

The launch site is on the east bank of the Housatonic, upstream of the West Cornwall covered bridge. From north or south, the easiest approach to the put-in is via US 7, which runs beside the river from Massachusetts through West Cornwall to New Milford, Connecticut. From east or west, CT 4 intersects US 7 at Cornwall Bridge, 4.0 mi south of West Cornwall.

For small groups of two or three cars, you can put-in about 100 ft upstream of the east end of the covered bridge. However, this is a quiet residential street, so cars must take turns unloading and then drive west across the covered bridge where a small parking area is located immediately left of the bridge. Sometimes a portable toilet is available here.

Larger groups should launch about a mile upstream on the east bank. Drive east on CT 128 a short block from the covered bridge and turn left on River Road before crossing the railroad tracks. Go north 1.2 mi to the river access on the left. Launch in the middle of the quickwater, called by the local residents "Push 'em Up Rapids." There is parking available for several cars.

Housatonic River: West Cornwall to Kent

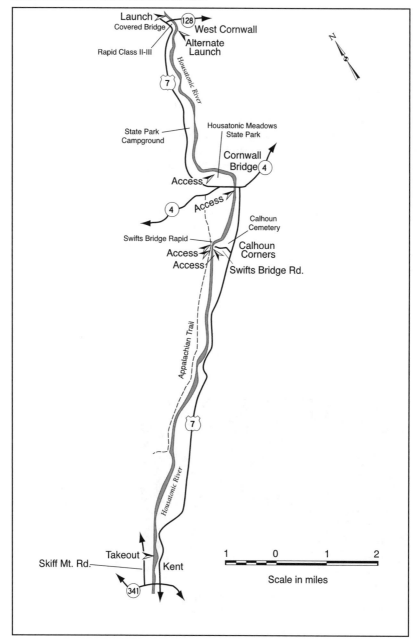

🛶 Description:

At medium water levels this is a delightful trip for Class II paddlers in open boats. The scenery is quite beautiful with wooded hills on both sides. Backpackers are often seen on the Appalachian Trail, which follows the west bank below Swifts Bridge. Although US 7 runs close to the river for the whole trip, it is seldom distracting. The river is broad and generally free of strainers. Total time, excluding breaks, is three to five hours, depending on how long you "play" in the waves and eddies.

Canoes and kayaks can be rented in West Cornwall from Clarke Outdoors (phone 860-672-6365 or e-mail: boatshop@bestweb.net). Clarke Outdoors will also provide information on river conditions. Camping facilities are located at the Housatonic Meadows State Park (4.5 mi below West Cornwall), Macedonia Brook State Park, and Lake Waramaug State Park near Kent.

The trip starts with a Class II–III drop beginning just upstream of the covered bridge. At high water this rapid is Class III. It is easily scouted from the bridge en route to the put-in. Most paddlers run right of center under the bridge with a shift to the left above the bend. For paddlers who want to avoid the rapid, an alternate put-in with a small parking lot is located on the east shore below the bend.

About a mile below the covered bridge there is a one-foot drop over a

ledge that is best run in the vee to the left of center.

About 4.5 mi and 1.5 hours into the trip, the river passes the Housatonic Meadows State Park campground, a convenient spot for a break or lunch. This is an easy place to beach the boats; there are flush toilets and fresh

Kayaking on the Hudson River   David Hough

water. A plaque on a prominent rock in the river is dedicated to Joe Baroni, 1906–1988, "a friend to the river." Another pleasant lunch spot is about 1.5 mi farther at the Housatonic Meadows picnic area on river right.

From the Housatonic Meadows picnic area, another 0.3 mi brings you to the imposing bridge at the town of Cornwall Bridge where CT 4 and US 7 cross the river. Access is available on river right just beyond the bridge for those who wish to begin or end at this point. To reach this point, drive north from the bridge on US 7, go right on River Road, and swing back under the bridge. Access is across from a state highway garage.

Rented boats are returned at Housatonic Meadows, so the remainder of the trip is less crowded. A mile below Cornwall Bridge the river swings sharply right, then left. The remnant of a bridge abutment is all that is left of Swifts Bridge. In moderate water, running on the left will avoid rocks and high waves. Low water may require running on the right.

There are three access points in the vicinity of Swifts Bridge Rapids. The first is on River Road, 1.2 mi south of the highway department garage at Cornwall Bridge. This is a steep and difficult takeout located on river right, just before the end of the rapid and down from a parking turnout. Although there are signs prohibiting motor vehicles beyond this point, River Road continues 400 yds or so to a fisherman's access spot indicated by a dip in the road and a small stream leading to a pulloff by the river. It is much easier to exit here, but cars should not be parked beyond the signs prohibiting motor vehicles. Therefore, one must carry the boat back up River Road to the designated parking area. A third access is at a sandy beach on river left below the rapids. Swifts Bridge Road turns right off US 7, south of the Calhoun Corners Cemetery. From the road to the beach is a carry of several hundred yards across tracks and through poison ivy infested brush. Be careful!

Below Swifts Bridge the Appalachian Trail parallels the river on the right. Bird sightings increase. It is worth a stop where a brook enters on the right to explore the stonework remnants of earlier times. Many wildflowers and unusual ferns can be found in this area. There is a pit outhouse further up the hill.

When houses become visible on the right there is a long Class II rapid with good surfing waves. After this rapid the river is mostly flat with a few stretches of quickwater and a short rapid just before the takeout at Kent.

🔺 Takeout:

Exit on river right, at the end of a short rapid, where the path from a fisherman's pulloff on Skiff Mountain Road comes to the river. Fix this spot in your mind when you run the car shuttle, because it is difficult to identify from the river. To drive to this takeout, go south on US 7 from West Cornwall. At Kent turn right on CT 341 and cross the bridge over the Housatonic. Take the first right, and go north on Skiff Mountain Road. The most desirable parking spot is in the largest of the several pulloffs on the right, about 0.7 mi upstream from CT 341. Beware, poison ivy flourishes here!

However you do it, have fun! This is a wonderful river!

Appendix A

Whitewater Trips

Upper Hudson River near Blue Ledge   Chet Harvey

Class Page

UPPER HUDSON WATERSHED

Hudson River and Tributaries

Newcomb Bridge to Indian River Confluence . . . II–III   15

Hudson Gorge: Indian River to North River . . . . III–IV   19

North River to North Creek . . . . I–II   23

North Creek to The Glen . . . . I–III+   25

The Glen to Thurman Station . . . . I–III   32

Cedar River

Indian Lake Village to Hudson River . . . . . . I–III+   66

Schroon River

Schroon Falls to Schroon Lake Village I   75

Starbuckville to Riverbank . . . . II–III   78

Riverbank to Warrensburg I   81

Sacandaga River, Middle Branch

Christine Falls to Auger Falls . . . . III–VI   84

Sacandaga River, West Branch

Whitehouse to Pumpkin Hollow . . . . II–III   95

Sacandaga River, Main Branch

Wells to Hope . . . . I–II 101

Stewarts Dam to Hudson River . . . . II–III 106

Class Page

Batten Kill
    Manchester, Vermont, to Arlington, Vermont . I–II 117
    Arlington, Vermont,
        to New York State Rest Area . . . . I–II 122
    New York State Rest Area to Shushan . . . . I 123
    Shushan to NY 22 Bridge . . . . I 124
    NY 22 Bridge to Battenville . . . . I 126
Kayaderosseras Creek
    Rock City Falls to Ballston Spa . . . . I–III 127
Hoosic River
    North Pownal, Vermont,
        to Hoosick Falls, New York . . . . I–II 141
    Hoosick Junction to Johnsonville Dam . . . . I 144
    Johnsonville Dam to Valley Falls . . . . I 149

LOWER HUDSON WATERSHED
    Lower Hudson Tributaries
    Kinderhook Creek
        Stephentown to West Lebanon . . . . I–II 160
        East Nassau to Chatham Center . . . . II 162
    Normans Kill
        Watervliet Reservoir to New Scotland Avenue I–II 166
    Catskill Creek
        Cooksburg to East Durham . . . . III 169
    Esopus Creek
        Allaben to Boiceville . . . . II–III 172

Class Page

MOHAWK RIVER WATERSHED
  Mohawk River Tributaries
    West Canada Creek
      Trenton Falls to Poland . . . . I 198
      Poland to Middleville . . . . II 201
      Middleville to Kast Bridge . . . . II–II+ 203
    East Canada Creek
      Stratford to Dolgeville . . . . II–III 206
    Schoharie Creek
      North Blenheim to Middleburgh . . . . I–I+ 211
      Middleburgh to Esperance . . . . I–I+ 214
      Esperance to Power House Road . . . . II–III 218
      Power House Road to the Mohawk River . . . . II 220
      Cobleskill Creek
        Cobleskill to Sagendorf Road . . . . II–III 224
    Alplaus Kill
      Charlton Road to Van Vorst Road . . . . I–II 229
      Kristel Falls to the Mohawk River . . . . I–II 230

LOWER CONNECTICUT AND HOUSATONIC WATERSHEDS
  Deerfield River, Massachusetts
    Fife Brook to Charlemont . . . . II–III+ 235
  Housatonic River, Connecticut
    Falls Village to West Cornwall . . . . I–II 239
    West Cornwall to Kent . . . . II–III 242

· · ·

Appendix B

Flatwater and Quickwater Trips

Page

UPPER HUDSON WATERSHED
Hudson River and Tributaries
Lake Luzerne to Corinth 34
Corinth Dam to Spier Falls Dam 37
Spier Falls Dam to Sherman Island Dam 40
Sherman Island to Big Boom Road 42
Big Boom Road to Feeder Dam 43
Fort Edward to Fort Miller 46
Fort Miller to Stillwater 49
Stillwater to Lansingburgh 54
Hudson River–Mohawk River Confluence 61
Cedar River Flow 63
Miami River 70
Cheney Pond and Boreas River
Cheney Pond and Lester Flow 72
Sacandaga River and Tributaries
Kunjamuk River (tributary) 88
Sacandaga River, West Branch
Route 10 Bridge to Shaker Place 90
Fall Stream (tributary) 99
Stewarts Bridge Reservoir 105
Moses Kill 112
Kayaderosseras Creek
Ballston Spa to Saratoga Lake 131

Page

Fish Creek
    Saratoga Lake to Grangerville 134
    Grangerville to Victory Mills 137
Round Lake and Anthony Kill 151
Grafton Lakes 153

LAKE CHAMPLAIN DRAINAGE
    Lake George, Northwest Bay Brook 179
    Poultney River 182
    Champlain Canal
        Whitehall to Fort Ann 186
        Fort Ann to Fort Edward 189
    Glens Falls Feeder Canal 192

Appendix C

Safety Code of American Whitewater

I. Personal Preparedness and Responsibility

1. Be a competent swimmer, with the ability to handle yourself underwater.
2. Wear a personal flotation device (PFD). A snugly fitting, vest-type PFD offers back and shoulder protection as well as the flotation needed to swim safely in whitewater.
3. Wear a solid, correctly-fitted helmet when upsets are likely. This is essential in kayaks or covered canoes, and recommended for open canoeists using thigh straps and rafters running steep drops.
4. Do not boat out of control. Your skills should be sufficient to stop or reach shore before reaching danger. Do not enter a rapid unless you are reasonably sure that you can run it safely or swim it without injury.
5. Whitewater rivers contain many hazards which are not always easily recognized. The following are the most frequent killers:
   A. High Water. The river's speed and power increase tremendously as the flow increases, raising the difficulty of most rapids. Rescue becomes progressively harder as the water rises, adding to the danger. Floating debris and strainers make even an easy rapid quite hazardous. It is often misleading to judge the river level at the put-in, since a small rise in a wide, shallow place will be multiplied many times where the river narrows. Use reliable gauge information whenever possible, and be aware that sun on snowpack, hard rain, and upstream dam releases may greatly increase the flow.
   B. Cold. Cold drains your strength and robs you of the ability to make sound decisions on matters affecting your survival. Cold water immersion, because of the initial shock and the rapid heat loss which follows, is especially dangerous. Dress appropriately for bad weather or sudden immersion in the water. When the water temperature is less than 50 degrees Fahrenheit, a wet suit or dry suit is essential for protection if you swim. Next best is wool or pile clothing under a waterproof shell. In this case, you should also carry waterproof matches and a change of clothing in a waterproof bag. If, after prolonged exposure, a person experiences

uncontrollable shaking, loss of coordination, or difficulty speaking, he or she is hypothermic, and needs your assistance.

C. Strainers. Brush, fallen trees, bridge pilings, undercut rocks, or anything else which allows river current to sweep through can pin boats and boaters against the obstacle. Water pressure on anything trapped this way can be overwhelming. Rescue is often extremely difficult. Pinning may occur in fast current, with little or no whitewater to warn of the danger.

D. Dams, Weirs, Ledges, Reversals, Holes, and Hydraulics. When water drops over an obstacle, it curls back on itself, forming a strong upstream current which may be capable of holding a boat or swimmer. Some holes make for excellent sport. Others are proven killers. **Paddlers who cannot recognize the difference should avoid all but the smallest holes.** Hydraulics around man-made dams must be treated with utmost respect, regardless of their height or the level of the river. Despite their seemingly benign appearance, they can create an almost escape-proof trap. The swimmer's only exit from the "drowning machine" is to dive below the surface when the downstream current is flowing beneath the reversal.

E. Broaching. When a boat is pushed sideways against a rock by strong current, it may collapse and wrap. This is especially dangerous to kayak and decked canoe paddlers; these boats will collapse and the combination of indestructible hulls and tight outfitting may create a deadly trap. Even without entrapment, releasing pinned boats can be extremely time-consuming and dangerous. To avoid pinning, throw your weight downstream towards the rock. This allows the current to slide harmlessly underneath the hull.

6. Boating alone is discouraged. The minimum party is three people or two craft.

7. Have a frank knowledge of your boating ability, and don't attempt rivers or rapids which lie beyond that ability.

A. Develop the paddling skills and teamwork required to match the river you plan to boat. Most good paddlers develop skills gradually; attempts to advance too quickly will compromise your safety and enjoyment.

B. Be in good physical and mental condition, consistent with the difficulties which may be expected. Make adjustments for loss of skills due to age, health, and fitness. Any health limitations must be explained to your fellow paddlers prior to starting the trip.

8. Be practiced in self-rescue, including escape from an overturned craft. The Eskimo Roll is strongly recommended for decked boaters who run rapids Class IV or greater or who paddle in cold environmental conditions.

9. Be trained in rescue skills, CPR, and first aid with special emphasis on recognizing and treating hypothermia. It may save your friend's life.

10. Carry equipment needed for unexpected emergencies, including foot wear which will protect your feet when walking out, a throw rope, knife, whistle, and waterproof matches. If you wear eyeglasses, tie them on and carry a spare pair on long trips. Bring cloth repair tape on short runs, and a full repair kit on isolated rivers. Do not wear bulky jackets, ponchos, heavy boots, or anything else which could reduce your ability to survive a swim.

11. Despite the mutually supportive group structure described in this code, individual paddlers are ultimately responsible for their own safety, and must assume sole responsibility for the following decisions:

    A. The decision to participate on any trip. This includes an evaluation of the expected difficulty of the rapids under the conditions existing at the time of the put-in.

    B. The selection of appropriate equipment, including a boat design suited to their skills and the appropriate rescue and survival gear.

    C. The decision to scout any rapid, and to run or portage according to their best judgment. Other members of the group may offer advice, but paddlers should resist pressure from anyone to paddle beyond their skills. It is also their responsibility to decide whether to pass up any walk-out or takeout opportunity.

    D. All trip participants should consistently evaluate their own and their group's safety, voicing their concerns when appropriate and following what they believe to be the best course of action. Paddlers are encouraged to speak with anyone whose actions on the water are dangerous, whether they are a part of your group or not.

II. Boat and Equipment Preparedness

1. Test new and different equipment under familiar conditions before relying on it for difficult runs. This is especially true when adopting a new boat design or outfitting system. Low-volume craft may present additional hazards to inexperienced or poorly conditioned paddlers.

2. Be sure your boat and gear are in good repair before starting a trip. The more isolated and difficult the run, the more rigorous this inspection should be.

3. Install flotation bags in non-inflatable craft, securely fixed in each end, designed to displace as much water as possible. Inflatable boats should have multiple air chambers and be test inflated before launching.

4. Have strong, properly sized paddles or oars for controlling your craft. Carry sufficient spares for the length and difficulty of the trip.

5. Outfit your boat safely. The ability to exit your boat quickly is an essential component of safety in rapids. It is your responsibility to see that there is absolutely nothing to cause entrapment when coming free of an upset craft. This includes:

   A. Spray covers which won't release reliably or which release prematurely.

   B. Boat outfitting too tight to allow a fast exit, especially in low-volume kayaks or decked canoes. This includes low-hung thwarts in canoes lacking adequate clearance for your feet and kayak foot braces which fail or allow your feet to become wedged under them.

   C. Inadequately supported decks which collapse on a paddler's legs when a decked boat is pinned by water pressure. Inadequate clearance with the deck because of your size or build.

   D. Loose ropes which cause entanglement. Beware of any length of loose line attached to a whitewater boat. All items must be tied tightly and excess line eliminated; painters, throw lines, and safety rope systems must be completely and effectively stored. Do not knot the end of a rope, as it can get caught in cracks between rocks.

6. Provide ropes which permit you to hold onto your craft so that it may be rescued. The following methods are recommended:

   A. Kayaks and covered canoes should have grab loops of 1/4"+ rope or equivalent webbing sized to admit a normal sized hand. Stern painters are permissible if properly secured.

   B. Open canoes should have securely anchored bow and stern painters consisting of 8–10 feet of 1/4" line. These must be secured in such a way that they are readily accessible, but cannot come loose accidentally. Grab loops are acceptable, but are more difficult to reach after an upset.

   C. Rafts and dories may have taut perimeter lines threaded through the loops provided. Footholds should be designed so that a paddler's feet cannot be forced through them, causing entrapment. Flip lines should be carefully and reliably stowed.

7. Know your craft's carrying capacity, and how added loads affect boat handling in whitewater. Most rafts have a minimum crew size which can be added to on day trips or in easy rapids. Carrying more than two paddlers in an open canoe when running rapids is not recommended.

8. Cartop racks must be strong and attach positively to the vehicle. Lash your boat to each crossbar, then tie the ends of the boats directly to the bumpers for added security. This arrangement should survive all but the most violent vehicle accident.

III. Group Preparedness and Responsibility

1. Organization. A river trip should be regarded as a common adventure by all participants, except on commercial instructional or guided trips as defined below. Participants share the responsibility for the conduct of the trip, and each participant is individually responsible for judging his or her own capabilities and for his or her own safety as the trip progresses. In other words, no person is responsible for the safety of other persons on the trip. Participants are encouraged (but are not obligated) to offer advice and guidance for the independent consideration and judgment of others.

2. River Conditions. The group should have a reasonable knowledge of the difficulty of the run. Participants should evaluate this information and adjust their own plans accordingly. If the run is exploratory or no one is familiar with the river, maps and guidebooks, if available, should be examined. The group should secure accurate flow information; the more difficult the run, the more important this will be. Be aware of possible changes in river level and how this will affect the difficulty of the run. If the trip involves tidal stretches, secure appropriate information on tides.

3. Group equipment should be suited to the difficulty of the river. The group should always have a throw line available; one line per boat is recommended on difficult runs. The equipment list may include: carabiners, prussick loops, first aid kit, flashlight, folding saw, fire starter, guidebooks, maps, food, extra clothing, and any other rescue or survival items suggested by conditions. Each item is not required on every run, and this list is not meant to be a substitute for good judgment.

4. Keep the group compact, but maintain sufficient spacing to avoid collisions.

If the group is large, consider dividing into smaller groups or using the "Buddy System" as an additional safeguard. Space yourselves closely enough to permit good communication, but not so close as to interfere with one another in rapids.

A. A point paddler sets the pace. When in front, do not get in over your head. Never run drops when you cannot see a clear route to the bottom or, for advanced paddlers, a sure route to the next eddy. When in doubt, stop and scout.

B. Keep track of all group members. Each boat keeps the one behind it in sight, stopping if necessary. Know how many people are in your group and take head counts regularly. No one should paddle ahead or walk out without first informing the group. Paddlers requiring additional support should stay at the center of a group and not allow themselves to lag behind in the more difficult rapids. If the group is large and contains a wide range of abilities, a "Sweep Boat" may be designated to bring up the rear.

C. Courtesy. On heavily used rivers, do not cut in front of a boater running a drop. Always look upstream before leaving eddies to run or play. Never enter a crowded drop or eddy when no room for you exists. Passing other groups in a rapid may be hazardous: it's often safer to wait upstream until the group ahead has passed.

5. Float plan. If the trip is into a wilderness area or for an extended period, plans should be filed with a responsible person who will contact the authorities if you are overdue. It may be wise to establish checkpoints along the way where civilization could be contacted if necessary. Knowing the location of possible help and preplanning escape routes can speed rescue.

6. Drugs. The use of alcohol or mind-altering drugs before or during river trips is not recommended. It dulls reflexes, reduces decision-making ability, and may interfere with important survival reflexes.

7. Commercial Instructional or Guided Trips. In contrast to the common adventure trip format, in these trip formats, a professional (i.e., paid) instructor or guide assumes some of the responsibilities normally exercised by the group as a whole, as appropriate under the circumstances. These formats recognize that commercial instructional or guided trips may involve participants who lack significant experience in whitewater, and who wish to place themselves under the care of professionals. However, as a participant acquires experience in whitewater, he or she takes on increasing responsi-

bility for his or her own safety, in accordance with what he or she knows or should know as a result of that increased experience. Also, as in all trip formats, every participant must realize and assume the risks associated with the serious hazards of whitewater rivers. It is advisable for professional instructors and guides or their employers to acquire trip or personal liability insurance.

A. A "commercial instructional trip" is characterized by a commercial (i.e., for-profit) enterprise and a paid instructor, where the primary purpose of the trip is to teach boating skills, and which is conducted for a required fee. This does not include a nonprofit organization conducting instruction with unpaid volunteers.

B. A "commercial guided trip" is characterized by a commercial enterprise and a paid guide conducting trips for a required fee.

IV. Guidelines for River Rescue

1. Recover from an upset with an Eskimo Roll whenever possible. Evacuate your boat immediately if there is imminent danger of being trapped against rocks, brush, or any other kind of strainer.

2. If you swim, hold on to your boat. It has much flotation and is easy for rescuers to spot. Get to the upstream end so that you cannot be crushed between a rock and your boat by the force of the current. Persons with good balance may be able to climb on top of a swamped kayak or flipped raft and paddle to shore.

3. Release your craft if this will improve your chances, especially if the water is cold or dangerous rapids lie ahead. Actively attempt self-rescue whenever possible by swimming for safety. Be prepared to assist others who may come to your aid.

A. When swimming in shallow or obstructed rapids, lie on your back with feet held high and pointed downstream. Do not attempt to stand in fast-moving water; if your foot wedges on the bottom, fast water will push you under and keep you there. Get to slow or very shallow water before attempting to stand or walk. Look ahead! Avoid possible pinning situations including undercut rocks, strainers, downed trees, holes, and other dangers by swimming away from them.

B. If the rapids are deep and powerful, roll over onto your stomach and swim aggressively for shore. Watch for eddies and slack water and use them to get out of the current. Strong swimmers can effect a powerful upstream ferry and get to shore fast. If the shores are obstructed with strainers or undercut rocks, however, it is safer to "ride the rapid out" until a safer escape can be found.

4. If others spill and swim, go after the boaters first. Rescue boats and equipment only if this can be done safely. While participants are encouraged (but not obligated) to assist one another to the best of their ability, they should do so only if they can, in their judgment, do so safely. The first duty of a rescuer is not to compound the problem by becoming another victim.

5. The use of rescue lines requires training; uninformed use may cause injury. Never tie yourself into either end of a line without a reliable quick-release system. Have a knife handy to deal with unexpected entanglement. Learn to place setlines effectively, to throw accurately, to belay effectively, and to properly handle a rope thrown to you.

6. When reviving a drowning victim, be aware that cold water may greatly extend survival time underwater. Victims of hypothermia may have depressed vital signs and look and feel dead. Don't give up; continue CPR for as long as possible without compromising safety.

V. Universal River Signals

These signals may be replaced with an alternate set of signals agreed upon by the group.

Illustrations provided by Les Fry and American Whitewater, www.americanwhitewater.org

STOP: Potential hazard ahead. Wait for "all clear" signal before proceeding, or scout ahead. Form a horizontal bar with your outstretched arms. Those seeing the signal should pass it back to others in the party.

HELP/EMERGENCY: Assist the signaler as quickly as possible. Give three long blasts on a police whistle while waving a paddle, helmet, or life vest over your head. If a whistle is not available, use the visual signal alone. A whistle is best carried on a lanyard attached to your life vest.

ALL CLEAR: Come ahead (in the absence of other directions proceed down the center). Form a vertical bar with your paddle or one arm held high above your head. Paddle blade should be turned flat for maximum visibility. To signal direction or a preferred course through a rapid around obstruction, lower the previously vertical "all clear" by 45 degrees toward the side of the river with the preferred route. Never point toward the obstacle you wish to avoid.

I'M OK: "I'm OK and not hurt, are you?" While holding the elbow outward toward the side, repeatedly tap the top of your head. Whenever this signal is seen, it should be answered with the same signal so that all involved know that everything is OK.

VI. International Scale of River Difficulty

This is the American version of a rating system used to compare river difficulty throughout the world. This system is not exact: rivers do not always fit easily into one category, and regional or individual interpretations may cause misunderstandings. It is no substitute for a guidebook or accurate first-hand descriptions of a run.

Paddlers attempting difficult runs in an unfamiliar area should act cautiously until they get a feel for the way the scale is interpreted locally. River difficulty may change each year due to fluctuations in water level, downed trees, recent floods, geological disturbances, or bad weather. Stay alert for unexpected problems!

As river difficulty increases, the danger for swimming paddlers becomes greater. As rapids become longer and more continuous, the challenge increases. There is a difference between running an occasional Class IV rapid and dealing with an entire river of this category. Allow an extra margin of safety between skills and river ratings when the water is cold or if the river itself is remote and inaccessible.

The Six Difficulty Classes:

Class I: Easy. Fast-moving water with riffles and small waves. Few obstructions, all obvious and easily missed with little training. Risk to swimmers is slight, self-rescue is easy.

Class II: Novice. Straightforward rapids with wide, clear channels which are evident without scouting. Occasional maneuvering may be required, but rocks and medium-sized waves are easily missed by trained paddlers. Swimmers are seldom injured and group assistance, while helpful, is seldom needed. Rapids that are at the upper end of this difficulty range are designated Class II+.

Class III: Intermediate. Rapids with moderate, irregular waves which may be difficult to avoid and which can swamp an open canoe. Complex maneuvers in fast current and good boat control in tight passages or around ledges are often required. Large waves or strainers may be present but are easily avoided. Strong eddies and powerful current effects can be found, particularly on large-volume rivers. Scouting is advisable for inexperienced parties. Injuries while swimming are rare; self-rescue is usually easy but group assistance may be required to avoid long swims. Rapids that are at the lower or upper end of this difficulty range are designated Class III- or Class III+ respectively.

Class IV: Advanced. Intense, powerful but predictable rapids requiring precise boat handling in turbulent water. Depending on the character of the river, it may feature large, unavoidable waves and holes or constricted passages demanding fast maneuvers under pressure. A fast, reliable eddy turn may be needed to initiate maneuvers, scout rapids, or rest. Rapids may require "must" moves above dangerous hazards. Scouting may be necessary the first time down. Risk of injury to swimmers is moderate to high, and water conditions may make self-rescue difficult. Group assistance for rescue is often essential but requires practiced skills. A strong Eskimo Roll is highly recommended. Rapids that are at the upper or lower end of this difficulty range are designated Class IV- or Class IV+ respectively.

Class V. Expert. Extremely long, obstructed, or very violent rapids which expose a paddler to added risk. Drops may contain large, unavoidable waves and holes or steep, congested chutes with complex, demanding routes. Rapids may continue for long distances between pools, demanding a high level of fitness. What eddies exist may be small, turbulent, or difficult to reach. At the high end of the scale, several of these factors may be combined. Scouting is recommended but may be difficult. Swims are dangerous, and rescue is often difficult even for experts. A very reliable Eskimo Roll, proper equipment, extensive experience, and practiced rescue skills are essential. Because of the large range of difficulty that exists beyond Class IV, Class V is an open ended, multiple level scale designated by Class 5.0, 5.1, 5.2, etc. Each of these levels is an order of magnitude more difficult than the last. Example: increasing difficulty from Class 5.0 to Class 5.1 is a similar order of magnitude as increasing from Class IV to Class 5.0.

Class VI. Extreme and Exploratory. These runs have almost never been attempted and often exemplify the extremes of difficulty, unpredictability, and danger. The consequences of errors are very severe and rescue may be impossible. For teams of experts only, at favorable water levels, after close personal inspection, and taking all precautions. After a Class VI rapid has been run many times, its rating may be changed to an appropriate Class 5.x rating.

Appendix D

River Level and Flow Information

Water levels and flow rates of many rivers are available on the Internet and by phone. Use the following services to decide if a particular river or stream is flowing at an appropriate level for your paddling skills.

Northeast River Forecast Center:
Web site: www.nws.noaa.gov/er/nerfc
Provided by the National Weather Service, this Web site gives hourly gauge readings, flow rates, and ratings of the current water level of each river on a scale ranging from flood to low. Click on Basin Maps and select a river system. Gauge stations on each river are color coded according to water level. Click on any gauge station for a detailed graph of current conditions.

Waterline:
Web site: www.h2oline.com
This is a national telephone hotline giving current river stage information 24 hours a day, 365 days a year. The toll free automated number is 800-452-1737. In order to get the current gauge reading or flow at a particular river location one must know the specific six-digit code; codes are available by calling customer service at 800-945-3376 Monday through Friday from 9:00 A.M. to 5:00 P.M. or on the Internet. Waterline is working on a book, *Waterline Guide to River Level and Flow Information,* which is not yet available.

USGS Water Resource of New York
Web site: http://ny.water.usgs.gov
Click on "stream flow" under the "Data Sources" button to get a chart, organized by county, giving current readings at gauges on rivers and lakes throughout New York State. Some locations record hourly whereas others record less frequently. Clicking on the station number provides graphs showing detailed historical data for the location.

The Hudson River/Black River Regulating District
A recorded phone message gives the water levels for the Hudson River at North Creek, the Sacandaga River at Hope, and the water elevations on Great Sacandaga and Indian Lakes. These recordings are made once a day Monday through Friday during the spring, summer, and fall seasons and once a week in winter. Call 518-465-2016.

National Weather Service's Automated Information Line in Albany, New York.
In addition to automated services, there is a specialist available at the Albany weather station from 9:00 A.M. to 4:00 P.M. on weekdays and from 9:00 A.M. to noon on weekends and holidays. This individual can usually access gauge levels and water flow information at specific locations. Call 518-435-9580.

Appendix E

Glossary

The following terms are used in defining difficulty of waterways:

drainage: The terms "watershed" and "drainage" can be used interchangeably to mean a region drained by a river or river system; both terms appear in this book, based on common usage.

flatwater: There is little or no current; the surface water is smooth and unbroken except when windy; paddling upstream poses no problem.

quickwater: Water moves fast; the surface is smooth and unbroken at high water, but may have riffles at medium and low water.

watershed: The terms "watershed" and "drainage" can be used interchangeably to mean a region drained by a river or river system; both terms appear in this book, based on common usage.

whitewater: Divided into classes ranging from I to VI according to the American Whitewater International Scale provided in Appendix C.

The following definitions may be useful in determining water levels:

low water: Water's edge is below the bank and clearly defined. Small rocky rivers may be uncanoeable. Large flat rivers and lakes will be navigable.

medium water: Water extends to or partway up the bank. Vegetation at the shoreline may be under water. Many medium and large whitewater rivers will be canoeable. For the whitewater enthusiast, the main sport will be rock dodging.

high water: Water extends close to the top of the defined bank; bushes along the shore may be partly under water. Most small whitewater rivers are canoeable at this level. Large whitewater rivers will have challenging rapids.

very high water: Water is at the top or over the bank. Many trees and bushes at the top of the bank have their roots and lower parts in or under water. It may be difficult for the paddler to reach shore. The current will be very strong and rapids may be a class above the difficulty rating given in this book. This water level is not recommended for most paddlers. Only experts who know the river should attempt it.

flood: Water is significantly over the banks and in the vegetation. The current is extremely strong. Along rivers the flow will pile up against trees that are normally on dry land. Controlling a boat will be extremely difficult, if not impossible. Rescue may be impossible. This level is very dangerous for everyone.

The following definitions used in discussions of waterways are for those new to paddling and those who wish to review:

above: Upstream of a boat or object.

below: Downstream of a boat or object.

braided: Divided into two, three, or more channels that spread out to flow around obstacles, such as islands, or through a marsh.

broadside: The boat length is perpendicular to the current. Broadsiding a downstream rock is a prescription for an upset!

carry or portage: To transport around an obstacle on foot or by vehicle; also used as a noun.

chute or vee: An obvious V pattern pointing downstream, formed by smooth water flowing between two obstacles such as boulders; provides a route through the obstacles; often leads to a series of standing waves.

confluence: Point at which two streams join; if one is much larger, then it is not a confluence, but the mouth of the smaller stream.

creek or stream: Used interchangeably and arbitrarily for small waterways; also known by the Dutch word, *kill*.

eddy: A quiet water or backcurrent (flowing upstream) located just downstream of an obstacle around which the main current flows; can serve as a resting place for paddlers who know how to maneuver across the eddy line.

eddy line: A visible line formed by the current differential between the main current rushing downstream and the eddy current flowing upstream.

eddy turn: A skillful maneuver which moves the boat quickly across an eddy line to either rest in the eddy or to re-enter the main current. A strong eddy line can easily upset an inexperienced paddler. Paddlers need instruction and practice to execute a successful eddy turn.

ferry: Paddling the boat across the current without drifting downstream by maintaining an upstream angle to the current of approximately 30 degrees (the faster the current, the steeper the angle); always done while paddling in the upstream direction at an angle to the current; may be done bow-first, paddling forward, or stern-first, paddling backward.

hole or souse hole: A hydraulic formed by water dropping steeply over a rock, ledge, or dam; water drops to the bottom, where it flows downstream, then rises and flows back upstream, thus creating a recirculating pattern; experienced paddlers play in holes that have side exits.

keeper: A very dangerous hole from which a boat and paddler(s) cannot escape because of the strong recirculation and lack of side exits; steep dams which extend all the way across a stream produce hydraulics which are keepers; many unwary people have drowned in these traps.

pillow: A raised convex wave formed by water pouring over the surface of a rock close to the surface.

pourover: Water flowing over an obstacle such as a rock or ledge; a steep drop results in a hole; a drop of a lesser angle results in a series of standing waves downstream.

riffle: A very small rapid.

rock garden: A rapid with many boulders (usually medium or small in size) around which paddlers must maneuver; often the water level is medium or low; usually there are a number of possible routes.

standing waves: A series of stationary waves (sometimes called haystacks) of gradually diminishing size found at the end of a chute or vee; indicate deep water channels.

surfing: Riding (playing!) the upstream slope of a wide standing wave; the boat remains on the wave when kept parallel to the current; experienced paddlers can position the boat sideways while surfing. These maneuvers provide many a thrill!

sweeper or strainer: A tree fallen across or into the waterway with branches through which water passes; boats swept by a strong current into sweepers are easily overturned; both boat and occupant(s) may be pinned against the branches. Sweepers are among the most common and dangerous obstacles on streams and rivers.

Appendix F

Resources

Paddling Instruction

There are many excellent paddling courses available in the northeast. To list them all is beyond the scope of this guide. We have elected to mention only those organizations and paddling schools that offer instruction within the geographic area covered by this book. Some organizations may ask you to bring your own equipment to class sessions. Paddling clubs usually offer a sequence of scheduled trips so that interested individuals may continue to participate with the group. Commercial outfitters that offer instruction require a fee.

Flatwater Instruction

The Albany Chapter of ADK offers several "Fundamentals of Canoeing" sessions during the winter months. Beginning in April and continuing into the fall, the club schedules early evening paddles once a week at various locations. Participants do not need to sign up and may paddle in tandem or solo boats. For information use the ADK Web site www.adk.org and click on the Albany Chapter. The address is P.O. Box 2116, ESP Sta., Albany, N.Y. 12220; phone 518-899-2725.

Adirondack Paddle 'N' Pole is a store devoted to paddling, cross-country skiing, and snowshoeing. Owner Rich Macha is actively associated with the Albany ADK paddling program and offers classes in beginning and intermediate paddling in both canoes and kayaks. The store is located at 2123 Central Avenue, Colonie, N.Y. 12304; phone 518-346-3180; www.paddlenpole.com.

The Northern New York Paddlers offer flatwater instruction once a week in the early evening on the Mohawk River. For persons who are interested in racing, this clinic provides instruction in special techniques for racers as well as basic paddling skills. The group publishes a monthly newsletter in conjunction with the Schenectady Winter Sports Club. For information write NNYP, P.O. 228, Schenectady, N.Y. 12301 or access the Web site at www.swc-nnyp.org.

The Berkshire chapter of the Appalachian Mountain Club offers an annual "Quiet Water Instruction" clinic every June. For information check the Web site www.amcberkshire.org or call 413-562-6792.

Whitewater Instruction

The Schenectady Chapter of ADK offers a whitewater clinic for novice paddlers with previous flatwater experience. The course is given once a year, usually in late May or early June. The program consists of an indoor lecture followed by a day on a Class I–II river with an experienced instructor. Periodically the chapter offers intermediate/advanced whitewater skill classes. For information on scheduling and contact persons write P.O. Box 733, Schenectady, N.Y. 12301 or check the ADK Web site www.adk.org and click on the Schenectady Chapter. You can access the chapter directly at www.geocities.com/schdyadk/.

The Albany Chapter of ADK offers indoor pool kayak clinics during the winter months. For information see Flatwater Instruction.

The Berkshire Chapter of the Appalachian Mountain Club (AMC) offers indoor pool rolling sessions during the winter and an annual two-day river training course. For information see previous entry on Flatwater Instruction.

Wild Waters Outdoor Center is a commercial outfitter that offers whitewater instruction in basic and intermediate canoeing and kayaking. Courses are held on the Hudson River near their headquarters at the Glen. Wild Waters offers two instructional programs at a discounted price for members of ADK. For information write Wild Waters, 1123 Route 28, Warrensburg, N.Y. 12885 or phone 800-867-2335 or 518-494-4984. The Web site is: www.wildwaters.net.

Zoar Outdoor is a commercial outfitter with waterfront property on the Deerfield River in Massachusetts where they offer basic, intermediate, and advanced classes in solo and tandem canoeing and kayaking. Headquarters is located at 7 Main Street on the Mohawk Trail (MA 2) in Charlemont, Massachusetts. Mailing address is P.O. Box 245, Charlemont, MA 01339; phone 800-532-7483. Access their Web site at www.zoaroutdoor.com.

Appendix G

Hudson River PCB Dredging Information

In 2002 the Environmental Protection Agency (EPA) announced its Record of Decision under Federal Superfund legislation approving a plan for removing an estimated 150,000 pounds of polychlorinated biphenyls (PCBs) from the upper Hudson River. The plan calls for dredging 2.6 million cubic yards of contaminated sediments from a forty-mile stretch of river from Fort Edward to Troy. A field office in the upper Hudson region will coordinate activities in cooperation with local communities.

An estimated 1.3 million pounds of PCBs were discharged into the Hudson River by General Electric capacitor plants in Fort Edward and Hudson Falls over a period of thirty years, ending in 1977 when the practice was banned. PCBs are suspected carcinogens that accumulate in the fatty tissues of fish and other river organisms. There is evidence of other detrimental effects, such as developmental abnormalities, in humans. Claiming that more harm than good would result from stirring up the contaminated sediments, GE waged an intensive media campaign against dredging. The cleanup will cost the company $500 million. GE lost that battle but is contesting the constitutionality of the Superfund law in the Federal District Court in Washington, D.C.

Although the EPA plan has been approved, it will probably be at least five years before any dredging can begin. Paddlers can call the headquarters of the Canal Corporation to check on the location of dredging activity that would interfere with navigation of river segments between Fort Edward and Troy. Call 518-436-2700. Another option is to call individual lock operators in each river segment. Phone numbers for locks are included in each write-up.

About the Authors

Chet Harvey and Kathie Armstrong have paddled canoes all their lives. When they met 25 years ago they became a tandem team and seriously began to hone their skills while paddling with the whitewater group of the ADK Schenectady Chapter. Although their paddling adventures have ranged north to the Northwest Territories in Canada and the Arctic Ocean, east to Norway, west to California, and south to Texas, the rivers and lakes of the Adirondacks remain their paddling home. Chet and Kathie have paddled almost every whitewater route described in this guide and many of the flatwater sections. They have served as leaders for many local ADK trips and have led several wilderness excursions in northern Canada. Their favorite whitewater run is between North Creek and The Glen on the historic and beautiful Hudson River.

Backdoor to Backcountry

ADKers choose from friendly outings, for those just getting started with local chapters, to Adirondack backpacks and international treks. Learn gradually through chapter outings or attend one of our schools, workshops, or other programs. A sampling includes:
- Alpine Flora
- Ice Climbing
- Rock Climbing
- Basic Canoeing/Kayaking
- Bicycle Touring
- Cross-country Skiing and Snowshoeing
- Mountain Photography
- Winter Mountaineering
- Birds of the Adirondacks
- Geology of the High Peaks ... and more!

For more information:
ADK Member Service Center
(Exit 21 off the Northway, I-87)
814 Goggins Road, Lake George, NY 12845-4117

ADK Heart Lake Program Center
P.O. Box 867, Lake Placid, NY 12946-0867

Information: 518-668-4447
Membership: 800-395-8080
Publications and merchandise: 800-395-8080
Education: 518-523-3441
Facilities' reservations: 518-523-3441
E-mail: adkinfo@adk.org
Web site: www.adk.org

Join Us

We are a nonprofit membership organization that brings together people with interests in recreation, conservation, and environmental education in the New York State Forest Preserve.

Membership Benefits

- **Discovery:**
  ADK can broaden your horizons by introducing you to new places, recreational activities, and interests

- **Enjoyment:**
  Being outdoors more and loving it more

- **People:**
  Meeting others and sharing the fun

- *Adirondac* **Magazine**

- **Member Discounts:**
  20% off on guidebooks, maps, and other ADK publications; discount on lodge stays; discount on educational programs

- **Satisfaction:**
  Knowing you're doing your part and that future generations will enjoy the wilderness as you do

- **Chapter Participation:**
  Brings you the fun of outings and other social activities and the reward of working on trails, conservation, and education projects at the local level. You can also join as a member at large. Either way, all Club activities and benefits are available.

Membership

To Join

Call **800-395-8080** (Mon.–Sat., 8:30 A.M.–5:00 P.M.), visit **www.adk.org**, or send this form with payment to:

Adirondack Mountain Club
814 Goggins Road
Lake George, NY 12845-4117

Check Membership Level:

☐ Individual — $45
☐ Family — $55*
☐ Student (full time, 18 and over) — $35
☐ Senior (65 or over) — $35
☐ Senior Family — $45*
☐ Lifetime Individual — $1200
☐ Lifetime Family — $1800*

School _____

*Includes associate/family members
Fees subject to change.

Name _____
Address _____
City _____ State _____ Zip _____
Home Telephone ( ) _____

☐ I want to join as a Chapter member*
☐ I want to join as a member at large

List spouse and children under 18 with birthdates:

Spouse _____
Child _____ Birthdate _____
Child _____ Birthdate _____

Bill my: ☐ MASTERCARD ☐ AMERICAN EXPRESS
          ☐ VISA   ☐ DISCOVER   Exp. date

_____
Signature (required for charge)

* For details, call **800-395-8080** (Mon.–Sat., 8:30 A.M.– 5:00 P.M.)

ADK is a nonprofit, tax-exempt organization. Membership fees, excluding $10 for membership benefits, are tax deductible, to the extent allowed by law.

Adirondack **ADK** Mountain Club

CG4

The Adirondack Mountain Club, Inc.

814 Goggins Road, Lake George, NY 12845-4117
518-668-4447/Orders only: **800-395-8080** (Mon.–Sat., 8:30–5:00)
www.adk.org

BOOKS

Adirondack Canoe Waters: North Flow
Adirondack Mountain Club Canoe and Kayak Guide: East-Central New York State
Adirondack Mountain Club Canoe Guide to Western & Central New York State
An Adirondack Passage: The Cruise of the Canoe *Sairy Gamp*
An Adirondack Sampler I: Day Hikes for All Seasons
An Adirondack Sampler II: Backpacking Trips
Catskill Day Hikes for All Seasons
Climbing in the Adirondacks: A Guide to Rock & Ice Routes
Forests & Trees of the Adirondack High Peaks Region
Guide to Adirondack Trails: High Peaks Region
Guide to Adirondack Trails: Northern Region
Guide to Adirondack Trails: Central Region
Guide to Adirondack Trails: Northville-Placid Trail
Guide to Adirondack Trails: West-Central Region
Guide to Adirondack Trails: Eastern Region
Guide to Adirondack Trails: Southern Region
Guide to Catskill Trails: Catskill Region
Kids on the Trail! Hiking with Children in the Adirondacks
Our Wilderness: How the People of New York Found,
Changed, and Preserved the Adirondacks
Ski and Snowshoe Trails in the Adirondacks
The Adirondack Reader
Views from on High: Fire Tower Trails in the Adirondacks and Catskills
Winterwise: A Backpacker's Guide

MAPS

Trails of the Adirondack High Peaks Region
Trails of the Adirondack Northern Region
Trails of the Adirondack Central Region
Northville-Placid Trail
Trails of the Adirondack West-Central Region
Trails of the Adirondack Eastern Region
Trails of the Adirondack Southern Region

The Adirondack Mountain Club Calendar

Price list available on request

Index

Locations are listed by proper name with Camp, Lake, or Mount following and are in New York State unless otherwise noted.

A

Allaben to Boiceville, 172–176
  map, 175
Alplaus Kill, 228
  Charlton Road to Van Vorst Road, 229–230
    map, 233
  Kristel Falls to Mohawk River, 230–232
    map, 233
Anthony Kill and Round Lake, 151–153
  map, 150
Arlington, Vermont
  from Manchester, Vermont, 117–119
    map, 121
  to New York State Rest Area, 122–123
    maps, 120–121
Auger Falls from Christine Falls, 84–87
  map, 85

B

Ballston Spa
  from Rock City Falls, 127–131
    map, 129
  to Saratoga Lake, 131–134
    map, 133
Batten Kill, 115–117
  Arlington, Vermont to New York State Rest Area, 122–123
    maps, 120–121
  Manchester, Vermont, to Arlington, Vermont, 117–119
    map, 121
  New York State Rest Area to Shushan, 123–124
    map, 120
  NY 22 Bridge to Battenville, 126–127
    map, 120
  Shushan to NY 22 Bridge, 124–125
    map, 120
Battenkill Canoe, Ltd., 116
Batten Kill Railroad, 116
Battenville from NY 22 Bridge, 126–127
  map, 120
Big Boom Road
  to Feeder Dam, 43–46
    map, 44
  from Sherman Island, 42–43
    map, 44
Blenheim Bridge, 211
Boiceville from Allaben, 172–176
  map, 175
Boreas River and Cheney Pond
  Cheney Pond and Lester Flow, 72–75
    map, 73
Bow Bridge, 36
Bureau of Water Resources, 173

C

Canada Creek. *See East Canada Creek; West Canada Creek*

Catskill Creek
Cooksburg to East Durham, 169–172
  map, 171
Cedar River
Cedar River Flow, 63–66
  map, 64
  Indian Lake Village to Hudson River,
  66–68
  map, 69
Champlain, Lake, Drainage map, 178.
  See also Champlain Canal; Glens
  Falls Feeder Canal; Lake George;
  Poultney River
Champlain Canal, 12, 185–186
  Fort Ann to Fort Edward, 189–191
  map, 190
  Whitehall to Fort Ann, 186–188
  map, 187
Charlemont, Massachusetts, from Fife
  Brook, Massachusetts, 235–238
  map, 237
Charlton Road to Van Vorst Road,
  229–230
  map, 233
Chatham Center from East Nassau,
  162–164
  map, 158
Cheney Pond and Boreas River
Cheney Pond and Lester Flow, 72–75
  map, 73
Christine Falls to Auger Falls, 84–87
  map, 85
Church, Frederick Edwin, 12
Clarke Outdoors, 244
Cobleskill Creek
Cobleskill to Sagendorf Road, 224–227

map, 225
Cold Brook Canoes, 173
Colden, Verplanck, 11
Cooksburg to East Durham, 169–172
  map, 171
Corinth Dam to Spier Falls Dam, 37–40
  map, 38
Corinth from Lake Luzerne, 34–37
  map, 35
covered bridges, 36, 125, 211

D
Deerfield River, Massachusetts
  Fife Brook, Massachusetts, to
  Charlemont, Massachusetts, 235–238
  map, 237
Dolgeville from Stratford, 206–209
  map, 207

E
East Canada Creek
  Stratford to Dolgeville, 206–209
  map, 207
East Durham from Cooksburg, 169–172
  map, 171
East Nassau to Chatham Center, 162–164
  map, 158
eels, 228
Elm Lake from Lake Pleasant, 88–90
  map, 89
environmental issues, Hudson River, 13,
  272
Esopus Creek
  Allaben to Boiceville, 172–176
  map, 175
Esperance
  from Middleburgh, 214–216
  map, 215

to Power House Road, 218–219
  map, 217

F

Fall Stream
  Piseco Lake to Vly Lake, 99–101
  map, 100
Falls Village, Connecticut, to West
  Cornwall, Connecticut, 239–241
  map, 240
Fife Brook, Massachusetts, to
  Charlemont, Massachusetts, 235–238
  map, 237
Fish Creek
  Grangerville to Victory Mills, 137–138
  map, 139
  Saratoga Lake to Grangerville,
  134–137
  map, 136
Flatwater and Quickwater Trips, 251–252
Fort Ann
  to Fort Edward, 189–191
  map, 190
  from Whitehall, 186–188
  map, 187
Fort Edward
  from Fort Ann, 189–191
  map, 190
  to Fort Miller, 46–49
  map, 48
Fort Miller
  from Fort Edward, 46–49
  map, 48
  to Stillwater, 49–53
  map, 51

G

George, Lake

Northwest Bay Brook, 179–181
  map, 180
Glen, The
  from North Creek, 25–30, 32
  map, 27
  to Thurman Station, 32–34
  map, 31
Glens Falls Feeder Canal
  Feeder Dam to Martindale Avenue,
  192–195
  map, 193
Grafton Lakes
  Long Pond, Second Pond, Shaver
  Pond, Mill Pond, and Martin-Dunham
  Reservoir, 153–155
  map, 154
Grangerville
  from Saratoga Lake, 134–137
  map, 136
  to Victory Mills, 137–138
  map, 139

H

Hinckley Reservoir release, 200, 201
Hoosick Falls from North Pownal,
  Vermont, 141–144
  map, 143
Hoosick Junction to Johnsonville Dam,
  144–147
  map, 145
Hoosic River, 140
Hoosick Junction to Johnsonville Dam,
  144–147
  map, 145
  Johnsonville Dam to Valley Falls,
  149–151
  map, 148

North Pownal, Vermont, to Hoosick
  Falls, 141–144
  map, 143
Hope from Wells, 101–104
  map, 103
Housatonic River, Connecticut, 239
  Falls Village, Connecticut, to West
  Cornwall, Connecticut, 239–241
  map, 240
  River Phone for, 244
  West Cornwall, Connecticut, to Kent,
  Connecticut, 242–246
  map, 243
Hudson, Henry, 11
Hudson Gorge, 12
  Indian River to North River, 19–23
  map, 20
Hudson Point Preserve, 43
Hudson River, 11–13
  Big Boom Road to Feeder Dam, 43–46
  map, 44
  Corinth Dam to Spier Falls Dam,
  37–40
  map, 38
  Fort Edward to Fort Miller, 46–49
  map, 48
  Fort Miller to Stillwater, 49–53
  map, 51
  Glen to Thurman Station, 32–34
  map, 31
  Hudson Gorge: Indian River to North
  River, 19–23
  map, 20
  from Indian Lake Village, 66–68
  map, 69
  Lake Luzerne to Corinth, 34–37

  map, 35
  –Mohawk River Confluence, 61–63
  map, 57
  Newcomb Bridge to Indian River
  Confluence, 15–18
  map, 14
  North Creek to The Glen, 25–30, 32
  map, 27
  North River to North Creek, 23–25
  map, 24
  PCB dredging and, 13, 272
  Sherman Island to Big Boom Road,
  42–43
  map, 44
  Spier Falls Dam to Sherman Island
  Dam, 40–42
  map, 41
  from Stewarts Dam, 106, 108–111
  map, 109
  Stillwater to Lansingburgh, 54–60
  maps, 56–57
Hudson River Whitewater Derby, 12, 26
hypothermia, 4

I
Indian Lake Village to Hudson River,
  66–68
  map, 69
Indian River Confluence from Newcomb
  Bridge, 15–18
  map, 14

J
Johnsonville Dam
  from Hoosick Junction, 144–147
  map, 145
  to Valley Falls, 149–151
  map, 148

K

Kast Bridge from Middleville, 203–206
  map, 204
Kayaderosseras Creek
  Ballston Spa to Saratoga Lake,
  131–134
    map, 133
  Rock City Falls to Ballston Spa,
  127–131
    map, 129
Kinderhook Creek, 157
  East Nassau to Chatham Center,
  162–164
    map, 158
  Stephentown to West Lebanon,
  160–162
    map, 159
Kristel Falls to Mohawk River, 230–232
  map, 233
Kunjamuk River
  Lake Pleasant to Elm Lake, 88–90
    map, 89

L

Lansingburgh from Stillwater, 54–60
  maps, 56–57
Lester Flow and Cheney Pond, 72–75
  map, 73
locks
  federal, 60
  state, 50, 58, 185
logging, 45
Long Pond, Second Pond, Shaver Pond,
  Mill Pond, and Martin-Dunham
  Reservoir, 153–155
    map, 154
Lower Connecticut and Housatonic

Watersheds map, 234. See also
  Deerfield River; Housatonic River
Lower Hudson Watershed map, 156. See
  also Catskill Creek; Esopus Creek;
  Kinderhook Creek; Normans Kill
Luzerne, Lake, to Corinth, 34–37
  map, 35

M

Manchester, Vermont, to Arlington,
  Vermont, 117–119
    map, 121
maps
  legend for, 7
  sources of, 6
Martindale Avenue from Glens Falls
  Feeder Dam, 192–195
    map, 193
Martin-Dunham Reservoir, Long Pond,
  Second Pond, Shaver Pond, and Mill
  Pond, 153–155
    map, 154
Melville, Herman, 62
Miami River, 70–72
  map, 71
Middleburgh
  to Esperance, 214–216
    map, 215
  from North Blenheim, 211–214
    map, 212
Middleville
  to Kast Bridge, 203–206
    map, 204
  from Poland, 201–203
    map, 202
Mohawk River
  –Hudson River Confluence, 61–63

map, 57
from Kristel Falls, 230–232
   map, 233
from Power House Road, 220–223
   map, 222
Mohawk River Watershed map, 196. *See also Alplaus Kill; East Canada Creek; Schoharie Creek; West Canada Creek*
Moses Kill, 112–115
   map, 113

N

National Guard Rifle Range, 167
Newcomb Bridge to Indian River
   Confluence, 15–18
   map, 14
New Scotland Avenue from Watervliet
   Reservoir, 166–168
   map, 165
New York State Rest Area
   from Arlington, Vermont, 122–123
   maps, 120–121
   to Shushan, 123–124
   map, 120
Normans Kill
   Watervliet Reservoir to New Scotland
   Avenue, 166–168
   map, 165
North Blenheim to Middleburgh,
   211–214
   map, 212
North Creek
   to The Glen, 25–30, 32
   map, 27
   from North River, 23–25
   map, 24
North Pownal, Vermont, to Hoosick Falls,

141–144
   map, 143
North River to North Creek, 23–25
   map, 24
Northwest Bay Brook, 179–181
   map, 180
NY 22 Bridge
   to Battenville, 126–127
   map, 120
   from Shushan, 124–125
   map, 120

P

paddling, in general
   instruction resources, 270–271
   physical disabilities, 7
   private property, 4
   safety, 2–4, 253–263
   seasonal water levels, 1–4, 264–265
Peebles Island, 62
Pleasant, Lake, to Elm Lake, 88–90
   map, 89
Poland
   to Middleville, 201–203
   map, 202
   from Trenton Falls, 198–200
   map, 199
Poultney River
   West Haven, Vermont, to Whitehall,
   182–184
   map, 183
Power House Road
   from Esperance, 218–219
   map, 217
   to Mohawk River, 220–223
   map, 222
private property, 4

Pumpkin Hollow from Whitehouse,
95–99
map, 97

R

Railroad Rapids, 174
Riparius
The Glen from, 29–30, 32
North Creek to, 28–29
map, 27
River Level and Flow Information,
264–265
Riverbank
from Starbuckville, 78–81
map, 79
to Warrensburg, 81–84
map, 82
Rock City Falls to Ballston Spa, 127–131
map, 129
Round Lake and Anthony Kill, 151–153
map, 150
Route 10 Bridge to Shaker Place, 90–94
map, 91

S

Sacandaga Outdoor Center, 108
Sacandaga River, Main
Stewarts Bridge Reservoir, 105–106
map, 107
Stewarts Dam to Hudson River, 106,
108–111
map, 109
Wells to Hope, 101–104
map, 103
Sacandaga River, Middle Branch
Christine Falls to Auger Falls, 84–87
map, 85
Kunjamuk River, Lake Pleasant to Elm

Lake, 88–90
map, 89
Sacandaga River, West Branch
Fall Stream, Piseco Lake to Vly Lake,
99–101
map, 100
Route 10 Bridge to Shaker Place,
90–94
map, 91
Whitehouse to Pumpkin Hollow,
95–99
map, 97
safety
cold temperatures, 4
obstacles in water, 3–4
Safety Code of American Whitewater, 3,
253–263
water levels, 1–4, 264–265
Sagendorf Road from Cobleskill Creek,
224–227
map, 225
Saratoga Battlefield, 52
Saratoga Lake
from Ballston Spa, 131–134
map, 133
to Grangerville, 134–137
map, 136
Saratoga Spa State Park, 132
Schoharie Creek, 210
Cobleskill Creek, Cobleskill to
Sagendorf Road, 224–227
map, 225
Esperance to Power House Road,
218–219
map, 217
Middleburgh to Esperance, 214–216

map, 215
North Blenheim to Middleburgh,
211–214
map, 212
Power House Road to Mohawk River,
220–223
map, 222
Schoharie Reservoir releases, 173
Schroon Falls to Schroon Lake Village,
75–76
map, 77
Schroon Lake Village from Schroon Falls,
75–76
map, 77
Schroon River
Riverbank to Warrensburg, 81–84
map, 82
Schroon Falls to Schroon Lake Village,
75–76
map, 77
Starbuckville to Riverbank, 78–81
map, 79
Schuyler, General Phillip, 138
Second Pond, Shaver Pond, Long Pond,
Mill Pond, and Martin-Dunham
Reservoir, 153–155
map, 154
Shaker Place from Route 10 Bridge,
90–94
map, 91
Shaver Pond, Long Pond, Second Pond,
Mill Pond, and Martin-Dunham
Reservoir, 153–155
map, 154
Sherman Island Dam from Spier Falls
Dam, 40–42

map, 41
Sherman Island to Big Boom Road,
42–43
map, 44
Shushan
from New York State Rest Area,
123–124
map, 120
to NY 22 Bridge, 124–125
map, 120
Spier Falls Dam
from Corinth Dam, 37–40
map, 38
to Sherman Island Dam, 40–42
map, 41
Starbuckville to Riverbank, 78–81
map, 79
Stephentown to West Lebanon, 160–162
map, 159
Stewarts Bridge Reservoir, 105–106
map, 107
Stewarts Dam to Hudson River, 106,
108–111
map, 109
Stillwater
from Fort Miller, 49–53
map, 51
to Lansingburgh, 54–60
maps, 56–57
strainer, 3
Stratford to Dolgeville, 206–209
map, 207

T
Tear of the Clouds, Lake, 11
Thurman Station from The Glen, 32–34
map, 31

Trenton Falls to Poland, 198–200
  map, 199

U

Upper Hudson Watershed map, 10. *See
  also Batten Kill; Cedar River; Cheney
  Pond; Fish Creek; Grafton Lakes;
  Hoosic River; Hudson River;
  Kayaderosseras Creek; Miami River;
  Moses Kill; Round Lake; Sacandaga
  River branches; Schroon River*

V

Valley Falls from Johnsonville Dam,
  149–151
  map, 148
Van Vorst Road from Charlton Road,
  229–230
  map, 233
Verrazano, Giovanni, 11
Victory Mills from Grangerville, 137-138
  map, 139

W

Warrensburg from Riverbank, 81–84
  map, 82
water levels, 1–4, 264–265
Watervliet Reservoir to New Scotland
  Avenue, 166–168
  map, 165
Wells to Hope, 101–104
  map, 103
West Canada Creek, 197–198
  Middleville to Kast Bridge, 203–206
  map, 204
  Poland to Middleville, 201–203
  map, 202
  Trenton Falls to Poland, 198–200
  map, 199

West Canada Creek Campground, 197
West Cornwall, Connecticut
  from Falls Village, Connecticut,
  239–241
  map, 240
  to Kent, Connecticut, 242–246
  map, 243
West Haven, Vermont, to Whitehall,
  182–184
  map, 183
West Lebanon from Stephentown,
  160–162
  map, 159
Whitehall
  to Fort Ann, 186–188
  map, 187
  from West Haven, Vermont, 182–184
  map, 183
Whitehouse to Pumpkin Hollow, 95–99
  map, 97
Whitewater Trips, 247-250